THE SECOND HOMEOWNER'S HANDBOOK

A Complete Guide for Vacation, Income, Retirement, and Investment

By

Jeff Haden

THE SECOND HOMEOWNER'S HANDBOOK
A Complete Guide for Vacation, Income, Retirement, and Investment

Copyright © 2006 by Atlantic Publishing Group, Inc.
1210 SW 23rd Place • Ocala, Florida 34474 • 800-814-1132 • 352-622-5836–Fax
Web site: www.atlantic-pub.com • E-mail sales@atlantic-pub.com
SAN Number: 268-1250

ISBN-13: 978-0-910627-74-0   ISBN-10: 0-910627-74-6

Library of Congress Cataloging-in-Publication Data

Haden, Jeff (William Jeffrey), 1960-
   The Second Homeowner's Handbook : A Complete Guide for Vacation, Income,
Retirement, and Investment / Jeff Haden.
      p. cm.
   Includes index.
   ISBN-13: 978-0-910627-74-0 (alk. paper)
   ISBN-10: 0-910627-74-6
   1. Second homes. 2. Real estate investment. I. Title.

   HD7289.2.H33 2006
   643'.12--dc22
                              2006013814

EDITOR: Jackie Ness • jackie_ness@charter.net
EDITOR: Ann Brown • Virtual Admins Plus • 800-320-5159 • Info@VirtualAdminsPlus.com • www.VirtualAdminsPlus.com
ART DIRECTION, FRONT COVER & INTERIOR DESIGN: Lisa Peterson, Michael Meister • info@6sense.net
GLOSSARY COMPILED BY: Christina Mohammed

Printed in the United States

CONTENTS

CHAPTER 3: DEVELOP A GREAT RELATIONSHIP WITH AN AGENT

CHAPTER 4: CHOOSING THE RIGHT LOCATION

CHAPTER 5: ANALYZING PROPERTIES

CHAPTER 6: MORTGAGE BASICS

CHAPTER 7: SHOPPING FOR A LOAN

CHAPTER 8: CREATIVE FINANCING

CHAPTER 9: BUYING A SECOND HOME FOR A RESIDENCE

CHAPTER 10: BUYING A REHAB OR "FIXER-UPPER"

CHAPTER 11: BUYING RENTAL PROPERTIES

CHAPTER 12: FINDING GREAT DEALS FROM OWNERS

CHAPTER 13: HOLDING PROPERTY

CHAPTER 14: PROPERTY MANAGEMENT

Chapter 15: Basic Improvements for Quick Profits

Chapter 16: Increasing Rental Property Profits

Chapter 17: Maximize Your Resale Price

DEDICATION

"To my father, who taught me everything I know about construction, and who was kind enough not to hang up the first time I said, 'Hey, I bought a house – but it needs some work….'

And to my wife Cynthia, who has the sharpest eye for real estate I know, and who constantly gives me confidence to set goals I could never reach on my own."

FOREWORD

I became a REALTOR® almost 20 years ago and I looked for advice and guidance wherever I could find it. I still vividly recall an experienced agent telling me, "The less your clients know about real estate, the better off you are." His point was that the less a potential buyer knows about real estate and real estate investing, the easier it is to sell him or her a home.

I've never forgotten his advice because it couldn't be more wrong. Great real estate agents don't sell homes; they find the right home for an individual buyer — at that point the home sells itself. Great real estate agents thrive because they help their clients find perfect homes for their needs. Buying the right home means two things: you bought the right home for your family's lifestyle and you made a wise investment. And the only way to buy the right home is to have a solid understanding of your needs and of real estate in general.

Interest in second homes has boomed nationally in the last five years. The number of second homeowners has grown by almost 50 percent. Why? Many homeowners purchase second homes to diversify investments, since real estate gains have beaten stock market results. For example, from 2000 to 2004, home prices increased 55 percent while the S & P 500 index fell by 15 percent. More and more investors see real estate as a smart investment choice — and there's an additional advantage. As a client of mine likes to say, "You can't spend a few weeks living in your stock certificates, but you can spend a few weeks at your vacation house at the beach." Second homes offer a unique opportunity: not only can they be great investments, but you can also actually enjoy them.

Buying a home (and buying a second home) is the biggest investment most people make; the perfect home is one that you not only enjoy living in but that also offers you the potential to build wealth. That's even truer when you buy a second home.

If you purchase a second home for investment purposes, you'll need to understand the business side of the transaction. You'll need to understand local market trends, vacancy rates, current pricing, and the effect of future housing trends in your area. If you purchase a second home for vacation purposes or to live in part-time, you'll still need to understand the business side of the transaction since it's likely you'll be renting the home to others for some portion of the year.

Here's the key: the more you know about real estate and about the unique opportunities found in second homes, the better choices you'll make and the greater the likelihood your investment will pay off – both in enjoyment and as an investment.

This book will help you make better choices. You'll learn how to assess your personal skills and determine your goals, and about developing good working relationships with real estate agents, evaluating properties, and getting the best deal on financing. You'll learn about property management, increasing rental income, creative financing, and quick fixes you can make to a distressed property. You'll learn how to add value to your second home and how to maximize its investment potential. In short, you'll learn everything you need to know to make a smart investment in a second home.

The agent who gave me advice years ago was wrong: the best clients are knowledgeable and informed clients. With this book, that's exactly what you'll be.

Jayne P. Schlabach, Realtor
Coldwell Banker Funkhouser Realtors
401 University Boulevard
Harrisonburg, Virginia 22801
540-434-2400
jayneps@cbfunkhouser.com
www.cbfunkhouser.com

INTRODUCTION

If you have ever considered buying a second home, now is the time, before prices climb even higher. Recent statistics from the National Association of REALTORS® show an upward trend in the number of second homes purchased for investment purposes. Second homes accounted for more than a third of residential real estate transactions in 2004, and investing in a second home now will be a great way to increase your net worth when you retire. There is no better time than now to buy that second home you have been thinking about for getaways, vacations, investment, or retirement. Low interest rates, tax benefits, rising appreciation, and effortless financing make it simple to profit from a second home if you go about it the right way.

Let us take a step back. Why should you invest in real estate? It is simple: real estate investing can be extremely profitable and is a relatively safe way to boost your net worth. Real estate investments should be a part of any investment portfolio, even if the only real estate you currently own is your home. In fact, the largest investment most Americans ever make is buying the home they live in. However, why stop with your primary home? Buying a second home lets you enjoy even greater benefits, both as an investment and as a way to improve your lifestyle.

Have you ever heard someone say, "I wish I had invested in real estate years ago. Just look at property values now." I am sure you have, and it is not a statement that is just being used today. A friend came across a letter written in the 1800's in which the author made the same statement! Prices rise because the population continues to increase, and people will always need somewhere to live. You can bet that years from now people will be saying that same thing.

Why? Real estate offers a wide variety of moneymaking opportunities. It is a finite commodity, and as the old cliché goes, "God is not making any more land." You can invest in your own home and then in a second vacation home. You can find an under-valued or foreclosure property and profit from a quick resale. You can invest in rental properties, and in many cases, use little or none of your own cash. Best of all, real estate is one of the most stable investments you will find. If you do your homework and follow the advice in this book, the risks you face will be far less than in the stock market, and the gains can be just as good. Real estate investing will take time and effort, but it is worth it.

This book explains how to invest profitably in a second home, whether you wish to live in it, re-sell it for a profit, use it as a vacation property, or convert it into a rental property for monthly income. The same steps can be easily applied to buying additional properties if you would like to continue to grow your real estate portfolio. How you use your second home is up to you, but this comprehensive guide presents proven tactics to make your second home purchase a smooth and profitable transaction.

BUILD YOUR FOUNDATION

Everyone wants to build wealth, and there are a number of great ways to do so. For many, real estate investments form a major portion of their investment portfolio. Steve Bange explains why investing in a second home was the right choice for both his investment and his personal goals.

"I've had money in stocks since I first got out of college, and like everyone I've had ups and downs. It never occurred to me to buy a second home – I thought that was something only wealthy people did. When I realized I could leverage my savings and my credit rating to buy another home, I jumped at the chance, and I'm glad I did. Not only has my property appreciated, but someone else, my tenant, is paying my mortgage, and I've gotten tax advantages I never would have. I like to think of my second home as a big part of my retirement plan with an added bonus. If I have an emergency, I can sell the home and get my hands on the capital. I cannot sell my pension plan."

P ossibly, you have heard someone say, "Real estate investing is not right for everybody." The answer to that statement is, "Well, it should be." Real estate investing is a great way to build wealth. Before we look at exactly how to go about purchasing a second home, let us look at some of the benefits of real estate investing.

THE BENEFITS OF REAL ESTATE INVESTING

The Risks Are Minimal

Real estate prices have risen dramatically in recent years, especially in major metropolitan areas like New York, Chicago, and Los Angeles. Here is an example: a couple bought a home in 2001 for $219,000 in Scotch Plains, New Jersey, a commuter town across the river from Manhattan. Two years later, they sold it for $344,000. They then moved to Harrisburg, Pennsylvania, where they bought a home for $319,000. Twelve months later, they sold that home for $358,000. While it is true that in some areas of the country home prices have stayed relatively flat, most areas of the country have seen double-digit increases over the past three to five years.

As a result, some experts predict that the real estate market "bubble" will burst soon, and prices will fall dramatically. Others predict that interest rates are bound to rise in the near future. If it sounds scary, it is not. You can make money in any real estate market: rising, falling, or flat. No matter what the current conditions are, you can profit from them. Here are some examples:

- If prices are rising quickly, you can buy properties that need cosmetic repairs and flip them for easy profits. ("Flip" is a word used to describe the process of buying and then quickly selling a property, hopefully for a tidy profit.)

- If prices are rising quickly, you can take cash out by refinancing your loan. It is a simple process: if a $100,000 property has risen in value by 20 percent, you can refinance the loan on the property for 90 percent of its value, keeping the other 10 percent as cash that you can use to invest in other properties or investment vehicles. ("Cash out" is a term used to describe the process of refinancing and taking equity out of the property in the form of cash.)

- If interest rates fall, you can refinance your properties at a lower rate, reducing your monthly payments to improve cash flow and make money available for other investments.

- If interest rates rise, home prices typically fall. You can buy under-valued properties and assume lower-rate mortgages from owners eager to sell, or take advantage of seller financing options at lower than market rates.

- If interest rates rise, new construction rates typically fall. Builders are less likely to build "spec" homes when they have to pay higher interest rates on construction loans. Less new construction decreases the supply of homes, and when the market picks up again, supply is usually out-stripped by demand, and prices rise. Real estate, like many other investments, is cyclical in nature, but what is not cyclical is the fact that the population continues to increase, and as a result, the demand for housing will continue to increase.

Appreciation

Think about it: are real estate prices higher now than they were ten years ago? Absolutely! Think about what your parents paid for their house. If a retired couple paid $12,600 for their home in 1963, their home is worth $245,000 today.

Rent prices also continue to rise. Years from now, the price you will pay for the average home will be much higher than it is today.

In 2003, the U.S. government published statistics regarding median home prices. Look at how rapidly the average home has appreciated over the past 35 years:

1970	$23,000
1975	$35,300
1980	$62,200
1985	$75,500
1990	$95,500
1995	$113,100
2000	$138,400
2005	$182,000 (estimated)

What is interesting to note is that while prices have certainly boomed in the past five years, prices have risen at double-digit levels in every five-year period. Very few investments can match that level of appreciation over the long-term.

Real estate prices are likely to continue rising. There are a number of reasons why; let us look at just a few. Over the next twenty years, the following is expected to happen:

- The U.S. population is expected to grow by more than 40 million people.

- The U.S. median income is expected to increase by 50 percent.

- Ten million people will choose to buy vacation homes in the U.S.

- More than sixty million children and grandchildren of baby boomers will enter the housing market.

- Environmental restrictions and land shortages will tighten property development in popular areas, causing a decrease in supply and an increase in housing prices.

- More than 60 million baby boomers will seek retirement income, and many will sensibly turn to real estate investments.

- Minorities and immigrants will continue to buy homes in record numbers. Currently 75 percent of whites live in their own homes, while only 40 percent of Hispanics and Asians own their homes. As their rate of home ownership increases, demand for housing will increase.

So what is the end result? Real estate prices should continue to rise, making smart real estate investing and investing in a second home a great way to grow wealth.

Income

There are two basic ways to get income or cash from real estate investing: buying and selling properties for a profit, commonly known as "flipping," or by collecting rent from tenants who occupy your properties. Most successful real estate investors do both. As the owner of a second home, you can choose either method of increasing your income.

If you "flip" properties, the profits can be either used as income for living expenses or to invest in more properties. The average real estate investor does not seek to earn an income from their properties, at least not at first. Most try to increase their net worth, but over time, you can do both.

For example, let us say you buy a house for $150,000 for use as a rental property. If your mortgage payments, taxes, insurance, etc. add up to $1,200 per month, but you are only collecting $1,300 per month in rent, you are generating very little monthly income. Nevertheless, you are building wealth.

Each year, more of your principal is paid off, and as the property appreciates, your equity grows. In effect, your tenants are paying your mortgage for you. If interest rates fall and you refinance your loan, you may be able to widen the gap between your expenses and your rental income. On the other hand, you may choose a "cash out" refinancing in order to free up capital for other investments. Whether you leave the equity in the property or take cash out, you are building wealth.

As years pass, you will grow significant equity in the property. If you hold the property long enough, you will eventually pay off your mortgage, and the money you were putting towards mortgage payments can now be seen as "income" or to fund other investments.

If you are a "buy and hold" investor, then your short-term income potential is low, but your long-term wealth potential is high. Your income potential is high once your properties are paid off. If you "flip" properties, you can still build wealth by continually reinvesting profits, or you can use some of the profits as income. In either case, real estate investing is profitable and financially rewarding.

Tax Advantages

Unlike investing in stocks or other traditional investment

vehicles, there are a number of tax advantages you can benefit from when you invest in real estate. Here are four of the most widely used and effective:

- **Investing in your own home**. Not only is mortgage interest paid tax-deductible, but so is the profit you make when you sell your home. When you sell your personal residence, defined as a home where you have lived for at least two of the past five years, up to $250,000 in profits for an individual and $500,000 for a couple is tax free. You can buy and sell your personal residences every two years and continue to avoid taxes on your gains. By definition, if you are interested in buying a second home you already own your first, so you should already be taking advantage of the tax advantages from owning a home.

- **Investing in rental properties**. You can also avoid taxes on capital gains of rental properties you own as long as you follow the IRS Section 1031 Exchange regulations. You are not really exchanging your property with someone else. As long as you buy another investment property within a few months, your gains are tax-deferred. We will look at Section 1031 Exchanges in a later chapter.

- **Depreciation**. If the income you receive from a rental property exceeds your expenses, you have to pay taxes on that income, right? Not necessarily. Investment properties can be depreciated over a number of years, which means that each year you can offset your income by a percentage of the value of the property. If you depreciate a $100,000 property over twenty years, you can offset up to $5,000 in income each year by depreciating your property, meaning that $5,000 in income is tax-free. After twenty years, you will no longer be able to depreciate the property, but in the meantime, you have sheltered significant amounts of income.

- **Retirement plans**. If you think your IRA funds can only be invested in stocks or bonds, think again. You can also invest your IRA dollars in real estate. IRA funds invested in real estate enjoy the same tax advantages as funds invested in stocks, bonds, mutual funds, etc.

Investing in real estate offers unique opportunities to grow wealth and gain income tax-free. To understand the specific tax implications for your situation, make sure to consult with a qualified accountant or financial services professional.

Leverage

Another unique feature of real estate investing is that you can buy properties using little or even none of your own money.

Leverage is a simple concept to understand: if you buy a $100,000 house and only put $5,000 down on a twenty-year mortgage, your $5,000 investment has allowed you to control and invest in a $100,000 property. That is leverage. Do you now own $100,000? Of course not, but you do control it, and you can take advantage of it.

Let us say you rent the property to other people for twenty years and pay off your mortgage. While you will have had expenses such as upkeep, maintenance, occasional repairs, etc., along the way, hopefully your rental income has at the least matched your expenses. In effect, your tenants have paid your mortgage and expenses for you. We will stay conservative and say the property rose in value by twenty percent, a figure that historically is well below average appreciation rates. So now, you own a $120,000 property, and you have only spent $5,000 of your own money. Moreover, each month it continues to bring in income for you.

If you do sell, your profit is $115,000. That is twenty-three times what you invested; try finding that rate of return anywhere else. That is the power of leverage.

Leverage can allow you to buy more and more properties. As your property values rise, you can borrow against those properties to make further investments.

Here is the bottom line: most successful investors use the power of leverage to maximize their returns on their investments.

Keep in mind, though, that leverage can increase your level of risk. If you borrow too heavily and do not have sufficient cash reserves, you can find yourself forced into foreclosure or bankruptcy. Unexpected events will occur, so make sure you have sufficient cash on hand to weather small storms. If you have borrowed so heavily that having a tenant fall a month behind on rent will cause you to miss making your mortgage payment, you are too heavily leveraged. If you are living above your means already, borrowing more money to buy properties only increases your risk.

There are a number of reasons to invest in real estate. Like all investments, though, there is an element of risk and unpredictability. You should always seek the help of competent legal and tax advisors.

Assess Your Skills and Interests

Before you start looking for a second home, you will want to look at your goals, your motivations, and your personal resources. Understanding your skills and your goals for the second home will help you make smart decisions and will save you time and money.

Why? Real estate investing of any kind takes time and effort. You will need to do your homework. If you are investing in rental properties, you will also have to decide whether you have the time and skills to tackle major or minor maintenance and repairs or whether you will need to hire someone else to handle those items for you. You will also need to evaluate your financial situation to determine what types of real estate investments are right for you. If you are interested in buying a vacation home that you will also rent to others, the same considerations apply. Even if you are buying a second home and you will be the only tenant of the home, you will still need to take into account the fact that your home maintenance responsibilities will double.

Personal Skills

If you like what you are doing, you will be more successful at it. It is that simple. If you do not, you will hate every minute of it, even if you are successful at it.

Look at your own personality first. Do you enjoy working with people? If you do not, then becoming a landlord probably is not right for you. You can still invest in a rental property, but you will just need to factor in the cost of using a property management firm to deal with your tenants.

Do you deal effectively with stress? If you do not, taking on too much risk might not be the best move for you. You should probably avoid owning a large vacation property or buying foreclosure properties, at least at first. After you become more experienced, you may find that taking on more risk is not stressful at all, because you have the capital and expertise to work through problems as they come up.

Look at the time you have available. If you are already extremely busy, buying fixer-upper houses with the intent that you will do the refurbishing work yourself probably does not make sense. The more work you do yourself, the more money you can make, but not if you do not have time to actually do the work. If you are already extremely busy, buying rental properties and turning over the day-to-day management to a property management firm may be right for you.

If you are married, does your spouse support your decision to purchase a second home? Investing in real estate takes time, and if your spouse is not interested or supportive, you will find it tough to devote the time you need to your investment. If you decide to manage a rental property yourself, you can expect late-night calls on occasion from tenants. If your spouse is not supportive, that can cause huge problems. Some investors have a "fourteen unit divorce rule." They like to joke that if they own more than fourteen rental properties, their marriage probably will not survive. Even though you are just considering a second home, there will be additional responsibilities involved. Make sure you discuss your goals with your spouse before you get started.

Do you have any mechanical, electrical, or carpentry skills? If you do not, you will have to pay someone to repair or refurbish your properties. If you have the skills, keep in mind you will have to have the time available to do the work.

Financial Abilities

If you find it hard to balance your checkbook, investing in real estate will be hard for you. You will need to understand the basics of personal and mortgage finance and have a general understanding of taxes and other accounting issues. If you do not, you will have to be willing to hire professionals to help you in those areas.

You can also take basic real estate classes at most community colleges. Some people even take the real estate agent preparatory class, one that is required for prospective real estate agents, in order to gain knowledge about real estate investing. You do not have to become a real estate agent if you take the class, but you can still learn a lot from it.

Your Personal Credit

How good your credit rating is will seriously affect your ability to get financing and to get it on the best terms possible.

If you have poor credit, your options will be limited at first while you work to repair your credit. You can still qualify for owner financing, you can assume a mortgage, or you can qualify for financing targeted to individuals with poor credit.

Getting and maintaining an excellent credit rating is critical to investment success. You can get better terms and rates, and you can more easily leverage your properties if you want to continue to grow your real estate portfolio. If you have poor credit, you can still invest. People do it every day, but you will have to be more creative or you will have to accept less favorable terms.

PUT YOUR FINANCIAL HOUSE IN ORDER

If your goal is to purchase a second home, you will probably have to change some of your priorities. At the very least, you will need to get your finances in order, so you can purchase the home you want on the best terms possible.

If you want to build wealth, you will probably need to be willing to do the following:

- **Cut your spending and increase your savings**. Eliminate "nice to" or "want to" spending and stick to "have to" spending.

- **Improve your credit rating**. At the very least, that means paying your bills on time and meeting your financial obligations.

- **Start looking closely at the real estate listings in your "local" papers, as well as at any sales flyers or brochures that "local" real estate firms produce**. "Local" could mean in your area if you are buying close to home, or in the area where you may want to purchase a vacation home. Your goal is to start getting a sense of the market or markets where you intend to purchase.

- **Start looking at properties that interest you, even if you are not ready to invest**. You will start to get a sense of what is available, and you will meet local real estate professionals. Hopefully, you will find professionals with whom you are comfortable working.

- **Talk to a lender about your investment goals, and see what type of financing for which you qualify**. Do not wait until you are ready to make an offer to find out if you even qualify for a loan under terms you can accept.

Improve Your Debt-to-Income Ratio

Lenders will evaluate the total amount of debt you have in relation to your income. If the ratio is too high, they will be unwilling to loan you money. However, you can still explore seller-financing options.

Decreasing your debt-to-income ratio can help you qualify for better loan terms. How do you decrease the ratio? Pay off existing debt. If you need to decrease the ratio quickly, consider selling some assets and using the proceeds to pay off an existing debt or to get out from under the debt. Do you have a boat in the driveway you almost never use? Sell it. You will get more enjoyment from a second home than you will from an occasional boat ride.

Gather Down Payment Funds

While it is possible to invest without putting any money down, in most cases you will still need cash for closing costs and other initial expenses. In addition, you will need some amount of cash in case of emergencies.

Mortgage terms for investment properties are not as liberal as for owner-occupied properties. Why? Investment properties carry more risk. Owner-occupants are more likely to take care of the property than renters are. Even if you will be the only resident of the second home, most lenders view financing second homes differently than primary homes. The terms usually, but not always, are not as favorable.

If you have available cash, that is great! If not, there are still options to generate cash. You can sell assets, you can borrow against a 401(k) plan, or you can seek funding from friends or family who wish to be partners with you.

You can even go so far as to generate cash using your credit cards, but understand the risks involved. The interest rates tend to be high, and you will be increasing your debt-to-income ratio, making it harder for you to borrow money. Unless, of course, you quickly flip the second home, pay off the credit cards, and use the additional profits to finance your next investment.

Here is a key tip: start accumulating cash now. Cash is king, and access to cash can make even the most complicated deals go smoothly.

Build Lending Relationships Now

Get a copy of your credit report, and make an appointment with a loan officer at your local bank. Bring your own copy so the loan officer will not have to pull one; this will avoid a new credit inquiry on your credit report. Once you are there, show the loan officer your credit report, and discuss your interest in buying a second home.

The loan officer will review your credit report and can tell you what types of financing of which you qualify. He or she can also give you advice about what you can do to qualify for better terms, bigger loans, etc. The easiest way to learn about what types of financing you can qualify for is to ask a person who evaluates potential loan candidates every day.

Now make an appointment with a local mortgage broker, and do the same thing. You may get the same answers, or you may not. Regardless, you will be learning. In effect, you will get free advice and guidance. You will walk away with a good sense of what you need to do to strengthen your financial position, improve your credit, and decide what types of properties and investments you can make through traditional financing means.

You will also establish rapport with local loan professionals, and this will give you a sense of whether you are comfortable dealing with them. This can be a valuable relationship later on, because you are a known quantity, not a stranger.

Perform a Self-Assessment

Now that you have a sense of your skills and financial situation, let us determine the best course of action for you. This book will show you a range of purposes and methods for buying a second home, and you can choose the best option based on your skills and on what you like to do. Real estate is an industry with so many aspects that anyone can find a profitable way to build wealth that is suited to his or her particular talents and interests.

Should you focus on one particular area when you buy a second home? You can, but you do not have to. Many people specialize in types of real estate that generate positive cash flow: single-family houses, apartments, or rooming houses. Others find a particular niche and focus exclusively on that, for instance, rehabs and fixer-uppers. You can choose to start with one type of purchase, especially if you are operating with limited capital, and expand into other areas as you generate cash and equity. Before you make a decision, though, you should read the entire book to make sure you understand all the options available to you.

Let us assume you are relatively new to real estate investing, and you have to start somewhere. The following is a breakdown of how you can get started based on your financial situation, your skills, and your personal interests. Use this as a guide to determine the best ways to invest in real estate and some of the best investment options, based on your individual skills, capabilities, and interests. We will cover these topics in detail in later chapters.

1. **Do You Have a Down Payment and Good Credit?**

   Yes: Consider bank financing. You can probably qualify for excellent terms, and in addition, you will build a business relationship with a lender that will be beneficial in the end.

   No: Consider seller financing or lease options. Sellers often are much more flexible in offering terms to buyers with poor credit. In addition, work hard to improve your credit rating. Pay all of your bills on time, and work to pay down your debts. The better your credit rating, the more readily you can get financing, and the easier it will be to invest in real estate.

2. **Do You Have Carpentry Skills?**

   Yes: Consider rehabs and fixer-uppers. Instead of paying others to do the work, you can do it yourself. In effect, you will be paying yourself a wage in addition to increasing the value of the property. Keep in mind, though, that rehabs can take considerable time to renovate, so make sure you have that time available.

   No: Focus on buying rental properties, on wholesaling

properties, or on other investments where your personal "sweat equity" is not required. Find skilled craftsmen who can do the work for you on rehabs or fixer-uppers.

3. **Do You Like Working With People?**

   Yes: Consider buying and managing your own rental property. You will save on property management fees, and you will build relationships with local lenders, government officials, and craftsmen. You may even rent to tenants who will later become buyers of other properties you invest in or of this property. In addition, you can consider selling your properties yourself instead of using the services of a real estate agent.

   No: If you invest in a rental property, use the services of a property management firm. You will probably also want to use a real estate agent to sell your properties. Landlords have a number of interpersonal dealings with tenants. If you do not like working with people, managing your own properties will be frustrating and stressful.

4. **Do You Have Solid Financial Management Skills?**

   Yes: Consider handling your own accounting and bookkeeping. You will have a better sense of the day-to-day state of your business. On the downside, if your investments are substantial, you will find yourself spending a lot of time handling the clerical tasks necessary to run your real estate "empire." At that point, you may decide you are better off handing the clerical duties to someone else while you focus on finding and making great investments.

No: Educate yourself by attending seminars or taking classes. The more you know, the better you will do. Alternatively, you can utilize the services of an accountant you trust.

5. **Do You Want or Need a Steady Stream of Monthly Income?**

   Yes: Consider an income-generating rental property. A property with a positive cash flow in which your income exceeds your expenses can provide you with extra income each month. Many investors specialize in investments of rental properties. They increase their monthly income, and over time, they build equity as they pay down the mortgages on those properties and as the value of the properties increases.

   No: Consider rehabs, fixer-uppers, options, and other shorter-term investments. Buying a house in poor condition, making improvements, and selling it for a profit will generate income, but not on a steady, predictable basis. If your goal is to build wealth instead of increasing cash flow, you can also invest in a property with longer-term appreciation potential.

6. **Do You Have a Source of Capital to Invest?**

   Yes: Use your capital to make down payments, to purchase options, and to help obtain necessary financing. You can also use your capital to finance improvements of your property.

   No: Focus on investing in a property where limited capital is necessary. Look for little or no money-down loans, seek owner financing, and guard the capital you have closely. Do not sink all of your capital into one property unless you plan to sell the property quickly. If you buy a rehab or a fixer-upper, you may have to finance the repairs and renovations using outside financing like credit cards, personal loans, etc.

7. **Is Your Current Income Level Low?**

Yes: Invest in a property that yields a positive cash flow. Under no circumstances should you purchase a second home with negative cash flow if you cannot afford that drain on your finances.

No: Invest in a property to build wealth or to make a shorter-term profit. Of course, you can still invest in a rental property that generates a positive monthly cash flow. You can also rent a portion of your home to a third party if you want to increase your income, especially if you only plan to live in your primary home for part of the year.

8. **Do You Have a Real Estate License?**

Yes: List your own properties, and buy properties too. You will save on commissions when you sell one of your properties, and you will be in a position to negotiate a better deal when you buy a property. As the buying agent, you earn a commission, which essentially goes right back into your pocket.

No: Consider getting a license for the reasons mentioned above. In most states, you will simply need to take a three-month class and pass a licensing test. Once you have passed, you can place your license with a local real estate agency. You do not have to sell real estate full-time; in fact, many agencies will allow you to handle your own transactions. Of course, you may also occasionally decide to list homes for friends or relatives, generating additional income for yourself.

ESTABLISH YOUR GOALS

Most people spend a lot more time dreaming about success than they do planning for it. Dreaming is simply dreaming. Planning requires taking an active role in setting goals for your life and taking appropriate action to achieve those goals. Remember the saying, "The average person doesn't plan to fail; most failures occur as a result of a failure to plan."

It is true, and setting goals is an important part of planning.

There are two basic ways to set a goal. One way is to look at your current situation, decide what you can do, and then set a realistic goal based on the present. That certainly works, but a better way to set a goal is to decide what you want to achieve. Then, work backwards to determine what steps you will need to take to reach that goal.

For example, if you currently have a full-time job, you might say, "I have an hour or so a night to devote to real estate, so in six months, I might be in a position to buy a second home." Contrast that approach to the person who says, "I would like to own a second home by the end of May, so what do I need to do to make that happen? I will need to get my credit in order, start talking to lenders, scour the papers for possible deals, find a contractor who is willing to work with me if repairs are needed, and find an agent who might be able to help me locate good deals. Okay, then my short-term goal is to get those things in place in two weeks. Then, I will be ready to start making offers on properties I think are right for me."

The difference is critical, and the best way to set goals is to decide where you want to be in six months, a year, five years, and ten years. Then, develop action plans that allow you to reach those goals. You will have to make changes to your life to reach your goals, but owning a second home will be worth that effort.

CHAPTER TWO

UNDERSTANDING THE PROCESS

From an experienced real estate agent's point of view, working with a buyer looking for a second home requires a different approach than working with a buyer looking for a new primary residence. Jayne Schlabach, an award-winning REALTOR® with Coldwell Banker Funkhouser REALTORS® in Harrisonburg, VA, explains how.

A buyer looking for a primary residence focuses on the location, the size of the house, the school system, the home's convenience to work and shopping… all the things that make a house perfect for their family's needs. A buyer looking for a second home has a somewhat different set of interests depending on his or her goals: whether the house will be an investment property, a rehab to sell for a quick profit, a second residence, a vacation home, or even a blend of these goals. Identifying buyers' goals is a critical step towards making sure I find the right homes for them to look at. In many cases, the buyer of a primary residence often focuses on what they need; the buyer of a second home frequently has the luxury of focusing on what they want. It is my job to make sure I fully understand not only what they need and can afford, but also what they really want from their second home.

———

E ven though you have bought at least one house in the past, it is helpful to have a thorough knowledge of the steps of a house purchase, especially some of the unique aspects of buying a second home. Let us walk through a second home transaction from start to finish so you can see how the process works. At the end of this chapter, you will have a solid understanding of how the process of buying a second home works, and how it will work for you.

ONE: IDENTIFY THE PROPERTY

Here is a brief summary of how to perform due diligence on an income property you are considering purchasing. Which property you purchase, of course, is an individual choice based on your goals and resources. When you do find a property you are interested in, you will want to inspect it thoroughly to make sure it meets your requirements. Keep in mind that some of the following may not apply, depending on the type of property you are purchasing. To perform due diligence, make sure you do the following:

- **Property inspections**: Get a professional evaluation of the condition of the property and estimates of any necessary repairs or upgrades.

- **Tenant review**: Talk to current tenants, neighbors, and contractors or tradesmen, if you can identify them. Look for problems with tenants or with the property that may be cause for concern.

- **Personal property identification**: Make sure you have a full listing of all property that stays: appliances, furnishings, window treatments, etc.

- **Current lease inspections**: Make sure that all the leases contain terms of which you are comfortable. Once you have purchased the property, you are bound by the terms of those leases.

- **Security deposit verification**: Ensure that all security deposits will be turned over to you at closing. Once the property is purchased, the security deposits belong to you, not the previous owner. In fact, they ultimately belong to the tenants, provided they do not violate the terms of their lease agreement.

- **Zoning and code verification:** Make sure that the property conforms to all zoning, building, and occupancy regulations.

Once you have done these things and you have identified a property you would like to purchase, it is time to make an offer.

Two: Make an Offer

To make an official offer, you will need to create a written contract. A contract is simply a voluntary, legally enforceable promise between two parties to perform some legal act in exchange for consideration. In this case, the legal act will be the transfer of real estate, and the consideration will be the purchase price you pay.

You can make verbal offers, but you should never do so. Some oral agreements are enforceable, while others are not. In either case, oral agreements can lead to messy and complicated disagreements. Make all your offers in writing, and you will avoid any uncertainty, confusion, or misunderstandings.

There are basic elements in a contract:

- Offer and acceptance

- Consideration

- Legally competent parties

- Consent

- Legal purpose

If you make an offer using a real estate agent, the agent will ensure that the offer is written using a valid form and that it contains appropriate language. Note that the language will be appropriate, but not necessarily advantageous to you. It is up to you to make your specific conditions known on the offer. Remember that the real estate agent has a vested interest in seeing the transaction completed, and you have a vested interest in getting the best possible deal. Therefore, it is up to you to specify the terms that are important to you. We will discuss a few of those terms in a moment.

Consideration is a part of any contract. Consideration is both the final price established for the sale and the "earnest" money that is put down with the contract. In most cases, you will make a small deposit when you make an offer, typically $500 or $1,000. The intent is to show your seriousness in making the offer, since if you back out of the contract, you could forfeit that earnest money, unless you back out due to a contingency that you insert in the contract. For instance, the sale is contingent upon your qualifying for particular financing terms. If you do not qualify for financing under those terms, the contract becomes void, and you get your earnest money back.

A real estate sales contract contains the complete agreement between parties. If you make an offer and it is accepted, you cannot go back later and request additional concessions or changes. You will want to be sure your contract contains the exact details of the purchase that you are willing to agree to. Here are key details that should appear on any contract:

- Purchaser and seller names.

- Sales price and terms, including any earnest money deposited.

- How long the contract is good for, usually expressed in hours or days.

- A legal description of the land or property, and any covenants or restrictions that apply to the deed.

- Additional items that convey, like appliances, light fixtures, window treatments, outside buildings, etc.

- A statement of the kind and condition of the title, and the form of deed to be delivered to the seller.

- The kind of title evidence required, who will provide it, and how many defects in the title will be eliminated.

- A statement of all the terms and conditions of the agreement between the parties and any contingencies.

- The method that will be used to prorate real estate taxes, rents, fuel costs, etc.

- Remedies available in the case of default.

- Signatures of all pertinent parties.

Most of the above information will appear in standard language on the contract template. Take the time to read it all to make sure you understand what you are agreeing to. If you are confused about anything or have any questions, have an attorney review the contract first. Once you have signed the contract, it becomes a legally binding agreement. Saying you did not understand what you were signing is unlikely to help you.

It is improbable your first offer will be accepted. Most sellers will assume you have started at a lower price, because you expect to do some haggling. If the seller does not accept your price, he has a choice either to ignore the offer or to make a counteroffer. If the seller ignores your offer and the contract period passes, you are released from any obligation. If you give the seller three days to consider your offer, he or she can accept the offer at any time up until the three-day period has passed. Most experts recommend specifying a forty-eight hour offer acceptance period, because that is enough time for the seller to consider your offer and counter-offer if he or she wishes.

If the seller rejects your offer, he or she can still make a counteroffer by making changes to the original contract. For instance, the seller may change the price, eliminate one of the contingencies, add contingencies, or any combination of things. Once a counteroffer is made, the original offer ceases to exist, because it has been amended. The process of offer and counteroffer can continue indefinitely.

Your goal in the negotiation phase is to find ways to reach win-win agreements. Try to determine what the critical issue is for the seller, and find ways to meet that need without compromising your needs. For instance, the seller may ask for $1,000 more than you wish to pay. Instead of haggling over price, possibly you could offer to let him or her keep a storage building that was originally included as part of the property. On the other hand, if the seller wishes to wait sixty days to move but you need to close in forty-five days due to a possible 1031 Exchange, offer to rent back the property for fifteen days after closing takes place.

If a real estate agent is involved, you can also ask that agent to cut his or her commission if the price difference is relatively small. Many agents will do so if it means making the sale; a smaller percentage of something is better than 100 percent of nothing.

If you or the seller agrees to an offer or counteroffer in the form it was made, in other words, with no amendments, then the contract is considered to be accepted. Duplicates of the contract are provided to both parties, and in states where contract review is required, a copy of the contract is forwarded to attorneys.

If you made an earnest money deposit, the money will be held in escrow until the closing. If your offer was not accepted and you do not choose to counteroffer, your earnest money is returned to you. In most cases, the check is not even cashed by the real estate agent until an offer is accepted.

Most contracts contain contingencies. Even if you have both signed the contract, it will not be legally binding unless all contingencies are satisfied. Common contingencies are:

- **Financing**: The buyer must obtain suitable financing at terms specified on the contract. The terms you stipulate can be very specific. For instance, you could state, "Financing at an interest rate of less than 6 percent for thirty years with five percent down."

- **Inspection**: Inspections can include pests, lead-based paint, structural or mechanical systems, sewage facilities, and radon or other toxic materials. Inspections can also entail the assessment of certain documents, like leases or expense statements.

- **Property sale:** You can make the sale contingent on the sale of another property you own within a specified time. For instance, if you are purchasing a residence to replace your current residence, you can make the purchase contingent on your selling your residence within sixty or ninety days.

These are the most common contingencies, but any contingency can be inserted if both parties agree. You can also add an escape clause, which permits the seller to continue marketing the property until all of the buyer's contingencies have been met. In the event the seller gets a better offer, you as the buyer have the option of letting the contract go or of waiving your contingencies. That is why you will often see a house stay on the market even after it is under contract. If there are a number of contingencies, the seller may have retained the right to keep marketing the house.

After a contract is signed, addendums or amendments can be made if both parties agree. An addendum is an additional agreement made between parties, and an amendment is a change to an existing agreement. For instance, if your original agreement called for closing in sixty days and you agree to change the closing to ninety days, you have amended the contract. If you later agree to split the cost of repairs found in a home inspection, you will have created an amendment to the contract.

Amendments and addendums cannot be made in a one-sided way. Both parties must agree in order for them to take effect.

THREE: OBTAIN FINANCING

We will cover financing thoroughly in later chapters. Hopefully you are pre-approved, and completing your financing is a breeze. If not, you will have to scramble, because most contracts require that financing be in place by a certain date or the contract can be voided.

While you are completing the financing transaction, your lender will also order any required inspections, like an appraisal or termite inspection, and will ensure that you get a suitable fire and accident policy to cover the property.

FOUR: CONDUCT INSPECTIONS

In addition to any lender-mandated inspections, you will want to conduct other inspections you specified in the contract, including a home inspection. Most contracts will allow you a specified amount of time to conduct the home inspection; if you fail to inspect the property within that time period, you can lose your right to do so.

Once the inspection is complete, there will likely be problems found by the inspector. After all, it is the inspector's job to find problems, and almost every inspector finds something. If the problems are relatively minor, simply ask the homeowner to make the repairs to your satisfaction. Most will gladly spend a few hundred dollars to avoid losing the sale. If the problems are more extensive, you will have to negotiate a settlement of the issue in question.

Remember that the homeowner was required to disclose problems that he or she was aware of prior to the inspection. That is why you ordered an inspection; you do not want to trust that the homeowner was aware of all of the potential problems, because many are not.

Once problems are identified by an inspection, the homeowner is now aware of them. If you back out of the contract, the homeowner is required to disclose the newly discovered problems to any future buyers.

Because of that fact, in most cases the seller will have either to discount the price or fix the problems to satisfy a new buyer. The result is that the seller, in all likelihood, will be motivated to reach an agreement with you. You will have to evaluate the nature of the problems and the cost to remedy them as you decide what you are willing to agree to.

While you are performing inspections, either your attorney or the title company performing the closing will conduct a title search to ensure the title is clear.

Other inspections may be necessary. For example, most lenders require a survey of the property. Typically, surveys are considered "buyer" expenses, but that can be negotiated. In some cases if a survey has been done recently, the lender may waive the survey, but not all will. Lenders will also typically require an appraisal, so they can be sure the value of the property is suitable for the amount of the loan they are making.

FIVE: GET READY FOR CLOSING

About one to two weeks before closing, check in with all parties to make sure everything is on track for closing. Check with your lender, with the seller, with the title company, with your attorney, and with any real estate agents involved. Do not assume that everyone is proceeding on pace, so it is a good idea to be proactive in order to deal with any problems early.

SIX: PERFORM YOUR FINAL WALK-THROUGH INSPECTION

Always do a final walk-through inspection of the property before closing. If possible, conduct the walk-through the day of closing, after the owner has moved out of the property. Make sure the condition of the home is the same as when you signed the contract and that all structures and other items that are supposed to stay have remained. Also, make sure that the owner has removed any trash, debris, or junk from the property. Once you close on the property, you have limited means to remedy any discrepancies. Note any problems during the walk-through so you can deal with them at the closing. If any repairs were made due to problems found during the home inspection, make sure that they were made correctly and to your satisfaction.

SEVEN: CLOSING

The closing is when the property changes hands, and the title is transferred from the seller to the buyer. Once closing takes place, the property has officially changed hands.

Your lender will provide two main documents to you while your loan is processed: a good faith estimate of anticipated settlement costs and a HUD-1 or "Uniform Settlement Statement" that itemizes all the charges and expenses incurred by the buyer and the seller.

The good faith estimate of anticipated settlement costs breaks down all the different charges for which you will be responsible: loan fees, origination fees, inspections, points, interest rate, and terms. (We will discuss rates, fees, terms, etc. in a later chapter.) The good faith estimate is your protection against changes to the agreement that an unscrupulous lender may try to make at a later date.

The HUD-1 statement is a form that settlement agents, like title companies, are required to use to process mortgages. The rules require you to be furnished a copy of the HUD-1 statement at least one day before settlement, but sometimes that does not happen. There could be delays due to inefficiency on the part of the lender or the title company or simply because last-minute items like repairs have not been completed.

In any case, you should ask for a copy of the statement ahead of time so you can review it before you go to closing. Once you are at the closing, you will feel pressure to hurry up and complete the transaction. You are much better off taking the time to review it completely for accuracy and to make sure no agreements or terms have changed. Even though many HUD-1 statements detail transactions involving hundreds of thousands of dollars, you would be surprised how often mistakes are made. Review your statement carefully for any errors. It is a good idea to go so far as to check all the mathematical calculations, as mistakes can happen.

If you do not get a copy ahead of time, resist the temptation to rush and take time to review it thoroughly, even if the other parties are impatient. It is your money and your investment, and it has to be right for you. If they grow impatient, that is not your problem.

Once the closing is complete, the property is yours. The title officer or attorney will file the appropriate paperwork with the local government office, and in a few weeks, you will receive a copy of the deed to keep for your records.

Now that you understand the basic process of a real estate transaction, let us look a little more closely at a few of the key components and milestones of a real estate transaction.

OFFERS AND PURCHASE CONTRACTS

Whether you are selling a property or buying a second home, the price negotiations will be handled using "offers" or "purchase contracts." An offer is simply a document that states the terms of the transaction, such as personal information, price, the amount of time the offer is good for, time until closing, financing requirements, additional items contained in the purchase, and any contingencies. If you are using an agent to buy or sell a second home, he or she will use standard forms and will put the offer in writing for you.

Offers are not official contracts until both parties agree to them. If you make an offer on a property and it is not accepted, you are under no obligation to purchase the property. If, for instance, you state that your offer is good for three business days, at the end of three business days you are no longer required to purchase the property under the terms you originally stated. You can change any terms you like and make another offer.

If you are buying a house, in all likelihood the seller will counter-offer. Alternatively, if you are selling a house, you will probably counter the original offer from a potential buyer unless the buyer agrees to your initial price. The counter-offer is simply a change to the original offer. It can be a change in price, time until closing, contingencies, or it can be additional terms that were not included in the original offer.

Most offers also include contingency clauses. Contingencies are terms stating events that must take place for the sale to take place. If those events do not take place, the party is under no obligation to consummate the contract and faces no penalties for doing so.

The most common contingency seen on real estate contracts is that the buyer must qualify for financing under terms specified in the contract. For instance, a buyer may say the contract is contingent upon his qualifying for 6 percent conventional financing for a term of thirty years. If he is unable to qualify for financing, the sale will not take place, and the buyer is released from the contract and refunded his earnest money.

Contingencies can involve events that must take place or questions that must be answered. A contract could be contingent upon a property passing a home inspection by a qualified professional. Other contingencies can include radon testing, the sale of another property, an appraisal that shows the property value exceeds a certain amount, etc. Every offer to purchase real estate is unique, and unusual contingencies can and do come up. You, of course, have a choice to accept or reject those contingencies in your counter-offer.

In short, offers and purchase contracts are written statements of the terms under which you are willing to buy or sell a property.

FINANCING

Once an offer is accepted and both parties have signed, the buyer must seek financing, unless he is fortunate enough to be able to pay cash for the property. This is still unlikely since an investor with sufficient cash to purchase the property outright is generally savvy enough to leverage his or her capital by borrowing to purchase multiple properties.

The contract should specify that the buyer has a certain amount of time to seek and qualify for financing before the contract is invalid.

Many buyers will attempt to insert unreasonable financing contingencies in their contracts, such as qualifying for below market-rate financing. They can back out of the contract later if they do not qualify, which of course, is not likely. As a seller, you should not accept unrealistic contingencies, especially in regards to financing.

INSPECTIONS

Some inspections are required by state or local law, and others can be negotiated within the offer. Most lenders require a pest inspection, and many state or local governments require testing for radon levels, mold, lead paint, and other hazardous items. As a buyer, you can also require a home inspection by a qualified professional.

Home inspectors evaluate the structure of the house, identifying any issues with the roof, plumbing, electrical systems, heating and air conditioning units, appliances, windows and doors, chimneys, and other components of the property. Commercial inspectors fulfill the same role on commercial properties.

If problems are found during the inspection, you have two choices: either you can continue with the sale, or you can re-negotiate the contract. If the problems are minor, most sellers will agree to fix them to your satisfaction, so they do not lose the sale. If the problems are major, you can either renegotiate or go ahead and buy the property knowing that certain repairs will need to be made once you are the owner.

The period during which inspections must be completed should be noted on the purchase contract. If you are a buyer and you fail to meet the time frame for the home inspection, the seller is under no obligation to allow you to back out of the contract if a later inspection finds problems. To protect yourself, always make sure your inspections take place in a timely fashion per the agreed-upon time frames in the contract.

You will also want to do a final walk-through inspection as close to closing as possible to make sure the property is in the same condition it was in when you agreed to purchase it. If you can, conduct your final walk-through after the owners have vacated the property, so you can make sure no damage occurred during the moving process.

TITLE

In its simplest form, the title to a property is simply the proof of ownership. If you have title, you own the property.

As you probably guessed by now, it is not quite that simple. If you borrowed money to buy the house, you do not own it outright until you pay off the loan. Depending on the state you live in, your title is encumbered either by a deed of trust or by a mortgage.

Roughly speaking, they both amount to the same thing. If you do not make your payments per your agreement in a mortgage state, the lender has the right to sell the property to recover the money. In a deed of trust state, an attorney must go to court to get the right to sell the property, so the lender can recover his money. The distinction between deed of trust states and mortgage states is unimportant. All you need to know is that you do not truly own the property until you have paid off your loan.

To ensure that the seller's title to the property is valid, a title search or title examination will be conducted. Most people use the term "clear title" to describe a case where the owner has full right and privilege to sell a property. The examiner, typically a paralegal or lawyer, will look at past deeds, wills, and trusts to make sure all past owners have released their claims to the property. The examiner will also try to verify that any mortgages, judgments, or other liens have been paid and officially released.

TITLE INSURANCE

If you need a mortgage, you will have to purchase title insurance, because all mortgage lenders require it for an amount equal to the loan. The policy stays in effect until the loan is repaid.

The buyer pays the premium at the time of closing. Title insurance protects against loss arising from problems connected to the title to your property. Before you purchased your home, it may have gone through several ownership changes, and the land on which it stands might have gone through many more. There may be a weak link in that chain which could pop up and cause trouble. For example, someone along the way may have forged a signature in transferring title, or there may be unpaid real estate taxes or other liens. Title insurance covers the insured party for any claims and legal fees that arise out of such problems.

Title insurance protects against losses arising from events that occurred prior to the date of the policy. Coverage ends on the day the policy is issued and extends backwards in time for an indefinite period. This is in stark contrast to property or life insurance, which protect against losses resulting from events that occur after the policy is issued for a specified period into the future.

The title insurance required by the lender protects the lender up to the amount of the mortgage, but it does not protect your equity in the property. For that, you need an owner's title policy for the full value of the home. In many areas, sellers pay for owner policies as part of their obligation to deliver good title to the buyer. In other areas, borrowers must buy it as an add-on to the lender policy. Many experts recommend doing this because the additional cost, above the cost of the lender policy you have to get, is relatively small.

Protection under an owner's policy lasts as long as the owner or any heirs have an interest in or any obligation with regard to the property. When they sell, however, the lender will require the purchaser to obtain a new policy. That protects the lender against any liens or other claims against the property that may have risen since the date of the previous policy. In other words, it protects the lender against something you may have done.

For example, if the contractor you failed to pay for remodeling your kitchen places a lien on your home, you are not protected by your title policy, because the lien was placed after the date of the policy. You will probably be required to get the lien removed before you can sell the property. In the event the lien has not been removed and a search has failed to uncover it, the new lender will be protected by a new policy.

You can shop around for title insurance. Unlike mortgage insurance, where the lender always selects the carrier, borrowers can select the title insurance carrier. However, most leave it up to one of the professionals with whom they are dealing: the real estate agent, the lender, or their attorney. This means that competition among title insurers is largely directed toward the professionals who can direct business rather than toward borrowers.

In addition, it can pay to shop around. It is difficult to generalize because market conditions vary state by state and sometimes within states. It makes sense to shop in states that do not regulate title insurance rates. These states are Alabama, District of Columbia, Georgia, Hawaii, Illinois, Indiana, Massachusetts, Oklahoma, and West Virginia.

You would be wasting your time shopping in Texas and New Mexico, because these states set the prices for all carriers. Florida also sets title insurance premiums but not other title-related charges, which can vary.

In the remaining states, it may or may not pay to shop around. Insurance premiums are the same for all carriers in "rating bureau states:" Pennsylvania, New York, New Jersey, Ohio, and Delaware. These states authorize title insurers to file for approval of a single rate schedule for all carriers through a cooperative entity. Yet in some, there may be flexibility in title-related charges. More promising are "file and use" states, all those not mentioned above, that permit premiums to vary between insurers.

It is a good idea to ask an informed but disinterested person whether it pays to shop in the area where the property is located. Just keep in mind that those likely to be the best informed are also likely to have an interest in directing your business in the direction that is to their advantage.

Title insurance protects against losses that might occur due to another party claiming ownership of the property, and it covers:

- Issues missed by the title examiner.

- Issues missed when a deed or other public document is determined to be invalid or forged.

- Liens from unpaid taxes or from a former owner.

Title insurance will pay your legal fees if you have to go to court to defend the deed. If you lose the property, the title insurance will cover your loss up to the amount of the policy.

Keep in mind that if you have owned the property for a few years and it has risen in value, the title insurance policy you purchased at closing will only reimburse you for the original amount, not for the new value of the property.

You may be thinking, "Wait a minute. If I pay an attorney to perform a title search, why do I need title insurance? Is not it the attorney's job to make sure the title is clear?" Yes, it is, but unexpected problems can pop up, and title insurance is a cheap way to avoid the cost of major problems that could occur.

CHAPTER THREE

DEVELOP A GREAT
RELATIONSHIP WITH
AN AGENT

While finding a real estate agent to partner with is not essential, it can save you considerable time and effort if you can build a positive business relationship. Lisa Chandler explains why.

My husband and I have owned a series of second homes. We enjoy using them as get-aways, but our main reason for buying and selling second homes is to make a profit. We've developed a great connection with a specific agent, and it helps us avoid the hassles of looking for the right property, sifting through all the homes that do not fit our needs, and just the hassles of working with different agents whom we do not know. There is another benefit to finding an agent to work with. Not only can the agent help you find a great house, but he or she is also the perfect person to list that house when the time comes to sell. Plus, our agent knows us. She knows what we like and do not like, what we're willing to spend, and what fixer-upper projects we're willing to take on. Since we do repeat business, she is very motivated to service us well, too. I will admit it has taken time to build that connection, but it has been worth it.

———

E very real estate sale requires two parties: the buyer and the seller. There is a third party involved in most real estate transactions, and that is the real estate agent. A good real estate agent can save you time, money, and effort.

Can you invest in real estate without the services of an agent? Of course you can, as long as you understand the pros and cons involved.

A real estate agent can play two basic roles: as a seller's agent or as a buyer's agent. In some states, a real estate agent can be a dual agent. By far the most common role an agent will play is that of a seller's agent. A seller's agent acts on behalf of the seller of the home to sell the property. Because he works for the seller, he cannot disclose confidential information to buyers of the property.

Let us take a closer look at the types of real estate agents and the role they can play to help you purchase a second home.

SELLER'S AGENTS

In the past, many buyers were not aware that the agent was not working on their behalf. After all, they may have seen a house they liked and called the agent, so shouldn't the agent be working for them? No. Some buyers would tell the agent the maximum they were willing to pay for the house, unaware that the agent could and would pass that information on to the seller.

As a result, agents are now required to disclose that they are agents for the seller, and in most cases, the disclosure must be in writing.

While seller's agents are working on behalf of the seller, they are required to disclose "material" facts. They must disclose material facts about property condition, for instance. If, for example, the roof is leaking, appliances are broken, or the heating system has failed, the agent is required to disclose those facts to potential buyers. Disclosure is also required if the property fails to meet zoning requirements or building codes.

Agents are not required to disclose personal information about the sellers, though. The agent does not have to tell a buyer how motivated the sellers are, what their bottom-line price is, why they reselling the home, etc.

BUYER'S AGENTS

Buyer's agents agree to work on the behalf of a buyer. They do not operate on behalf of the seller, so in effect the confidentiality relationship is reversed.

Most buyer's agents will require you to sign an exclusivity contract stating you will work only with them for a specified amount of time. In fact, some agreements state that you are required to pay the buyer's agent a commission even if you purchase a house using another agent. Why do they require an agreement? They will put a lot of work into finding a house for you and representing you, so they want some amount of guarantee their hard work will pay off.

Buyer's agents can be very helpful. They also are required to disclose material facts about properties. They can research past sales to help you determine how much to offer for a property, they can help you negotiate with the sellers and the seller's agent, and they can help walk you through the closing process.

Why are there fewer buyer's agents than seller's agents? It is simple. If an agent lists a house for sale, as long as the house sells, he or she is paid a commission. It does not matter whether the agent found the buyer or not, although the commission is higher if he does. A buyer's agent has to hope that you find the right house and complete the purchase; otherwise, his or her odds of earning a commission are lower.

If you use a buyer's agent, you can negotiate the terms of your agreement. For instance, you can specify:

- **The geographic area**. If you are looking at properties in a broad area, you can limit your agreement with the buyer's agent to a particular city or county.

- **The time period**. You can agree to a long-term relationship (thirty, sixty, or ninety days) or to a time period as short as one day or even the showing of one house. Keep in mind that the longer the term, the longer you are required to work with the agent. In general, the longer the term, the harder the agent will work for you.

- **Basic exceptions**. For example, you could negotiate that if you find a property that is being sold by its owner, you have the right to purchase it without paying the buyer's agent a commission.

If you use a buyer's agent, make sure you understand all the terms of the agreement. The contract can state any terms you both agree to, so make sure you fully understand what you are agreeing to.

DUAL AGENTS

A buyer's agent is a dual agent when showing a property listed by his or her real estate agency. Some states will not allow dual agency, as it is a little confusing, because the agent has responsibilities to both parties. The agent cannot disclose personal information to either client about the other, but still must make sure to meet the needs of both. It is a tight line to walk for the agent.

It is easier to work with a dual agent if he or she is not the person who actually listed the property. In that case, the agent may not be aware of personal information about the sellers, so confidentiality is easier to maintain. If you have a buyer's agent agreement with a particular agent and she wants to show you a home she has listed, many firms will require the agent to "hand you off" to another agent in the firm for that showing and possible transaction.

Dual agency must be disclosed to both sellers and buyers in writing.

AGENT COMMISSIONS

If you are selling a home using an agent, you will pay a commission as a fee for the agent's services. If you buy a home, you pay no commission, even if you are using a buyer's agent. The seller will pay the commission.

Typical agent commissions range from 5 percent to 7 percent. That means if you sell your house for $100,000 and the agreement with your agent specifies a 6 percent commission, you will only net $94,000, because you paid the agent a commission of $6,000.

Your agent does not pocket the entire commission. He or she only gets a portion. While some agreements vary, especially for newer or inexperienced agents, a typical commission agreement works like this:

Your agent listed the house you are selling. We will say the commission rate you have agreed to is 6 percent. No matter who represents the buyer, your agent's company (agency) will get half of the commission, or 3 percent. The agent representing the buyers gets the other half. If your agent or his agency manages to find the buyer for your house, the agent's company gets the entire 6 percent.

Your agent will then split his company's share of the commission with the owner of the company. For instance, if your agent works for Century 21, the agent will split the 3 percent commission with the owner of his local agency. "Split" implies the 3 percent will be shared equally, and that is not always the case. Some agents get slightly more than half, and new agents typically get much less than half, sometimes as little as 30 percent.

For the sake of this exercise, pretend your house sold for $100,000. Let us look at three basic scenarios:

- **The buyer was represented by an agent from Coldwell Banker**. Coldwell Banker gets half of the 6 percent commission, or $3,000. Your agent's company, Century 21, gets the other half. Your agent's agreement with Century 21 is that he will receive half of the agency's share, so he gets $1,500. The owner of his local agency keeps the other $1,500. Therefore, even though the commission totaled $6,000, your agent received $1,500.

- **The buyer was represented by an agent from your agent's company**. It does not matter to your agent, though. He or she gets half of the 3 percent share of the commission, the other agent gets half of 3 percent, and the owner of the agency gets 3 percent, half from each side. Agencies like when their listings are sold by agents in-house, because that maximizes their return. In these cases, sometimes an agency will agree to lower an agreed-upon commission rate when the contract is being finalized, if that helps to sell the house.

- **The buyer is represented by your agent, who is the same agent who listed your house**. This is the dream scenario for both the agency and the agent. The agency still gets its 3 percent, and your agent keeps 3 percent. By selling your house himself, your agent doubled his commission. That is why agents invariably show potential buyers their own listings first.

Commission rates are negotiable by law. Let us say you are talking to an agent about listing your house, and she says her commission is 7 percent. You say you would only like to pay 6 percent. No law compels her to stay at 7 percent, but her agency may have rules that she is guided by. Some agents will automatically negotiate down to 6 percent or even 5 percent depending on how eager they are to list your house.

An estimated four out of five agents will negotiate their fee downwards. They want your listing, and it is how they earn a living. Five percent of an actual sale is a lot better than 6 percent of nothing.

Some agents will say that accepting a lower commission rate will affect their ability to market your home properly. If you are told that, find another agent. Others may try to convince you that if you will accept, say, a 7 percent commission rate, they can do a lot more marketing, and your home will have a better chance of selling.

Maybe some agents will actually spend more on marketing, but it is unlikely. The average firm has marketing guidelines for their agents to follow, and you should ask for a marketing plan as part of the requirements for an agent to list your house. Most agents will do similar things in terms of marketing. Skilled agents are good at finding and working with qualified buyers, and more advertising is not a guarantee of a greater likelihood of sale. In fact, more houses sell due to multiple listing services, which agents use to find out about all the properties available in their area, than due to newspaper or other print advertising.

Agents will sometimes say that if they accept a 5 percent commission rate that will keep other agents from showing your house, because if they find a buyer the commission rate is not worth it. That is also not true. Again, an agent would rather have a reduced share of something than a full share of nothing.

Agents will also reduce commission rates as part of the negotiation to list your home. Say you are selling your second home, and a buyer comes within $1,500 of your price. Your price is a bottom-line price, though, and you are not willing to go any lower. Your agent knows that, so she gets together with the buyer's agent and they agree to reduce the overall commission rate. The $1,500 comes out of their commission, the buyer gets the price he wants, and you get the price you want. Many times, agents will lower their commission if it means salvaging a deal they may otherwise lose. Again, most agents realize that a reduced share of something is better than a full share of nothing.

Feel free to negotiate commission rates. There is a saying many real estate professionals use: "List or die." Agents live by their listings. If the house sells, they are paid even if they did not find the buyer. Most agents will negotiate the commission rate downwards even if it is only by a half of a percent. Moreover, that half percent is worth it to you, because if your house sells for $200,000 and you have negotiated a commission rate .5 percent lower, you will have put $1,000 more in your pocket.

FINDING THE RIGHT AGENT FOR YOU

If you choose to use a real estate agent to help you purchase a second home, you will need to find the right agent. If you later decide to sell your second home or your primary home, you will want to find the right agent. Finding the right agent for you is critical.

Rarely do people actively look for the right agent. They usually just stumble over them. Perhaps they mention they are selling their house to a friend or relative, and that person recommends an agent. Typically, the process of selecting an agent is haphazard at best. That is a shame, since finding the right agent is one of the keys to maximizing your sales price if you are a seller and to weeding through all the properties for sale to find the right one for you.

One way people typically find an agent is at an open house. You walk in, look around, the agent seems nice, and you decide to use him or her. However, how do you know if the agent is skilled, experienced, and right for you?

Based on statistics from the National Association of REALTORS®, the typical agent makes less than $10,000 a year. That is due in part to how many part-time agents there are, but it is also because selling real estate is a tough business. It is hard to get started and even harder to succeed.

Many times people will start selling real estate part-time and hope to get established so they can quit their full-time jobs. The problem is they cannot dedicate themselves full-time to selling real estate, and they may be unable to show your house when it is convenient for a potential buyer. On the other hand, they may not be able to show a house to you when it is convenient for you.

Ideally, you want a full-time agent, and there are very few exceptions to this rule. You need someone working for you who makes his or her living selling real estate. The more motivated and committed agents are, the harder they will work for you.

The following are ways to find the best agent for you.

Get Recommendations

When you look for representation or an agent to work with, you should not just trust that the right person will appear. You are hiring someone. You would not hire the first person who asked for a job in other situations. Ask your friends and neighbors. Do they know a good REALTOR®? Is there anyone that they would specifically recommend? Do they know any that you should avoid? If they have had bad experiences, they will be sure to tell you about them. Ask for input, and consider all recommendations. That should help you arrive at a better decision. It will at least increase your odds of getting a better agent than if you randomly choose someone. Unfortunately, it is still no guarantee. Sometimes a "good" agent is still not the right agent for you.

Ask people if they know of any good real estate companies in the area. You are not looking for an agent yet. Once you have resolved in your own mind that the information on the best companies has been supplied to you, call one high on the list. Ask to speak to the manager or the broker owner. Ask, based on your particular set of circumstances, whom he or she would recommend if they were in your shoes. That is your best shot at getting the best match for your needs.

You might think the owner or manager will steer you to an inexperienced agent, but that is unlikely to happen. The owner makes money when houses sell, and does not have a vested interest in which agent makes the sale. He or she will want to place you with the best person, because that maximizes the chance of a sale.

Look for Expertise

Not all agents are experts in the area you need. They may be great, but they may be working a different geographical market entirely. They may be the best commercial specialists in town, but you need a good residential broker. They might be the best high-end agent you can find, but might be weak when working with buyers looking for investment properties or for vacation homes.

With real estate agents, just like with doctors, there are specialties within specialties. Just as one doctor will recommend another doctor, a good agent will not hesitate to recommend another agent if he thinks another agent's expertise is better suited to the task. These agents will be smart enough to put themselves in for a little referral fee, but do not kid yourself on that point. Some brokers will tell their agents, especially with respect to geography, to "refer out" leads. As a rule of thumb, the advice they gives agents is, "If you do not know where it is and you cannot easily find it on the map, you should probably look for an agent who knows that market better than you do."

Does the agent who makes the referral lose money? Some, but in all likelihood that agent would not have sold the house anyway, and most will receive a referral fee from the agent they refer your listing to.

Expertise also has to do with time in the business. Is the agent new to the business? It is not your job to help a new agent get started. It is your goal to find a great second home and to negotiate a great price. You want someone who is highly recommended and has been involved in a number of transactions. You want someone who can deal with complications and obstacles and has a track record of making and closing sales.

Look for a Good Reputation

Reputations are earned by doing good work and having good credentials. In terms of credentials, many agents have acronyms like GRI or CRS after their names. The first one denotes they are graduates of the Real Estate Institute, and they have taken and passed an extra five courses of study in real estate beyond the statutory requirement. The GRI courses are excellent, and agents are given special credit they can use to fulfill any continuing educational requirements they may have. Oddly enough, most states have very low educational requirements to become a licensed real estate agent. New York's is relatively difficult, and yet it still only insists on a minimum of forty-five hours of pre-licensing training.

Agents with the GRI designation are well regarded in the business. It is no guarantee of performance, though. Objectively speaking, the GRI courses are valuable and offer very good training for those who want to improve themselves in the business.

Another designation is the CRS or Certified Residential Specialist. This is the next degree up from the GRI, as the GRI is a prerequisite for the CRS. Once again, the designation is not a clear guarantee of performance.

A good way to determine an agent's reputation is to review any letters of recommendation or commendations the manager may have with respect to a particular agent.

Assess the Agent's Drive

"Drive" refers to determination, motivation, and commitment. Many agents have a number of awards and plaques on their walls, which is usually a good sign and means they are top performers. Be careful of a few things, however. Ask about the agent's performance not just based on volume, but on style. Many agents sell millions of dollars worth of real estate each year, but you might not want to work with them. They may be top producers who care nothing about the quality of their listing performance. In other words, they might sell three million worth of houses a year, but also have two million in properties they did not sell.

Again, it might seem odd to ask the owner of a real estate brokerage for a recommendation. Remember, they want to work through their firms, and very few people ask the owner for recommendations. You are very likely to get good input from a person who has a vested interest in your happiness, because the only way you will be happy is if you find the right house.

ESTABLISHING EXPECTATIONS

Once you have found the right agent, take the time to make your expectations clear. Describe the types of houses you are looking for. Be clear about your preferences in terms of location, school districts, number of bedrooms and bathrooms, size of yard, and everything that is important to you. In particular, make sure you give your agent the price range you are comfortable with or can afford.

Explain how you would like the agent to work with you. Some buyers prefer to have a listing sheet or a description of a property faxed or mailed to them ahead of time. They will review those sheets and select the properties they would like to view. Others are willing to let the agent create a list of appropriate properties without any input from the buyer. How you want to handle sorting through properties is up to you.

As you are looking at potential second homes, give your agent feedback. Let him or her know what you did and did not like about each house. The more the agent knows about your interests, the better job he or she can do. Do not expect an agent to find a perfect house right away, because it will not happen. The typical buyer looks at eight to ten houses before making an offer on one.

Unless you are using a buyer's agent, keep in mind that the agent really does not work for you. The agent works for the seller, but he or she wants to find the right house for you in order to make a sale. Let your agent know what you like and what you do not like, and put him or her to work for you. Your agent may not have a stake in ensuring you get the best deal possible, but he or she does have a vested interest in finding a

CHAPTER FOUR

CHOOSING THE RIGHT LOCATION

The words "dream vacation home" mean different things to different people, and sometimes different things to the same people as time goes by. Randy Mitzelfelt has owned second homes on the beachfront, at a ski resort, and in the mountains. Here is his take on the concept of a "dream vacation home."

We were so happy when we finally bought our home at the beach. We love the beach, and we could picture ourselves spending a few weeks every summer at our own home, not at someone else's house. And it worked out great, because we were able to cover almost all of our costs by renting the home to other vacationers. I never would have imagined it, but after a few years, we realized we did not like being tied to the beach for our vacations – it would be nice to go somewhere else sometimes and not feel bad that we were not using our second home. We couldn't afford a third vacation home, so after a lot of soul-searching we decided to sell the house and buy another home in the mountains. The experience taught me an important lesson. No matter how sure we are that we'll love to have a home in a certain location, things do change. We make sure the home we pick seems like a place with good appreciation potential, and that will hopefully be easy to re-sell. We learned not to ignore the thought of one day selling the home, because you never know.

E arlier we discussed setting goals for your second home. Will it be a vacation home, a second residence, a rental property, or an investment you hope to sell quickly for a profit? Choosing a location is based on what your goal is for your second home.

Once you have determined your goals, choosing a location is a little easier. If you are interested in a vacation home, choosing the location is not too hard, as you will pick an area where you enjoy vacationing. If you are interested in a second residence, the same thing is true. Where do you want to live? If you are buying a second home for income or as an investment, determining the right location has more to do with the financial possibilities of the investment than with your "enjoyment" of the property. In the end, your enjoyment will come from making a great investment.

VACATION HOME

Choosing the right location for a vacation home is completely up to you. Your primary consideration should be, "Where do I want to go on vacation?" You most likely already know where you would like a home. If you like the beach, you probably already have a favorite. If you like to ski, there is probably a ski resort you love. If you like to go boating or fishing, there is almost certainly a lake or river on which you have dreamed of living.

The key to picking a location for a vacation home is to keep in mind that you will be making a significant investment. Make sure the location you choose is one you can see yourself enjoying for years to come. Otherwise, and there's nothing wrong with this choice, you are buying an investment home in a resort or vacation area.

Most people combine the two. They buy a vacation home in an area they love, and they help finance the purchase by renting or leasing the property to others. The vast majority of people who buy a second home in a vacation area hope to rent the property for all but three or four weeks out of the year. During those "free" weeks, they vacation in the home.

Once you have decided on a location, you need to find the right property. If the location is far from your primary residence, house hunting can be a little trickier. Here are some tips to make house hunting a little easier from a distance:

- **Use a portion of every vacation you take to look at potential properties**. Check out the area, look at available homes, and talk to real estate agents. Get a sense of the market and the possibilities for you.

- **Spend time driving around the area**. Look for shopping centers, stores, schools, and recreation areas. Try to get a feel for different neighborhoods. Your goal is to try to find areas or neighborhoods in which you are comfortable.

- **Talk to people**. Ask them about the area. What do they like, what don't they like, and what are the schools like? If you want, tell them you are considering buying a home in the area. Ask them where they would look if they were you. You will be surprised at what information you can get.

- **Scan through the newspaper(s)**. Do not look only at the homes listed for sale, but also check the rental ads to get a feel for how many properties are available for rent and in what price ranges. Also, look for articles about new developments, housing trends, and other real estate information. If you are serious about the area, you may want to subscribe to the paper for a few months, but first check to see if the paper and its classified ads can be accessed online.

- **Talk to a few real estate agents**. Tell them what you are looking for and that you are in the early stages of your house hunting. Ask them to provide or send you information about the properties currently for sale. A good agent will keep in touch with you, even if you are not likely to buy a home in the near future.

Keep in mind that unless you can afford to make two house payments, a vacation home will also need to generate rental income. The majority of second homebuyers find themselves in this situation. The location you choose cannot be selected only by deciding where you want to live. You also need to take into account how attractive the property will be to prospective renters.

Once you have found a location you like, a real estate agent can be a tremendous help. The agent can provide you with information about other properties in the area, such as rental amounts, vacancy percentages, average property management costs for the area, and other information that helps you assess the income and investment potential of the house. We will look more closely at how to assess the investment potential, income potential, and financial implications of a second home purchase a little later.

SECOND RESIDENCE

If you are buying a second home to use as a second residence, the same considerations apply as for a vacation home. Where do you want to live? Where would you like to spend a portion, for some people even as much as half, of the year?

If you plan to rent the home while you are not in residence, the same considerations apply as well.

A major difference between a second residence and a vacation home is the amount of time you will spend living in the home. Many people live in their second home for months at a time. If that will be the case, it is even more important that you choose the right location. You are not just vacationing in the home, but you are living in the home.

To make sure you are comfortable with the area, consider taking a short-term lease on an apartment nearby. Living in the area will help you get a feel for shopping, traffic patterns, and neighborhood conditions, and this will go a long way toward confirming your choice of location. While a short-term lease may cost a little, see it as an investment. You are making sure the second home you buy is in a location and an area you will love. Look at a short-term lease as "better safe than sorry" insurance and a way to check out the area.

INCOME PROPERTIES

Simply put, the better the location, the more you can improve both the house and its value and the more income you can generate from rent. If the overall real estate market heats up, better areas appreciate more. In less desirable areas, you will not be able to get back your investment on anything other than basic improvements, unless you buy at extremely cheap levels. Even if you intend to live or vacation in the home, you still want it to increase in value. You are making an investment, and it should pay off. Happily, you can combine both of your goals. You can find a location you like and you can find a property with wealth building potential. The two are in no way mutually exclusive goals.

For example, there are older neighborhoods in nearly every city with small 900-square-foot homes built in the 1940's and 1950's. If they are near a university, downtown, or other desirable location, their value has probably soared. Yet, these same types of homes built near an airport or commercial center will sell for tens of thousands less and will be much harder to sell.

Here is an example. A couple found a 1950's two-bedroom, brick cottage near a private college and close to an upscale shopping area. The house was an estate sale and had not been upgraded, but they got a good deal on it and were excited at its potential.

Looking at other homes in the neighborhood, they noticed that most had been remodeled or upgraded. It turned out that their home was the least attractive on the street. It was a great opportunity, and they took advantage of it by painting, restoring the woodwork, and upgrading the kitchen, furnace, and wiring. A few years later, when they outgrew their home, they had accumulated enough equity to put a sizable down payment on their next home.

So what did they do correctly?

First, they focused on location. They looked for a neighborhood with homes likely to rise in value near a college, university, or popular shopping area. It was an area that would appeal to young professionals who did not like a long commute, where homes had charm, and where similar-minded homebuyers were moving in and renovating.

Second, they were careful about the money they put into the home. A large percentage of their upgrading required their own labor and cosmetic repairs. The money they did spend on a new furnace, roof, and kitchen went where it would give them the best return.

Third, they realized that eventually the house would be too small and they would have to sell and move to a bigger home. Their plan was to accumulate as much equity as possible, and they kept their eye on what homes were selling for in the area.

Choosing a second home in a good location has two major benefits. You will enjoy the home more because of the location. What makes a neighborhood "hot" are positives like good schools, well-kept homes, convenience, and livability. These things make the neighborhood or area a great place to live. Homes in good locations appreciate more quickly than homes in less desirable areas for the same reason, because people want to live there and are willing to pay more for the privilege. Choosing the right location lets you win twice. You will love the area, and your investment will be more likely to pay off.

One of the biggest contributors to the desirability of an area is the school system. The quality and reputation of local schools should be an important consideration for you even if you do not have children. However, if you are buying a vacation home, then proximity to the beach, ski resort, or local attractions is the most important factor. An area that has a reputation for good schools will have homebuyers actively seeking homes. REALTORS® will advertise that their listings fall within certain school boundaries knowing they will attract serious homebuyers.

When you can find a good area with desirable schools, you have a powerful combination for rapid home appreciation. In a seller's market, these homes will appreciate faster and will hold their value better in a down market. You can go to web sites like **SchoolMatch.com** and key in data for the schools in your area of interest to find out how they are rated. This, however, is only one tool at your disposal, and you will need to talk to parents in the neighborhood to get a realistic picture.

The bottom line is to go for the best location you can afford. A bigger house in a less desirable area is not as good a deal as a smaller home in a better area. In addition, always factor in the school system, because it influences an area's desirability and value. Even if the dog and cat are all the family you will ever have, it is still wise to buy in a good school district. Resale is easier and more profitable if the area has a reputation for good schools.

WHAT TO LOOK FOR – AND TO LOOK OUT FOR

What to Look For:

- Find areas close to colleges, upscale shopping, and cultural and sporting events. You will notice that people are spending significant sums remodeling older homes.

- Find out what areas have the best schools, and look for available homes within their boundaries.

- Look for areas that are close to where young professionals work and where they are moving. When it is time for you to sell and move up, these are the buyers you want to attract.

- If prices in your interest area have steadily increased over the past few years, that is a good sign. Reasonably priced starter homes may be hard to find.

- New areas and subdivisions can be a good way to go. Values will tend to go up in the long term.

What to Look Out For:

- Avoid buying on busy streets and in high traffic areas.

- If the schools do not have a good reputation, this may be an indication the area is going downhill. If so, home values will follow.

- Before you buy, check out what type of people live in the area. If they are low wage earners, you may have a problem selling for top dollar a few years down the road.

- If there are a lot of good deals and concessions, there is a reason. It is usually not too hard to find out why if you look around and talk to people in the area.

- If it is a new subdivision of starter homes and you plan to move on in about five years, others who bought at the same time may also want to move. This may put more homes up for sale than the market can handle, and prices can decline or at least stay flat in the short term.

EVALUATING PROPERTIES

If you have done your homework and have identified the area where you want to purchase a second home, you are ready to start evaluating properties. Looking at houses is a lot like prospecting, and you should take the time to prepare yourself before hitting the streets.

Use the property-listing sheet provided by the real estate agent or homeowner as the first step before touring the house. There is a tremendous amount of property information on a real estate listing sheet, even though at first glance it reads like a laundry list. Nevertheless, the more listing sheets you read, the more you begin to dissect the information and get an idea of what to expect when you tour the property. Before visiting any property, spend time reading between the lines of a listing sheet, and use it as a starting point for questions and investigation.

Real estate agents use the Multiple Listing Service (MLS) to electronically exchange listing information about properties. Years ago, the information was kept on paper in binders or on note cards. While earlier information was cryptic and often contained limited descriptions, agents today, and more importantly, you, can retrieve listing information instantly. Listing information contains the vital signs of a house, including approximate square footage, architectural style, the year it was built, sizes and numbers of rooms, type of heating and cooling system, type of siding, condition of windows and roof, school district where it is located, which appliances are included, and the asking price and yearly taxes.

In the "remarks" section of a listing sheet, you will find statements about features the listing agent wants to highlight such as "immaculate throughout this darling cottage." Depending on the writing skills of the listing agent, a listing sheet can exaggerate conditions with superlatives or provide no real details at all.

The listing sheet is your first exposure to a property, but it is basically a fact sheet used as a sales tool. You will not find negative information on the sheet, so it is up to you to inspect the property. Your first impression of a property is important, and your reaction will probably be similar to that of other prospective buyers. Make sure you do not overlook aspects of the property that cannot be changed economically. Here are some trouble spots of which to be aware:

- **Standing water on the lot**. Standing water on the property can be a sign of poor drainage, which can be the cause of a wet basement or a settling or cracked foundation. Be sure to walk around the lot and note any damp, mossy areas and places where grass does not grow. Some drainage problems are easy to fix, but if the lot seems damp or you see standing water, make sure you investigate further.

- **Water and moisture damage**. Rain, snow, and moisture can cause damage to several parts of a house, such as wood rotting in the soffits where there is no ventilation or moss growing on roof shingles or the siding on the north side of the house. These telltale signs are a tip-off to look for other indications of water damage throughout the house, such as in the attic for signs of rotten sheeting or rafters.

  Dampness can also promote the growth of mold and mildew, which means more trouble. Water damage can be prevented with proper maintenance, but if neglected over time, the damage can be expensive to repair. Any signs of neglect should cause you to take a second look.

- **Structural problems**. Major structural problems such as a cracked or settling foundation can be very expensive to fix. Unless you can get a firm estimate on the repair cost and use the amount to negotiate a lower purchase price, do not consider the property. Carefully explore the cause of large cracks in walls, especially in corners. Large horizontal cracks can be a tip-off to foundation movement.

- **Underground tanks**. Underground tanks of any type can become an environmental disaster if they have been leaking for years. Be sure to check the location of heating oil, propane, or gasoline tanks on the property. You do not want to discover when excavating the foundation for an addition that you have a large oil spill in the backyard.

- **Well and septic systems**. If the property does not have public water and sewer, ask about the condition of its well and septic system. Septic field failure can produce wet areas and poor drainage.

Evaluating Appliances

Once you have taken a high-level look at the lot and the house, do not forget to check out the appliances. Appliances have a useful life, and after that, it often is more expensive to repair than replace the unit. Carefully note the condition of each appliance. Even if you plan a kitchen makeover, many times you can reuse the appliances. Here is a guide to how long appliances typically last.

APPLIANCE	AVERAGE USEFUL LIFE
Air conditioner, room	2 years
Cook top, double, built-in	21 years
Cook top, single, built-in	13 years
Dehumidifier	11 years
Dishwasher	13 years
Disposal	12 years
Dryer	13 years
Oven, built-in	16 years
Range, double-oven	18 years
Range, drop-in, single-oven	11 years
Range, slide-in, single-oven	17 years
Refrigerator	14 years
Trash compactor	4 years
Washer, front-load	11 years
Washer, top-load	14 years

After your first pass through a property, you will have a good feel for whether it should stay on your list of homes to investigate further. Your goal is to find the right area, the right location, and then the perfect house for your second home. In many ways, it is a process of elimination, so take the time to work through the process, and you will find a home you love.

ANALYZING PROPERTIES

Unless you have unlimited funds, you will want to get the best deal possible on your second home. Determining the right price to pay is an equation that is part science and part art. Jeff Stanley explains how he solves that equation.

The key to deciding the right price is to know as much as you can about the market. I own a beachfront home that is four hours away from where I live. I didn't want to just use an agent's or an appraiser's advice. I wanted to listen to everyone's opinions but also use what my heart told me. It is hard to have a "gut feel" if you do not have a sense of the market. I subscribed to the local paper and looked at house listings for six months to get a feel for listing prices, and I also kept track of the sales transactions to see what houses actually sold for. I also checked the MLS real estate Web sites constantly. Within a few months, I thought I had a good feel for the market, and when I drove to the beach, I decided to test myself: I drove by different houses for sale and tried to guess the listing price before I checked the actual listing. It turns out I could come within three or four percent of the actual price, so I decided my "gut" had gotten a decent education. You can get all the advice you want, but you owe it to yourself to develop your own sense of the market. You are the one who will be writing the check, so make sure you are comfortable with the amount you are writing on it.

————

The last thing you want to do is overpay for your second home. While the "value" of any property is by definition what someone else is ready and willing to pay for it, real estate values can be estimated with reasonable certainty.

The value of a property is usually determined by an appraisal. There are three basic types of appraisals: sales comparison, cost, and income capitalization.

- **Sales Comparison**: The sales comparison method estimates a property's value by comparing it to similar properties that recently sold in the area. Those properties are called comparables or "comps." An appraiser will compare comps to the subject property to help determine its value. Sales comparison appraisals are typically used to evaluate single-family homes, townhouses, and duplexes. If you are buying a second home to use as a residence, the sales comparison appraisal method is the most appropriate to use.

  Appraisers are generally required to compare the subject property to at least three comps. Since very few houses are identical, the appraiser will adjust the values according to some standard formulas. For instance, if the subject property has a deck and a comp does not, the appraiser will adjust the value of the subject property upwards to compensate for the additional feature.

  Sales comparison appraisals are part "art" and part "science," because the appraiser has a fair amount of latitude within which to determine the value of the property. If two different appraisers evaluate a property, they will rarely agree on the property's value.

- **Cost**: The cost method determines a property's value
  by calculating how much it would cost to replace. The
  appraiser estimates the value of the property if it was
  new, then deducts an amount for depreciation based on
  the property's current condition. The value of the land is
  determined by using recent sales of comps. **Note:** There is
  no way to estimate land value by a cost method since the
  land cannot be replaced.

  Cost appraisals are more accurate when the property is
  fairly new, since it is easier to estimate the replacement
  cost. Cost appraisals are also useful when a property is
  unique and suitable comparables cannot be found.

- **Income capitalization**: Income capitalization appraisals
  place a value on a property based on its ability to
  produce income. If you are buying a second home as a
  rental property or as a vacation property where you hope
  to receive income, an income capitalization appraisal
  will help you determine its value. Income capitalization
  appraisals are most commonly used to estimate the
  value of office buildings, commercial real estate, and
  other rental properties. Very seldom does an appraiser
  do an income capitalization appraisal; they are done
  by investors. In effect, the investor is determining how
  much he or she is willing to pay, which becomes what the
  property is worth. You will see why investors perform
  this calculation in a moment.

  The process is simple. First, calculate the gross income
  (rent) for the property, and then subtract an amount for
  typical operating expenses like loan payments, taxes,
  maintenance, insurance, and other costs. The result is the

net income the property is expected to provide.

Let us use the following simple example:

Gross income $50,000

Expenses $40,000

Net income $10,000

You have calculated that the property will produce $10,000 per year in net income. Now you can decide how much you are willing to pay for the property.

You can calculate the value by using the formula:

Value = net income / capitalization rate

The capitalization rate is the expected rate of return. Let us say that in this case you want to get at least a 10 percent rate of return. If you do not, you would rather invest your money elsewhere. The math is simple:

Value = $10,000 / 10%

Therefore, the value of the property to you is $100,000. That is the most you can pay in order to get a 10 percent rate of return. In effect, that is the property's value, at least to you.

Say you are willing to accept an 8 percent rate of return. Here is the formula:

Value = $10,000 / 8%

The value of the property is now $125,000. That is the

most you can pay in order to receive the 8 percent rate of return you want.

As you can see, an appraiser is not the right person to perform an income capitalization appraisal, as the appraiser does not know what rate of return you are seeking. The appraiser can perform a cost approach appraisal to provide a different view of the property's value, but if you are investing for income, the income capitalization approach is the only way to be sure you will get the rate of return you seek.

In summary, appraisals are important to buyers, sellers, and lenders. Lenders use appraisals to make sure they do not loan more than the property is worth. Sellers use appraisals to make sure they are not over-paying for a property, and buyers use appraisals to help them properly value their properties for sale. When you are buying a second home, an appraisal is a good way to feel comfortable with the price you are paying and to assess the income and investment potential of a property.

FOR INVESTORS, CASH FLOW IS KING

When you are evaluating a residential rental property that you wish to use to generate income, you are guided by the same principles you used to evaluate a home you would live in. You look at the location, condition, attractiveness, and investment potential, and you also evaluate its potential cash flow.

If your goal in purchasing a second home is to generate monthly income, you will need to purchase a property where the rental income exceeds your operating expenses. If you are not generating a profit every month, you are not generating income.

So what do you look for? Because it is intended to be a rental property, do not look for new homes or for houses with lots of features like hot tubs, whirlpools, and other amenities. Renters typically will not pay more for those features, and they create more opportunity for repair and maintenance costs. The ideal home is a solid house in a well-maintained neighborhood. It does not need to be fancy, just clean, neat, and easy for you to maintain. If you are buying a vacation home, the same thing is true, unless it is intended to be a luxury home. Vacationers will rent the home because it is on the beach, on the slopes, or on the lake, not because it has the latest in kitchen technology. The ideal property is clean, neat, and easy to maintain.

You can also find a property in poor repair to refurbish before you rent it. We will discuss refurbishing and rehabbing later.

Here is an example of a good single unit rental investment. A young woman bought a small, three-bedroom brick ranch in an older neighborhood for $110,000. Unbelievably, in some areas, deals like that still exist. The neighborhood was well established, and most of the owners kept their homes in good repair. The house was also in a good school district. The roof had been replaced a few years earlier and so had the heating system. She anticipated very little expense in terms of maintenance costs, at least for the first few years.

Her "target" renter was a small family, possibly a couple with one child, or a single parent with two children, eager to live in a house instead of an apartment. Fortunately, that target market is reasonably extensive, because a large percentage of families do not have adequate credit or cash to purchase a home of their own.

Her anticipated expenses, including her mortgage, totaled approximately $675. After a survey of rental properties in the area, she determined he could easily rent the home for $775. That net operating income of $1,200 per year may not sound like a lot, but in her mind, it was enough to take on the risk of buying the property.

She also saw further potential. The home was located minutes from a local college where parking space was limited. The back of the lot had street access, and she created a parking area for three cars, renting each space for $40 per month to college students. In addition, the property contained a small garage, again at the back of the lot, that she rented as storage space to a local mechanic for $60 per month. Those two additions in revenue increased her net operating income to $2,400 per year, making her much more comfortable with the investment.

Some people buy more expensive houses with the intent to convert them to rental properties, but doing so carries more risk. The average person who can afford to rent a luxury home can probably afford to buy a luxury home. It is possible to make money by renting luxury homes to relocated executives while they purchase a home, but the chances of the property sitting vacant are much greater. If you pursue this option, make sure that the rent you net allows you to cover at least a few months per year worth of vacancies.

CHAPTER SIX

MORTGAGE BASICS

"The number of mortgage programs and packages available to second homebuyers has exploded in recent years, and it is likely there is a financing option available to fit your financial position. The only way to determine the best financing option for your needs is to make sure your mortgage provider understands your goals and intentions," explains Steve Runnells, President of America's First Home Mortgage in Frederick, Maryland.

The average second homebuyer intends either to live in the home as a second residence or to rent the home to generate income. Qualifying for financing for a second residence is similar to primary residence qualifying, and we look at your income, your current debt level, and your ability to repay the loan. If you are buying a second home as an investment property, the qualification process is a little different. We will not only evaluate your credit worthiness, but we will also look at the investment from a business perspective and take into account the anticipated rent, expenses you will incur, and other "business" factors. In general, you will get better and more flexible terms if the home will be a second residence, but there are a variety of ways we can structure the loan package depending on your particular situation.

Make sure you let the lender or broker know exactly what your intentions are for the home. Some clients are hesitant to detail their plans, so your best bet is to be as specific and detailed as possible. Mortgage brokers have a variety of tools and packages at their disposal, but without knowing your intentions and your situation, we cannot sift through the wide variety of programs to find the right loan for your needs.

———

T he price you pay for your second home is important, and you want to get the best deal you can.

However, getting an overall great deal does not end with the price you pay. If you cannot afford to pay cash for the home, then you will need to borrow the money, and the terms of the mortgage are extremely important. Getting a great deal involves negotiating a great purchase price and getting the best mortgage with the best terms possible. Understanding how mortgages work and how to find the best deal on your second home mortgage can save you thousands of dollars.

Let us start with the basics. Many borrowers begin looking for second homes with no idea of how much they can afford to pay for the home. You need to know approximately how much you can afford before you start to shop.

The amount you can spend on a house depends on your income, the amount of cash you can put down, and the mortgage terms available in the market at the time you are shopping. Terms include interest rates, points, length of the loan, down payment requirements, and the maximum allowable ratio of housing expense to income. In addition, affordability can be affected by your current level of debt if it is higher than the level that lenders are willing to accept. What you can afford is also affected by closing costs, which can vary from region to region.

There are three different calculations you can use to find out what you can afford. You should use all three and go by whichever result is the lowest.

CALCULATING HOW MUCH HOUSE YOU CAN AFFORD

The three methods you can use to determine how much house you can afford are the income rule, the debt rule, and the cash rule. To make the explanation easier, we will work through each method assuming you have already paid off your primary residence. If that is not the case, you will simply add together the debt you will incur between your first and your second homes.

If you ask a real estate agent how much you can afford, they will typically use a version of the income rule. The income rule says that your monthly housing expense (MHE), which is the sum of the mortgage payment, property taxes and homeowner insurance premium, cannot exceed a percentage of your income that is specified by the individual lender. Different lenders tend to have different thresholds. If the lender's maximum percentage is 28 percent, for example, and your monthly income is $4,000, your MHE cannot exceed $1,120. If taxes and insurance on the home are $200 per month, the maximum monthly mortgage payment you can handle is $920. At 7 percent interest for a 30-year loan, that payment will support a loan of $138,282. Assuming your down payment is 5 percent, the maximum price of the home you can afford would then be $145,561.

The debt rule says that your total housing expense (THE), which is the sum of the MHE plus monthly payments on existing debt, cannot exceed a percentage of your income specified by the lender. Using the same terms as above, if this maximum is 36 percent, for example, your monthly payment cannot exceed $1,440. If taxes and insurance are $200 a month and existing debt service is $240, the maximum mortgage payment you can afford is $1,000. At 7 percent interest and thirty years, this payment will support a loan of $150,308. Assuming a 5 percent down payment, the maximum price of the home you can afford would then be $158,218. This lets you buy a significantly higher-priced house than what we calculated using the income rule.

The cash rule says that you must have cash sufficient to meet the down payment requirement plus other settlement costs. If you have $12,000 and the sum of the down payment requirement and other settlement costs are 10 percent of the sale price, then the maximum sale price using the cash rule is $120,000. Since this is the lowest of the three maximums, it is the affordability estimate many experts recommend you use. Again, you are better off being safe than sorry.

When the cash rule sets the limit on the maximum sale price, as in the case above, the borrower is said to be "cash constrained." Affordability of a cash-constrained borrower can be raised by a reduction in the down payment requirement, a reduction in settlement costs, or access to an additional source of down payment, for example, from a relative.

When the income rule sets the limit on the maximum sale price, the borrower is said to be "income constrained." Affordability of an income-constrained borrower can be raised by a reduction in the maximum MHE ratio or access to additional income, like getting a second job or having your spouse enter the workforce.

When the debt rule sets the limit on the maximum sale price, the borrower is said to be "debt constrained." The affordability of a debt-constrained borrower, but not that of a cash-constrained or income-constrained borrower, can be increased by repaying debt.

How much house you can afford can be overestimated if you ignore one of the three rules and the one you ignored turns out to be the one generating the lowest maximum price. The affordability estimate will also be affected by changes in the assumed maximum MHE and THE ratios, which vary from loan program to program and can also vary with other characteristics of the loan, such as the down payment. Affordability may also be affected by changes in the assumptions made regarding settlement costs, taxes and insurance, interest rate, and term.

HOW MUCH YOU CAN AFFORD FROM A LENDER'S POINT OF VIEW

Individual lenders decide differently how much you can afford to borrow. They have a much different perspective than yours and will often be willing to lend you more money than you can realistically afford to pay back. Just because the bank is willing to lend you a certain amount of money does not mean that is the right thing for you to do. They are not saying it is a good idea for you to borrow that much. They are simply saying they are willing to do so, but the choice is still yours.

From a lender's point of view, a "good loan" is a borrower who can demonstrate both the ability and the willingness to repay it. Qualification has to do only with determining the borrower's ability to repay the loan. Your willingness to repay is determined largely by your past credit history.

For a loan to be approved, the lender must be satisfied as to your ability to repay and your willingness to repay. This is the difference between "qualification" and "approval." You may "qualify" if you have the ability to repay; you will be approved if you are also seen to be willing to repay.

Lenders ask two basic questions about a borrower's ability to pay. First, is the borrower's income large enough to service the new expenses associated with the loan, plus any existing debt obligations that will continue in the future? Second, does the borrower have enough cash to meet the up-front cash requirements of the loan? In other words, can you cover the down payment and closing costs? The lender must be satisfied on both counts for you to get approved for the loan.

In general, the lender assesses the adequacy of the borrower's income in terms of two ratios that have become standard in the business. The first is called the "housing expense ratio," and it is the sum of your monthly mortgage payment including mortgage insurance, property taxes, and hazard insurance, divided by your monthly income. The second is called the "total expense ratio," and it is the same, except that the numerator includes the borrower's existing debt service obligations. For each of their loan programs, lenders set maximums for these ratios, usually between 28 percent and 36 percent, which your actual ratios cannot exceed.

Maximum expense ratios actually vary from one loan program to another. Therefore, if you are only slightly over the limit, nothing more may be necessary than to find another loan program with higher maximum ratios. Usually that means you will pay a little more for the loan, too, because the greater the risk to the lender, the greater the cost of the loan will be to you. This is a situation where it is handy to be dealing with a mortgage broker who has access to loan programs from many lenders. We will discuss mortgage brokers a little later.

Even within one program, maximum expense ratios may vary with other characteristics of the transaction, and this can work against you. For instance, the maximum ratios are often lower, meaning more restrictive, for any of a long list of program "modifications." Some examples include:

- If the property contains two to four separate dwelling units.

- If the property is a co-op, a condominium, or a second home.

- If it is designed for investment rather than owner occupancy.

- If the borrower is self-employed.

- If the loan is a cash-out refinance.

- Combinations of any of these.

The maximum ratios are not carved in stone if the borrower can make a persuasive case for raising them.

Here are a few examples where the limits may be waived:

- The borrower is just slightly over the housing expense ratio but well below the total expense ratio, 29 percent and 30 percent, for example, when the maximums are 28 percent and 36 percent.

- The borrower has an impeccable credit record.

- The borrower is a first-time homebuyer who has been paying rent equal to 40 percent of income for three years and has a perfect payment record.

- The borrower is making a large down payment.

If expense ratios exceed the maximums, one possible option is to reduce the mortgage payment by extending the term. If the term is already thirty years, however, there is very little you can do, because few lenders offer 40-year loans.

If you have planned to make a down payment larger than the absolute minimum, you can use the cash that would otherwise have gone to the down payment to reduce your expense ratios. This can be done by paying off debt, paying points to reduce the interest rate, or funding a temporary buy-down.

A temporary buy-down is the most effective method. With a temporary buy-down, which some lenders allow on some programs, cash is placed in an escrow account, a deposit account maintained by the lender and funded by the borrower, from which the lender makes tax and insurance payments for the borrower as they come due. However, in this scenario, the cash is also used to supplement a borrower's mortgage payments in the early years of the loan.

For example, on a 2-1 buy-down, the mortgage payment in years one and two are calculated at rates 2 percent and 1 percent, respectively, below the rate on the loan. The borrower makes these lower payments in the early years, which are supplemented by withdrawals from the escrow account. The expense ratios are lower, because the payment used is a "bought-down" payment in the first month, rather than the total payment received by the lender. Borrowers sometimes can obtain the additional cash required to reduce their expense ratios from family members, friends, and employers, but the most frequent contributors in the United States are the home sellers, including contractors and builders. If the borrower is willing to pay the seller's price but cannot qualify for a loan, the cost to the seller of making the contribution the buyer needs to qualify may be less than the price reduction that would otherwise be needed to make the house saleable.

There may be circumstances where borrowers can change the income that the lenders use to qualify them for the loan. Lenders count only income that can be expected to continue, so they tend to disregard things like overtime and bonuses. The burden of proof is on you to show that such other sources of income can indeed be expected to continue. The best way to do that is to show that they have occurred over a considerable period in the past. If you can show that you have received bonuses consistently for the last few years, you have got a better chance of having that income included.

Borrowers who intend to share their house with another party can also consider the possibility of making that party a co-borrower. In that situation, the income used in the qualification process would include the co-borrower, too, and the co-borrower would be equally responsible for repaying the loan. If you and family or friends are purchasing a second home together, making them co-borrowers will increase your chances of qualifying for a loan and of being on favorable terms.

THE EFFECT OF DOWN PAYMENTS

To qualify for a loan, applicants typically need enough cash for the down payment and settlement costs. In the United States, however, mortgage insurance has substantially reduced down payment requirements, and the downside is the mortgage insurance premium, which is in effect like a higher interest rate.

On Federal Housing Administration (FHA) loans and Veterans Administration (VA) loans, down payment requirements have been largely eliminated, and all a borrower pays is an insurance premium to the government. On conventional (not FHA or VA) loans, borrowers who put down less than 20 percent have to pay for private mortgage insurance.

In general, lenders want borrowers who put less than 20 percent down to meet the requirement with funds they have saved, as opposed to gifts from family and friends. If relatives are willing to give or lend you a major chunk of the down payment, make sure the money is in your own account several months before you apply for a loan. The lender will not be thrilled that you have borrowed money for your down payment, because that is additional debt you will have to be able to pay back. If the money is in your account for more than three months, in all likelihood, the lender will not know where it came from, and the average lender only requires you to provide three month's worth of bank statements.

You can also get "zero-down" or 100 percent loans, as well as 107 percent and 125 percent loans. With these options, you do not even need money for closing costs. These loans carry higher interest rates in addition to mortgage insurance premiums, and they generally require that you have outstanding credit.

UNDERSTANDING CREDIT REPORTS AND CREDIT SCORES

When you apply for a loan, you will fill out a credit application. Initially the loan officer may take your information over the phone, but eventually you will need to complete the paperwork. The information you give will be used to obtain a credit report to determine your suitability for a loan.

Three large bureaus control America's credit information: Experian, TransUnion, and Equifax. Experian, the largest, maintains approximately 100 million credit files, processes over 35 million credit reports, and services hundreds of thousands of business subscribers. Banks, lenders, and nearly all businesses that extend credit pay a fee to obtain credit reports and credit scores. How you handled your debts in the past is a good indication of how you will handle future loans. Subscribers can also use your credit file to verify information on your credit application.

In short, lenders use your credit history and credit score to evaluate the amount of risk involved if they approve your loan.

What's on Your Credit Report

- **Identification information**: Full name, your last two addresses, social security number, date of birth, and place of employment.

- **Detailed information on listed accounts**: Name of the issuer, the date the account was opened, original balance or credit limit, the current balance, and the current status of the account.

- **Public record information**: Bankruptcies, tax liens, judgments, foreclosures, divorces, and other public filings.

- **Credit report requests**: Whenever someone requests a copy of your report, it is recorded and remains on your record for up to one year. Too many inquiries may cause a prospective lender to question why you were turned down so often, even though there are many possible reasons for inquiries.

- **Consumer statements**: You may challenge or explain any credit entry in your file with a 100-word maximum statement. The statement is then placed in your file and can be accessed by potential creditors.

How Your Score Is Calculated

Your credit score is one of the main factors any lender will use when deciding whether to approve your loan.

The three large credit bureaus use a ranking system called a FICO® score. For instance, the Equifax scoring system ranges from 300 to 850, and the average person has a score of around 700. The higher your score, the better the risk you are considered, and the more likely you are to receive loan approval. Statistically, individuals with scores less than 600 will default on a loan approximately 50 percent of the time.

Lenders use other factors, of course, to determine credit-worthiness, but your FICO® score is a commonly used tool that almost all lenders rely heavily on. What does it mean to you? People with higher FICO® scores get better rates on loans than those with lower scores.

Your score is broken down into five categories:

- Credit history

- Amount currently owed

- Length of credit history

- Type of credit used

- New credit obtained

Each category carries a different weight. The most important categories are your credit history and the amount you currently owe. If you have handled debt well in the past, you are a good risk to continue doing so, and how much you currently owe can greatly affect your ability to make payments on new loans.

Why You May Be Denied Credit

A low credit score is one reason you may not qualify for a loan. Here are some others:

- **Delinquent credit obligations**. Late payments, bad debts, or legal judgments make you a greater risk.

- **Incomplete credit application**. If you forget important information or make an error on your application, major discrepancies between your application and your credit file will raise a flag with a prospective lender.

- **Too many inquiries**. Creditor inquiries are noted on your report whenever you apply for credit. As few as four inquiries in six months may be considered excessive. Lenders can assume you are trying desperately to get credit and are being rejected frequently.

- **Errors in your file**. Credit bureaus handle millions of files, and they can make mistakes. The only way those errors can be found and corrected is if you review your credit file for accuracy and take steps to correct errors you find.

- **Insufficient credit file**. Your credit history may be too short for the type or amount of credit requested. For instance, if you have never had a loan or credit card, it may be difficult to quality for a home loan.

Your credit score is only one component of the final decision. Your income, employment history, assets, liabilities, and numerous other factors play a significant role in the decision to offer credit and the terms under which you receive that credit.

GET PRE-APPROVED, NOT JUST PRE-QUALIFIED

If you have looked at a home with a real estate agent before, you are familiar with the following scenario.

You meet the agent at the property. As you are walking through, the agent describes features of the home. The agent also casually asks you questions about yourself, like where you work, how long you have worked there, where you currently live, if you are renting or own your own home, etc.

Naturally, your agent is trying to get to know you. After all, they want to try to build a relationship, even if it is just a business relationship. But your agent is also determining if you are a serious buyer and if you will be able to qualify for a loan for the home you are visiting or for any home at all, for that matter. If you have noticed, the same thing happens when you visit a car dealership. Every agent is looking for serious, qualified buyers for the properties they show, and they will work harder for serious buyers.

An easy way to show you are a serious buyer and to improve your power in negotiations is to get pre-approved for a loan. You will immediately establish credibility as a serious buyer, and in a bidding contest between other buyers, your offer will carry more weight. Many people get pre-qualified, but pre-qualification is not the same thing as pre-approval.

Approval can take two forms:

- **Pre-qualified** simply means you have described your financial situation to a lender, and the lender is rendering an opinion about whether or not you will qualify for a loan. Pre-qualification is a lender's opinion based on information received. It does not mean the lender has reviewed your credit report, verified your information, etc.

  Simply put, a pre-qualification letter can be translated as, "I, the lender, feel this individual is probably qualified for a loan of this size if everything this individual told me about his or her financial situation is accurate. I have not tried to make sure the individual truly does qualify, however, so who knows how it will turn out in the end."

- **Pre-approved** means you have provided documentation proving income, assets, and liabilities, which is everything the lender needs to evaluate your credit-worthiness. The lender has checked your credit report, and most of the paperwork needed for your loan has been prepared. Sellers can be as certain as possible that a pre-approved buyer will be able to close on their home.

  A pre-approval letter can be translated as, "I, the lender, have reviewed all necessary documentation and have run appropriate credit checks to ensure that the individual will qualify for a loan of this size; therefore, I will make the loan to them."

As you can see, there is a big difference between being pre-qualified and pre-approved. Real estate agents know the difference, and some home sellers know it too. Getting a pre-approval letter provides several advantages that can save you time and money.

If you have been pre-approved:

- The seller can feel comfortable accepting your offer and taking his or her home off the market. In many cases a seller accepts an offer only to find out, sometimes weeks later, the buyer could not qualify for financing. That seller then has to put the home back on the market and lose valuable weeks of time and possibly miss a qualified buyer.

- A seller reviewing several offers will look more favorably upon your offer, because it is certain that you will be able to obtain financing. If an owner needs to sell a home quickly, for instance, many times he or she will accept a lower-priced contract from a buyer whom he or she knows can get financing.

- Completing the home purchase can be quicker. If you are pre-approved, much of the loan application work has already been done, possibly allowing your closing to take place sooner. Motivated sellers may further discount their home price if they know they can close quickly.

In short, you should shop for a loan and get pre-approved for financing before you start seriously looking at homes. At the very least, get pre-approved before you decide to make an offer on a property.

There are several reasons why most experts recommend being pre-approved before you start seriously looking at new homes:

- You will know exactly how much house you can afford, which will keep you from getting stretched too far when you are shown that house that you "just have to have."

- You will be in a better negotiating position when you do find the house you want.

- You will not be caught in the trap of hurriedly searching for a loan after you have found the house you want. Most home sales are contingent on your getting financing, and you are typically only allowed thirty days or so to get financing in place. It can be tough to shop around properly during that time, so if you do it ahead of time, you can find the best financing deal possible. The bigger hurry you are in, the more you will probably spend on your mortgage.

Keep in mind that getting pre-approved does not lock you into any one type of loan or even to working with a certain lender. It just lets sellers know that you can get financing if you make an offer on their house. You can still choose the right lender and the right loan later on. When you begin looking for a second home, it is important that you know exactly what you can afford and can make an offer on a house with the confidence that comes from knowing you can get financing. You will be in a better position to negotiate with the seller, and you will know exactly what price range of houses you should be looking for.

HOW THE LOAN APPROVAL PROCESS WORKS

Lenders will want documentation of your financial history, such as bank statements, pay stubs, W-2 forms, etc. Some loan types require lots of documentation and others, almost none. That is why they are called "no-doc" or no-documentation loans.

Here is a summary of each type:

- **Full documentation**. Both income and assets are disclosed and verified, and income is used in determining the applicant's ability to repay the mortgage. "Formal" verification requires the borrower's employer to verify employment and salary and the borrower's bank to verify deposits. "Alternative" documentation, designed to save time, accepts copies of the borrower's original bank statements, W-2s, and paycheck stubs.

  At one time, full documentation was the rule and it remained the standard. In recent years, however, other documentation programs have grown in use.

- **Stated income, verified assets**. Income is disclosed and the source of the income is verified, but the amount itself is not verified. You list how much you make, and your employer verifies that you are indeed employed, but the lender does not verify the amount you make. Assets are verified and must meet an adequacy standard, like six months of stated income and two months of expected monthly housing expense.

- **Stated income, stated assets**. Both income and assets are disclosed but not verified. However, the source of the borrower's income is verified.

- **No ratio.** Income is disclosed and verified but not used in qualifying the borrower. The standard rule that the borrower's housing expense cannot exceed some specified percent of income is ignored. Assets are disclosed and verified.

- **No income.** Income is not disclosed, but assets are disclosed and verified and must meet an adequacy standard.

- **Stated assets or no asset verification.** Assets are disclosed but not verified. Income is disclosed, verified, and used to qualify the applicant.

- **No assets.** Assets are not disclosed, but income is disclosed, verified, and used to qualify the applicant.

- **No income, no assets.** Neither income nor assets are disclosed. This is usually called a "no-doc" loan, because you are providing virtually no documentation to the lender.

While these categories are fairly well established in the lending market, there are many differences between individual lenders in the details. For example, under a stated income program, a lender may or may not require that an applicant sign a form authorizing the lender to request the applicant's tax returns from the IRS in the event the borrower defaults. Similarly, lenders differ in the amount of assets they require.

Why are there so many different documentation programs? Lenders have realized that many consumers with the potential for home ownership were shut out of the market by excessively rigid documentation requirements. It also dawned on lenders that documentation could be viewed as a risk factor that could be priced or offset by other risk factors. In other words, the less documentation you provide, the more risky your loan may be, but if the lender prices the loan high enough, who cares? If a borrower has excellent credit and is putting 25 percent down, for example, why should the lender worry too much about documentation?

Full documentation is the least risky to the lender, a no income/ no asset or no-doc loan is the most risky, and the others are in between. If the documentation level is riskier, the lenders will charge you more, will require a "risk offset," or will do both. The typical risk offsets are large down payments and high credit scores. The more risk, the more down payment the lender will want and the higher the credit rating they will expect you to have.

THE EFFECT OF YOUR CREDIT RATING

The change in lender attitudes toward documentation is similar to the change that occurred in connection with credit ratings. At one time, lenders would deal only with what are today classified as "A-credit" borrowers. Now, loans are available for "B-," "C-," and "D-credit" borrowers, but they are priced higher and may require offsets by other risk factors.

The change in attitudes toward both credit rating and documentation requirements has expanded the market. Here are some examples of borrowers who would not have qualified under full documentation requirements and how they qualify under current standards.

- Person A is a freelance writer with no fixed place of business who makes good money, but cannot document it. He can document his mutual funds, and his CPA can verify his self-employed status, so Person A qualifies under a stated income/verified assets plan.

- Person B is in the same business and uses the same CPA as Person A, but an uncle is gifting him with the cash he needs. Since Person B cannot document assets, he pays a little more under a stated income/stated asset program.

- Person C can document income and assets, but wants to allocate 58 percent of his income to housing expenses, which far exceeds conventional guidelines. Person C qualifies under a no-ratio loan.

- Person D is leaving her job to move to a new city where she has no job. She plans to buy a house when she gets there with money from the sale of her current house. She has no income and cannot document assets, because her old house will not be sold until after closing on the new one. Nevertheless, she qualifies under a no income/no asset program. If she has a contract of sale on the old house before closing on the new one, she will be able to document assets and can qualify under a no-income program.

A high credit score can help you qualify for a better loan, but how do you get one? Most people understand that if you do not pay your bills on time, your credit score suffers. There is a common misconception, however, that if you pay off these accounts, all will be forgiven. People assume that since the lender has been paid, their credit score will return to what it was before the delinquency occurred. However, it does not work that way.

Delinquencies reduce your credit score, because the credit-scoring models view delinquent accounts as evidence of a weak commitment toward meeting your obligations. The evidence is not wiped away when you repay the accounts. The delinquencies are still there and still impact your score. The only thing that will wipe them away is the passage of time and a better payment record.

A similar misconception is that consolidating credit card accounts into a smaller number of cards will improve your credit score. It will not if the consolidation of balances significantly raises the ratio of balances to available credit lines on the remaining cards. While the credit-scoring models do not like you to have many cards, the models look even less favorably on a high ratio of loan balances to maximum available lines, because it may indicate you are having financial difficulties.

Here is an example: Let us say you have five credit cards. Each card has a $5,000 limit, and you owe $1,500 on each card. Your total debt is $7,500. Each card has a 33 percent loan balance to available credit ratio. If you get a new credit card with a limit of $8,000, and transfer all the outstanding balances to that card, you still owe $7,500 total, but now your balance to available credit ratio is 93 percent.

To a credit bureau, it appears you have almost maxed out your credit power, and your rating will suffer.

If you have already consolidated and your credit score has been reduced, do not try to undo the damage by opening more accounts. The credit rating models look very unfavorably on multiple new accounts in a short period of time, because that can be another indicator of financial distress.

Credit inquiries affect credit scores negatively, because statistical studies show that multiple inquiries are associated with high risk of default. Distressed borrowers often contact many lenders hoping to find one who will approve them. On the other hand, multiple inquiries can also result from applicants shopping for the best deal.

To avoid penalizing loan "shoppers," credit ratings ignore inquiries that occur within 30 days of a score date. Suppose, for example, you shop a lender on June 30 and the lender has your credit scored that day. Even if you had shopped fifty other lenders in June and they had all checked your credit, none of those inquiries would affect your credit score on June 30.

However, inquiries from May and the previous eleven months would be counted on June 30. To avoid biasing the credit score from earlier shopping episodes, the scorers treat all inquiries that occur within any fourteen-day period as a single inquiry. If you shopped fifty lenders from June 1-14, they would count as one inquiry. If you spread them over June 1-28, they would count as two inquiries.

You will damage your credit if you spread your loan shopping over many months. The market can change from day to day, so it makes little sense to do so.

Circumstances can cause a consumer to shop, drop out of the market, and return later when conditions are more favorable. You minimize the adverse effect by concentrating each shopping episode within fourteen days or less.

Couples who purchase a home together often find that one of

them has good credit and the other one has the income required to qualify. Lenders, however, are concerned with the credit of the borrower(s) whose income is being used to qualify. Good credit on the part of a borrower without the means to pay is of no use. Income and credit cannot be separated, as they are both important.

BASIC FINANCING TERMS, FEATURES, AND COSTS

While loan types can vary, there are common terms and features to all. Let us look at each.

Interest Rate

An interest rate is the price of money, and a mortgage interest rate is the price of money loaned against the security of a specific property. The interest rate is used to calculate the interest payment the borrower owes the lender.

The rates you see quoted are annual rates. On most home mortgages, the interest payment is calculated monthly, so before calculating the payment, the rate is divided by twelve.

Take a six percent rate, for example, and assume a $100,000 loan. In decimals, six percent is .06 and .005 when divided by twelve. Multiply .005 times $100,000 and you get $500 as the monthly interest payment.

Suppose the borrower pays $600 this month. $500 of the payment covers the interest, and $100 is used to reduce the loan balance. One month later, when another payment is due, the balance is $99,900, and the interest is $499.50. The interest rate stays the same, but the interest payment portion is lower because the balance is lower.

The lower the interest rate you pay, the better off you are. However, you cannot say that about interest payments, which depend not only on the rate but also on the loan amount and the term. Reduce the loan amount and/or shorten the term, and interest payments will fall. Whether either is in your interest depends on the circumstances. Reduce the loan amount, and you need to come up with more cash for the down payment. Shorten the term and you have to make a larger monthly payment.

Points

Points are fees the borrower pays the lender at the time the loan is closed. They are expressed as a percent of the loan. On a $100,000 loan, three points means a cash payment of $3,000. Points are part of the cost of credit to the borrower, and part of the investment return to the lender.

Borrowers do not have to pay points if they do not want to. While the rate quotes you will see in the news media usually include points, virtually all lenders are willing to make no-point loans if you ask for them. Of course, the rate will be higher. The rate/point quotes you see in the news are what the lenders view as their "base" terms. However, they have other rate/point combinations they can pull out when they need to, especially if they are trying to land your business.

For example, a lender quoting 6.25 percent plus 2 points might also be offering 5.75 percent plus 4 points, 6.5 percent plus 0 points, and 7 percent plus a 1.5-point rebate. This means cash back to you, but you are paying a higher interest rate for the privilege of getting that rebate.

Points offer flexibility, but they also add complexity to a process that can already seem complicated enough. Most lenders can offer a wide variety of interest rate and points scenarios, but they typically do not show them to you unless you ask. It works out better for the lender that most people do not ask, as they do not have to give what they are not asked to give.

Some borrowers have little or no leeway, because they are "cash-short" or "income-short." If they are cash-short, they are required to avoid points in order to have enough cash to complete the deal. If they are income-short, they need to accept the lowest rate available so that the mortgage payment will not be viewed as excessive relative to their income.

If you have sufficient income and cash, you should be guided largely by how long you think you will keep the loan. If you expect to have the mortgage a long time, paying points to reduce the rate makes sense because you are going to enjoy the lower rate for a long time. If you plan on selling or refinancing in the near future, avoid points and pay the higher rate, because you will not be paying it for long.

The federal tax code treats points differently on purchase and refinancing transactions. Points paid in cash on a purchase transaction are fully deductible in the year the loan is closed. If the points are included in the loan, however, they are not deductible as points. The loan amount will be higher, and therefore interest deductions will be greater, but these deductions are spread over the life of the loan. If you finance the points and repay the loan early, much of the deduction derived from the points will be lost. The only way to deduct the full cost of points you pay is to pay them in cash, not finance them within the loan.

If you are refinancing, points paid in cash are deductible, but the deduction must be spread evenly over the term. If the points are $3,600 and the term is thirty years, for example, the deduction is just $10 a month. However, if you pay off the loan early, all unused deductions can be taken in the year of payoff. If the loan just mentioned is paid off after five years, for example, a deduction of $3,000 could be taken in the year of the payoff. In summary, points on a refinance that are included in the loan are treated in the same way as points on a purchase that are included in the loan.

Down Payment

In dollars, the down payment is the difference between the property value and loan amount. If value is $240,000 and the loan is $198,000, the down payment is $42,000.

In percentage terms, the down payment is one minus the LTV, the ratio of "Loan to Value." Since a loan of $198,000 is 82.5 percent of the value of $240,000, 1 minus .825 is .175, or 17.5 percent. When the LTV is above 80 percent, the down payment is less than 20 percent and the borrower must purchase mortgage insurance.

Many people confuse the down payment with the amount of cash they put into the transaction. In fact, the down payment amount is smaller because of settlement costs. For example, if you have $48,000 in cash and purchase a $240,000 house, your cash would be 20 percent of value. However, if settlement costs are $5,000, you are left with only $43,000 for the actual down payment.

If a house is appraised for more than the sale price, the difference cannot be counted as part of the down payment. The rule is that the property value used in determining the down payment and the LTV is the sale price or appraised value, whichever is lower. The only exception to this is when the seller provides a gift of equity to the buyer, who is usually a family member. In this case, the lender recognizes that the house is being priced below market and will accept the appraisal as the value. Most lenders in such cases will require two appraisals, and they will take the lower amount of the two.

A seller cannot help with a down payment, but the seller can pay some or all of the settlement costs as long as that arrangement is disclosed to the lender. That is just as good as having the seller give you money towards the down payment, since cash that you would have used to pay settlement costs is now available for the down payment. For this to work, the appraiser must say that the house is worth the higher price.

Here is an example: A seller offers his house to you for $200,000, and you are willing to pay that price. However, under the best financing terms available to you, you need $12,000 in cash, and you do not have it. You and the seller agree that he will raise the price of the house to $206,000, and he will gift you $6,000. Assuming the appraiser goes along with it, the amount of cash required of you drops from $12,000 to $6,360, making the purchase affordable if you have $6,360. The seller gets his price and you get your house, so everyone is happy, except maybe the lender.

If the house is actually only worth the original offer price of $200,000, the buyer has only $180 of real equity, the difference between the original property value and the higher loan amount, rather than $6,180. Less equity means greater loss for the lender if the loan goes into default.

For this reason, lenders and mortgage insurers limit seller contributions to buyers. The smaller the down payment requirement, the more critical the issue becomes. On conventional loans, it is common to restrict seller contributions to 3 percent of the sale price with 5 percent down and to 6 percent with 10 percent down. On FHA loans, sellers can contribute up to 6 percent of the price to the buyer's settlement costs, but nothing to the down payment.

PMI

Lenders require mortgage insurance on any loan that exceeds 80 percent of property value. Private mortgage insurance, usually called PMI, is that insurance. The larger the loan is relative to the value of the home, the higher the insurance premium will be. While the insurance premium is assessed against the entire loan, the cost should be allocated entirely to the portion of the loan that exceeds 80 percent of value.

Assume you can get a thirty-year fixed rate mortgage at 7.5 percent and zero points to purchase a $100,000 house. Without mortgage insurance, you could borrow up to $80,000, 80 percent of the property value, whereas with mortgage insurance you could borrow up to $95,000 or 95 percent of the property value. The insurance premium on the $95,000 loan is .79 percent of the balance per year for the first 10 years, after which it drops to .20 percent.

The best approach to measuring the cost of the insurance premium is to view the loan of $95,000 as two loans: one for $80,000, which has an interest cost of 7.5 percent consisting solely of the interest rate; and the other for $15,000, the cost of which includes both the interest rate and the insurance premium. The interest cost on the $15,000 loan turns out to be 12.7 percent if you stay in your house for up to ten years, declining slowly after that to 12 percent if you stay a full thirty years.

Since the insurance premium is only .79 percent, how can the cost of the $15,000 loan be 5.2 percent higher than the cost of the $80,000 loan? The reason is that while you are borrowing an additional $15,000, you pay the premium on the entire $95,000.

The cost calculation above assumes that you take a fixed-rate mortgage with a loan-to-value ratio of 95 percent and pay mortgage insurance for ten years. Change the assumptions, and you change the cost. For example, on 85 percent and 90 percent loans, the cost is 13.4 percent and 12.5 percent, respectively.

While the insurance premiums are smaller, the incremental loans are also smaller.

On smaller loans within the same mortgage insurance premium bracket, the cost is higher. For example, the cost of insurance on a 91 percent fixed-rate loan, which has the same premium as a 95 percent loan, is 14.3 percent.

Adjustable rate mortgages have higher insurance premiums and therefore higher costs than fixed-rate mortgages.

Mortgage insurance costs can be reduced if you manage to get the insurance removed early. For example, if the insurance on a 95 percent fixed-rate mortgage is removed in five years but you stay with the mortgage for ten, the cost falls to 10.8 percent. However, if you move in five years and pay off the mortgage, there are no savings.

Here is a handy rule of thumb for estimating the interest cost on the incremental loan made possible by mortgage insurance, assuming the loan runs ten years. Divide the total loan by the incremental loan and multiply the result by the annual insurance premium. For example, $95,000 divided by $15,000 equals $6.33, which when multiplied by .79 percent equals 5 percent. Adding that to the interest rate gives an estimated cost of 12.5 percent on the incremental $15,000 loan.

The choice between a smaller loan without insurance and a larger loan with insurance is an investment decision. Taking the smaller loan means investing $15,000 in a larger down payment that provides a risk free return of 12.5 percent.

If you do not have the $15,000, this is not an attractive investment. Even if you have it, you would be locking it up for an indefinite period, although you might borrow against it using a home equity loan. Alternatively, you may not be impressed with a 12.5 percent return if you can earn more than that in your business or are paying more on credit card loans. On the other hand, if you have a bond portfolio earning 7 percent, you might well want to liquidate it to invest in the larger down payment.

Avoiding PMI

In addition to putting 20 percent down, there are two other ways to avoid purchasing private mortgage insurance (PMI).

One way is to pay a higher interest rate instead of PMI. When a borrower accepts this option, the lender buys PMI for less than the borrower would have to pay. The higher interest rate covers the insurance cost to the lender plus a profit margin. Some but not all lenders offer this option.

Why would you consider this? The sales pitch for the higher

rate as a replacement for PMI is that interest is tax deductible whereas PMI premiums are not.

The other side of the coin, however, is that you must pay the higher interest for the life of your mortgage, while mortgage insurance will be terminated at some point.

In most experts' opinions, it is not a good move to make. On most loans closed after July 29, 1999, mortgage insurance must be cancelled at the borrower's request if the loan balance is paid down to 80 percent of the original property value. Further, insurance must be terminated automatically when the balance reaches 78 percent of the original value. In addition, subject to certain conditions, PMI on loans sold by lenders to Fannie Mae and Freddie Mac must be cancelled when the loan balance reaches 80 percent of the current property value, taking account of appreciation.

Broadly speaking, if you expect significant appreciation and monitor your property value so you can terminate PMI as soon as possible, the higher interest rate option is a poor choice, unless you expect to hold the mortgage a very short time.

The second way to avoid paying for PMI is to take a first mortgage for 80 percent of value and a second mortgage for 10 percent or 15 percent. These are known as 80/10/10's and 80/15/5's, with the last number as the down payment percentage. So, an 80/10/10 means you are getting an 80 percent first mortgage, a 10 percent second mortgage, and you are putting ten percent down.

In general, combination loans are more attractive the higher your tax bracket, the smaller the difference in rate between the two mortgages, and the shorter the term of the higher-rate second loan. Expected rapid price appreciation reduces the attractiveness of combination loans, because it means that mortgage insurance will terminate sooner.

FIXED TERM MORTGAGES

There are two basic types of loans, fixed term and adjustable rate mortgages. Let us look at fixed term mortgages first.

If you decide to get a fixed term loan, your first decision is whether you want a 15-year loan or a 30-year loan. There are also 20-year loans, but the decision-making process you will use is the same, so we will make it simpler by comparing 15-year and 30-year loans.

If you cannot afford the monthly payment on a 15-year loan, the choice is made for you, because monthly payments are naturally higher on 15-year loans.

If you can afford the 15-year loan, you will need to decide whether you are more concerned with minimizing your monthly payment or maximizing your ability to build wealth. The first is concerned mainly with the present and the second with the future.

For example, the mortgage payment on a $100,000, 30-year loan at 7 percent, is $665. On a 15-year loan at 6.75 percent, it is $885. If your main goal is to minimize your monthly payment, the 30-year loan is your best option.

On the other hand, after five years, the borrower who took out the 15-year loan has repaid $22,933, while the borrower who took out the 30-year has repaid only $5,868. That amounts to a difference in wealth accumulation of $17,065. To the person whose main goal is to build wealth, that makes a huge difference in a short period.

Some borrowers who can afford a 15-year loan choose a 30-year loan because of the flexibility it provides. You can make the larger payment of the 15-year, they argue, but you do not have to; if you get into a pinch, you can make the lower payment of the 30-year. Those who take a 30-year but make the larger payment of the 15-year, however, do not pay down the balance as rapidly as they would have if they had taken a 15-year, because they are paying the higher rate of the 30-year loan.

Many people who elect the 30-year option to obtain flexibility later find that they really do not want it after all. After a few years of being homeowners, they discover that what they really want is to build equity more quickly than the 30-year loan allows. They discover, in other words, that they want to build wealth.

At that point, some who have 30-year loans begin systematically making additional monthly payments in order to build their equity faster. Of course, they would have been better off taking the 15-year from the beginning and enjoying the lower interest rate, but it is still better late than never.

If the rates on the 30-year and 15-year were 7 percent and 6.75 percent, for example, a 10 percent investment yield would not put you ahead for sixty-three months. At investment yields of 12 percent, 14 percent, and 16 percent, the periods are 41, 30, and 24 months, respectively. If the rate on the 15 is 6.5 percent, the periods are almost twice as long.

ADJUSTABLE RATE MORTGAGES

Adjustable rate mortgages or ARMs are loans where the interest rate is tied to a specific economic index the lender will use to measure interest rate changes. If the index goes up, so does your interest rate and the amount of your monthly payments.

ARMs are described using figures like 1/1, 3/1, and 5/1. The first number refers to the initial period of the loan, and during that period, your interest rate will stay the same. The second number is the adjustment period, which tells you how often your rate can be changed.

Here are a couple of examples:

- A 1/2 ARM has an initial period of one year, and rates can change every two years.

- A 3/1 ARM has an initial period of three years, and then rates can change annually.

Therefore, here is how it works. At the end of the initial rate period, the ARM rate is adjusted. The adjustment rule is that the new rate will equal the most recent value of a specified interest rate index, plus a margin. This margin is specified in the original note and remains unchanged through the life of the ARM. For example, if the index is 5 percent when the initial rate period ends and the margin is 2.75 percent, the new rate will be 7.75 percent.

The rule is subject to two conditions. The first condition is that the increase from the previous rate cannot exceed any rate adjustment cap specified in the ARM contract. An adjustment cap, usually 1 percent or 2 percent but ranging in some cases up to 5 percent, limits the size of any interest rate change.

The second condition is that the new rate cannot exceed the contractual maximum rate. Maximum rates are usually five or six percentage points above the initial rate.

During the second phase of an ARM's life, the interest rate is adjusted periodically. This period may or may not be the same as the initial rate period. For example, an ARM with an initial rate period of five years might adjust annually after the five-year period ends. These are referred to as a "5/1 ARM." There are also 3/1, 7/1 and 10/1 ARMs. In some cases, the second adjustment period could be on a monthly basis, which means your payment could change every month.

The rate that is quoted on an ARM, on the news, and by loan providers, is the initial rate, regardless of how long that rate lasts. When the initial rate period is short, the quoted rate is a poor indication of the real interest cost to the borrower. The only significance of the initial rate on a monthly ARM, for example, is that this rate may be used to calculate the initial payment.

The index plus margin is called the "fully-indexed rate" or FIR. The FIR, based on the most recent value of the index at the time the loan is taken out, indicates where the ARM rate may go when the initial rate period ends. If the index rate does not change, the FIR will become the ARM rate.

For example, assume the initial rate is 4 percent for one year, the fully indexed rate is 7 percent, and the rate adjusts every year subject to a 1 percent rate increase cap. If the index value remains the same, the 7 percent FIR will be reached at the end of the third year.

The worst thing about adjustable rate mortgages, or ARMs, is not that they are so dangerous, but that they are so complicated.

Oddly enough, the complications come primarily from efforts to make them less dangerous.

ARMs in the United States differ from ARMs that are the standard instrument in most other countries in three major ways:

1. **The initial period during which the rate is preset is longer**. In South Africa, some banks offer "fixed-rate" mortgages, by which they mean that the initial rate can last as long as two years before lender discretion kicks in. In the United States, initial rate periods run as long as ten years.

2. **Rate adjustments are automated**. Rate adjustments on ARMs in the United States are determined not by the board of directors of the lending institution but by a computer that has been programmed to apply a set of adjustment rules that are stipulated in the ARM contract. The main rule is that the rate will be adjusted on pre-specified dates to equal the value on that date of an interest rate index over which the lender has no control. The lender has no discretion whatsoever.

3. **Rate adjustments are generally constrained**. The great majority of ARMs in the United States limit rate changes on any one adjustment date called an "adjustment cap," and also set a maximum rate over the life of the instrument called a "lifetime cap." There are some that have only adjustment caps and some with only lifetime caps, but almost all have one or the other.

BALLOON LOANS

Balloon loans are payable in full after a period that is shorter than the term. In the 1920's, most balloon loans were interest-only, and the borrower paid interest but no principal. At maturity, usually 5 or 10 years, the balloon that had to be repaid was equal to the original loan amount. Most balloon loans offered today, in contrast, calculate payments on a 30-year amortization schedule, so there is some amount of principal reduction. Assuming a rate of 6.5 percent, for example, a $100,000 loan would have a balance remaining at the end of the fifth year of $93,611. The interest-only variant has reappeared recently, however.

Borrowers often choose between a 5-year balloon loan and a 5/1 ARM or between a 7-year balloon loan and a 7/1 ARM. Both offer a rate in the early years below that available on a 30-year fixed-rate mortgage, and both carry a risk of higher rates later on. However, there are some important differences.

Advantages of a Balloon Loan

- Balloon loans are much simpler to understand and therefore easier to shop for.

- The interest rate on a 5-year or 7-year balloon is typically lower than that on a 5/1 or 7/1 ARM.

Advantages of an ARM

- The risk of a substantial rate increase after 5 or 7 years is greater on the balloon. The balloon must be refinanced at the prevailing market rate, whereas rate increases on most 5 and 7-year ARMs are limited by rate caps.

- Borrowers with 5-year balloons incur refinancing costs at term, whereas borrowers with 5/1 ARMs do not, unless they elect to refinance.

- Borrowers who are having payment problems may find it difficult to refinance balloons. The balloon contract allows lenders to decline to refinance if the borrower has missed a single payment in the prior year. This is not a problem with ARMs, which do not have to be refinanced.

- Borrowers may find it difficult to refinance balloons if interest rates have spiked. The balloon contract allows lenders to decline to refinance if current market rates are more than 5 percent higher than the rate on the balloon.

So is a fixed-term loan or an ARM right for you? It depends on your situation.

If you are happy with the current interest rate offered on a fixed-term mortgage and you are planning to keep your second home for more than a few years, go with a fixed-term mortgage. While interest rates may fall later, as long as you are comfortable with the loan you have gotten, you do not have to worry that in years to come your payments will go up because of interest rate spikes. In addition, if interest rates fall steeply, you can always refinance to take advantage of that situation.

If you are not planning to keep the home long, an ARM is the better way to go. Your monthly payments will be lower, and it does not matter that you are not paying down the principal much. In the first few years, you pay down very little of the principal on a fixed-term loan anyway.

Here is an example. Say you buy a second home in the

mountains. You only plan to live in the home for about a year, because you plan to then move to another state and start your own business. Your hope is that the house will appreciate during that time. Interest rates are low at the time, so you decide to take out a fixed-term mortgage. It is an expensive house, and your monthly payments are almost $2,000 per month. A year later, you sell the house.

If you had taken the interest-only ARM mortgage available at that time, your monthly payments would have been $400 less per month. You would have saved almost $5,000 in mortgage payments in one year. The lesson to be learned is that you would have been significantly better off getting an ARM instead of a fixed-term mortgage.

Why did you make the decision to take out a fixed-term mortgage? You probably decided on a fixed-term mortgage "just in case." Just in case you did not move, for example. You were trying to be safe, but you ended up spending a lot of money needlessly.

CHAPTER SEVEN

SHOPPING FOR A LOAN

N ow that you understand how mortgages work, it is time to go shopping! Before you do, however, here is some background information you need to know.

There are two main players in the mortgage business: mortgage lenders and mortgage brokers. Lenders are institutions like banks, which offer their own loan programs. If you go to your local bank to apply for a home loan, you are dealing with a lender. The loan officer will only be able to offer you loan packages that his or her bank has available.

Mortgage brokers deal with a large number of mortgage lenders. Most receive daily rate and term updates from dozens of mortgage lenders, and they can offer you any one of those programs. Since mortgage brokers are not restricted by one lender's rates or terms, they are free to seek out the best terms and rates for their clients and to find a lender with approval standards that meet the needs of the borrower. We will talk about the advantages and disadvantages of using lenders and mortgage brokers a little later.

When you are evaluating different mortgages, the two basic components you need to focus on are the interest rate of the loan and all the settlement costs. Interest rates are easy to compare. All other things being equal, you want the lowest rate possible, since that loan will cost you the least amount of money in interest payments. Settlement costs are a little tougher to evaluate.

EVALUATING SETTLEMENT COSTS

The best approach to take when evaluating settlement costs depends on whether you are dealing with a lender or with a mortgage broker. We will deal with the lender case first.

Settlement costs can be divided into the following categories:

1. Lender fees

2. Lender-controlled fees paid to third parties

3. Other fees paid to third parties

4. Other settlement costs

Lender fees, consisting of points and other fees, should be your major focus when you are comparing loans.

As already discussed, points are an up-front charge expressed as a percent of the loan amount, such as "one point" or "two points," meaning "1 percent of the loan" or "2 percent of the loan." An origination fee is "points" in disguise, because the fee is in effect the same as points, except that it is not related to the interest rate.

Dollar fees are fees specified in dollars, such as fees for

processing, tax service, flood certification, underwriting, wire transfer, document preparation, courier, and lender inspection.

Nevertheless, from a shopping perspective, what the fees are called and whether they are justified does not matter. For the purposes of your negotiation with the lender, all that matters is how much all those fees add up to. After all, it is your money you will be spending.

Shoppers typically pay close attention to points in selecting a lender, because lenders always report points alongside the interest rate. Dollar fees and origination fees, however, are not reported in the media and generally are not volunteered by lenders. For this reason, most shoppers often fail to consider them when selecting a lender. Do not make that mistake.

Always ask for dollar fees and expect the lender to guarantee them through to closing. In contrast to guaranteeing a rate and points, which exposes a lender to market risks, there is virtually no risk to the lender in guaranteeing dollar fees. The same is true of an origination fee.

Lender-controlled fees are paid to third parties for services ordered by the lender. These include the costs of appraisals, credit reports, and, when required, pest inspections. Lenders know the prices of these services and can easily guarantee them in addition to their own fees.

Other fees paid to third parties are not controlled by the lender, who may not know them. The most important of these are title-related services and settlement services. If you are in an area in which it can pay to shop for them, you can do that after selecting the lender.

Therefore, here is what you want to do. When you are shopping lenders, compare the total of points, including the origination fee, if any, dollar fees, and lender-controlled fees paid to third parties. Ask lenders if they will guarantee all fees, except points, in writing.

The common mistake that shoppers make is to select a lender without knowing any of the lender's charges except points, and then try to negotiate other charges afterwards. Typically, they do this after they receive a good faith estimate, or GFE, which itemizes all the settlement costs including all lender charges.

Challenging individual cost items is not an effective way to control lender fees. The typical borrower has little to no factual basis for challenging a cost item. Even if borrowers have such knowledge, their bargaining power is weak. Having already selected the lender, few are prepared to walk away from the deal, and the lender knows this.

In addition, even if a determined borrower succeeds in pushing the lender into making a change, a determined lender can and will get it back somewhere else. The costs shown on the GFE are estimates and can be different at closing than they were the day before closing. You as a borrower just cannot win this contest.

You should adopt a different strategy. After all, what matters are total settlement costs, so you should select a lender based on which offers the lowest total settlement costs. Instead of shopping individual lender fees, just shop total settlement costs.

Now let us look at evaluating settlement costs with a mortgage broker.

If you are dealing with a mortgage broker rather than a lender, the process is two-fold. It is more complicated in the sense that there is one more significant fee to consider, the broker's fee. It is simpler in the sense that the broker keeps the lender honest on fixed-dollar fees.

While some retail lenders view fixed-dollar fees as an easy way to generate additional revenue from unwary borrowers, wholesale lenders do not, because it would cause problems for their brokers. For this reason, lender fees differ very little from one wholesale lender to another. Dealing with a mortgage broker pretty much eliminates fixed-dollar lender fees as an issue to the shopper. Mortgage brokers can also help borrowers find third-party services at competitive prices.

The result is that shoppers who deal with a mortgage broker can shift their focus from shopping settlement costs to negotiating with the broker. Just make sure that the broker fee includes any payment to the broker from the lender. For example, if you agree on a fee of $3,000 and the broker gets $1,500 from the lender, your payment should be the difference of $1,500.

You can also shop for mortgages on the Internet. While in most cases you are entering data into dialogue boxes instead of talking to a person, at least at first, the result is similar. You will eventually receive quotes, estimates, etc, that you can evaluate just as if you talked to your local banker.

Internet referral sites provide price information for a large number of lenders and mortgage brokers and are usually listed by state. They also provide quick entry to the Web sites of each loan provider listed. In theory, a borrower can sort through the list of loan providers, identify those with the lowest prices, and visit the individual websites to make a final selection. The problem is, the lenders quoting the best prices on the referral sites often either are quoting higher prices on their own sites or are not providing complete price information. Using referral sites is probably no better than using the phone book.

NOW LET'S REALLY GO SHOPPING

How do you start shopping? First, make a list. Look in your phone book under "mortgages," and start calling. Call each firm listed, whether it is a lender or a mortgage broker. Be up front with them: tell them you are going to buy a second home in the near future, and you are looking for the best deal on financing you can find. Make a list and write down all the pertinent information from each, such as interest rates, points, length of loans, settlement costs, other fees, etc. Get as much detail as you can from each, and later you can narrow your list down to the best deals.

Some people you call will be lenders, and others will be mortgage brokers.

Remember the difference: A mortgage broker offers the loan products of different lenders, but does not actually lend. A lender makes the final decision regarding loan approval and provides the money to the borrower at the closing table. Mortgage brokers counsel borrowers on any problems involved in qualifying for a loan, including credit problems. Brokers also help borrowers select the loan that best meet their needs and shop for the best deal among the lenders offering that type of loan.

Brokers take applications from borrowers and lock the rate and other terms with lenders. They also provide borrowers with the many disclosures required by the federal and state governments.

In addition, brokers compile all the documents required for transactions, including the credit report, property appraisal, verification of employment and assets, and so on. Not until a file is complete is it handed off to the lender, who approves and funds the loan.

The main advantage mortgage brokers have over lenders is their access to loan programs from many lenders. The mortgage market is complex and subdivided into countless segments, and no one lender offers loans in every segment. For example, many lenders will not offer loans to borrowers with poor credit, to borrowers who cannot document their income, to borrowers who cannot make any down payment, to borrowers who want to purchase a condominium as an investment, to borrowers with very high debts, to borrowers who need to close within 72 hours, or to borrowers who live overseas. Nevertheless, there are lenders in every one of these segments and brokers can find them.

Brokers are also experts at shopping the market. They receive price updates every day on all major programs from all the lenders they deal with. Many mortgage brokers receive price quotes from over 50 different lenders each day and some, twice a day.

Price differences from lender to lender in the wholesale market in which they operate are much smaller than comparable differences in the retail market.

Here is an important point: Some mortgage brokers will spend very little time on the phone with you once they realize you are "shopping," and that is okay. You will not want to do business with them anyway, because some mortgage brokers try to maximize their profit on each transaction. They do not want to deal with consumers who are shoppers. They want to deal with consumers who will simply accept whatever deal is offered to them. If you talk to a loan officer at local bank, in most cases he or she is paid on a salary basis. They want your business, but they are not dying for it.

Mortgage brokers are only paid when they "sell" a mortgage, so they need your business badly. Here is how they are paid:

The lenders that mortgage brokers deal with quote wholesale prices, leaving it to the brokers to add a markup. The wholesale price plus the markup equals the retail price the broker quotes to you. For example, one wholesale price on a particular program might be 7 percent and 0 points, to which the broker adds a markup of 2 points, resulting in a retail price to the customer of 7 percent and 2 points. In other words, that is what you would pay, and in this case, the borrower pays the 2 points.

Another wholesale price on the same program might be 7.25 percent and a 1.5-point rebate or negative points, which when marked up would be 7.25 percent plus .5 points. In this case, the borrower pays the broker .5 points, and the lender pays the broker 1.5 points. Brokers have a fair amount of discretion in terms of the markup they apply to a loan program.

Why use a mortgage broker? The wholesale prices that lenders quote to brokers are lower than the retail prices lenders quote to borrowers because of the work that brokers do for them that lenders would otherwise have to do themselves. In addition to getting a wholesale price, borrowers benefit from the brokers' superior ability to shop the market.

If the wholesale-retail price spread plus the savings from better shopping exceeds the broker's fee, you pay less dealing with a broker.

There can be disadvantages to using a mortgage broker. Some borrowers find comfort in dealing with a large lender with a recognizable name. Brokers are not known nationally, although they may be well known locally, especially by the real estate agents from whom they receive referrals. The perception is that brokers are more likely than lenders to be unscrupulous, but there is no clear data to support that. Sadly, unscrupulous people are everywhere.

There are disadvantages to using a "brand name" lender, too. Many borrowers go to lenders whose name they recognize, because in a complex market, name recognition provides comfort. The logic of this approach is that a lender with a reputation to protect is not going to jeopardize it by exploiting borrowers.

On the other hand, name lenders tend to price a little above the market. They like to say that they provide better service than bargain-basement lenders. What they are really saying is that borrowers should be willing to pay something more for the comfort of dealing with them.

How much more is difficult to say, because it varies across products, and it depends on how well you deal with the loan officer. While the lender may be known worldwide, you still have to negotiate your deal with a local loan officer who has some discretion in pricing loans. If he or she picks you out as unknowledgeable and timid, you may well pay an "overage," which is amount above the price listed on the loan officer's price sheet. In many lending institutions, the lender and the loan officer share overages.

On the other hand, if you are smart and forceful, you might negotiate an "underage," a price below the listed price. This could be as good a deal as you might get anywhere else, but there are many more overages than underages.

The bottom line is that you may pay a premium price dealing with a name lender, especially if you pay an overage. However, name lenders cap the size of overages, so the overpayment will not be outrageous.

SHOPPING MORTGAGE AUCTION SITES

Mortgage auction sites pull together a group of up to four lenders who bid for your loan. They are really lead-generation sites, because from a lender's perspective, that is what they do. A lead is information about a consumer in the market for a loan. Lenders pay for leads, and auction sites are an important source of leads.

All of mortgage auction sites basically work the same way. You fill out a questionnaire covering the loan request, property, personal finances, and contact information. The sites use this information to select the lenders to whom the information is sent. Lenders then prepare an offer to you based on the same information.

Most sites send the information provided by applicants to "up to four" lenders. Lenders are selected based on prior information provided by the lenders regarding the types of loans, borrowers, and properties that they are prepared to consider.

For example, an applicant with poor credit who wants to purchase a condominium would not be referred to a lender who has told the site it only wants loans to A-quality borrowers purchasing or refinancing single-family homes. Similarly, an applicant who does not want to document income or assets would not be sent to a lender who always requires full documentation.

In principle, the lender selection function performed by auction sites should be particularly valuable to borrowers with one or more challenging features, such as poor credit, incomplete documentation, or little cash. Such borrowers can avoid wasting time soliciting lenders who will not deal with them. How well the sites perform this function, however, is hard to determine.

The lender-screening process employed by the auction sites also provides some protection against falling into the hands of unscrupulous lenders or mortgage brokers out to extract as much revenue as possible from every customer. The sites have every reason to drop a lender who attracts multiple complaints from borrowers.

Auction sites may be useful in screening out unscrupulous lenders and allowing borrowers with poor credit, incomplete documentation, or little cash to find lenders that deal in those market segments. With few exceptions, single-lender sites do not quote prices that apply to those borrowers. Strong borrowers who can find their desired loans priced on single-lender sites will probably do better shopping those sites.

Here are some suggestions for using an auction site effectively:

- Before using the site, decide whether you want a fixed or adjustable-rate mortgage, as well as your preferred loan term, down payment, and points. Auctions cannot work if the item being sold is not precisely defined. If necessary, do some homework. If you would rather not bother, see a mortgage broker.

- Fill out the questionnaire as accurately and completely as you can. The information you provide is used with information the site has on the preferences of its lenders to match you with the lenders most likely to be interested in your loan.

- Remember that mortgage price information comes not from the site, but from the lenders who contact you. The amount of price information they give you may depend on what you ask for. On fixed-rate mortgages, you need the interest rate, points, and dollar fees. While some lenders are not in the habit of providing their dollar fees in initial price quotes, you should insist upon it. On adjustable-rate mortgages, you need to know more than the rate, points, and loan fees. Also, ask the lenders for the interest rate index, margin, all rate adjustment caps, and maximum rate.

- Ask lenders to e-mail or fax their prices to you. Receiving price quotes over the telephone is a problem, because you have nothing in writing.

- Remember that the interest rate and points quoted to you by a lender apply only on the day you receive them. The lender is not bound to them the following day since the market may have changed. For the same reason, it is not safe to compare a price received on Monday from one lender with a price received on Tuesday from another.

- Keep in mind the prices that really matter are those quoted to you on the day you lock the loan with the lender. The lock means that the lender is committed to the prices.

- Understand the lender's requirements to lock. Since locking imposes costs on lenders, they want some evidence of your commitment to the deal before they will lock. Their requirements vary widely, however, ranging from a signed application to a signed application plus a nonrefundable payment. You are entitled to know exactly what each lender's requirements are and how long it should take if you do everything expected of you. All you have to do is ask.

- Since you selected the lender based on the initial price quote and the locked price is what you are going to pay, you have a right to know how the lender will set the price on the day you lock. You need not accept a statement that the new price will be "at the market." The answer you want is that the lock price will be the same as the price the lender is quoting to new customers on the identical loan on the same day. Ask if the lender has a Web site that contains up-to-date prices that you can use to monitor your price day by day. If it does not, ask the loan officer how he or she intends to prove that you have received the correct price.

- Unlike rates and points, loan fees are not market-driven. Unless you change one or more of the loan characteristics, there is seldom a good reason for these fees to change between the time you receive the initial price quote and the time you close. Some lenders will guarantee these fees in writing if you ask. They may even be willing to include appraisal fees and credit charges in the guarantee, because they order them and know how much they cost.

The best way to get the best deal is to shop aggressively. Get as many quotes as you can. You will learn more as you go, you will be a better consumer, and your chances of saving the most money on your mortgage will go way up. Do not be lazy, because you can save thousands of dollars by hunting for the best mortgage.

CHAPTER EIGHT

CREATIVE FINANCING

Seller financing offers a number of advantages, and you will learn about them in a moment. Advantages exist for the seller, too. Understanding a few of those advantages will help you to understand the deal from the seller's side. Glenwood Jones discusses why he offered seller financing.

I had owned a second home for over forty years, and I had paid it off a long time ago. I finally decided I did not want to be a landlord anymore, but the problem was I did not want to just sell the house and face the capital gains taxes. So, I decided to offer financing to the buyer. That way, the new owner of the house took over the responsibility of being a landlord, I still get monthly checks, and the only taxes I pay are on the gain I get from the interest on the loan. I was willing to accept a little lower price for the house since offering financing was good for me. I put a balloon clause on the loan so I can cash out after eight years if I want to or I can decide to refinance the loan and keep getting the monthly payments. If I do not cash out eventually, my son will inherit the loan, and he can decide whether he wants to keep getting monthly income or whether he wants to cash out when the balloon is due.

"T raditional" or conventional financing is used for over 95 percent of all real estate transactions. "Creative" financing refers to situations where the borrower makes arrangements other than simply through a bank or other lending institution. "Creative" does not mean illegal, unethical, or shady. It simply means the purchaser is taking advantage of other options to finance the purchase. Most successful real estate investors have taken advantage of creative financing options, and under the right circumstances, so should you. Creative financing may make it possible for you to purchase a second home, and under better terms than a lender or broker could have offered you.

Here are a few ways you can use creative financing to help you purchase a second home.

SELLER FINANCING

Seller financing is an important and popular tool that can help buyers purchase a property they otherwise would not be able to buy. Sellers are sometimes willing to become "banks" for the buyer, taking payments just as a bank would until the loan is paid off. In all other respects, the transaction is the same as through traditional financing. The deed is transferred to your name, and you simply make your payments to the seller instead of to a bank.

More and more sellers are offering financing, because the rate of return they can get is better than through income-producing investments like certificates of deposit, money market accounts, or other "safe" investment vehicles. A seller will be much happier receiving 7 percent interest on the mortgage he offers you rather than receiving 2 or 3 percent from a money market account.

For buyers, seller financing can be a cheaper alternative. You will not pay loan fees or PMI premiums, and in many cases, the credit checks and underwriting requirements are much lower. Some sellers will not even check your credit. In general, the closing costs involved in seller financing are much lower than with traditional financing.

Why would the seller be willing to finance your purchase of their property? There are a number of possible advantages, and the seller may be willing to offer financing if:

- The property type is difficult to finance through traditional third party lenders.

- The property has been on the market for 90 or more days.

- An "as-is" closing is desired on a property in need of repairs.

- The owner has not met minimum holding time or title seasoning requirements required by traditional lenders.

- An immediate closing is required due to imminent foreclosure or other financial burdens.

- A quick closing is preferred by the seller to free up investment capital.

- The seller desires long-term interest income.

The last situation listed is especially common, and this is why. Let us say you have owned a rental property for a number of years and have paid off the mortgage. You enjoy the monthly income you receive from rental payments, but you are not interested in being a landlord any more. By selling the property and offering owner financing, you still get the monthly income you want, but you avoid all the duties of being a landlord, since that is now the new owner's role. In addition, you have avoided any capital gains taxes that might be due if you sold the property outright.

Here is why seller financing can be advantageous to buyers:

- **You can often put little or no money down**. Some sellers will require ten, twenty, or thirty percent down, but many will accept less than ten percent, especially if their goal is to receive monthly income from the property in the form of mortgage payments.

- **You will face lower credit requirements**. Some sellers will not check your credit at all. Most will simply make sure you have had no bankruptcies or foreclosures in your past.

- **Sellers will not require you to have an underlying or qualifying income**. If it is an investment property you are buying, a traditional lender will expect you to have sufficient income to cover at least some of the monthly payments on the property in case your house is vacant for a period of time. Sellers assume your income will be derived from rent payments. As long as the rent you will receive covers the monthly payments, the typical seller will not ask about your monthly income from other sources.

- **The terms can be more flexible**. You and the seller agree on terms, and you can decide on any terms with which you are comfortable. Price, interest rate, terms, and any other loan requirements are all up for negotiation. If you have unusual needs, you and the seller may be able to reach an agreement that a traditional lender will not. For instance, let us say you work on commission, and at year-end, you always receive a lump-sum payout. If the seller agrees, you could make lower monthly payments for eleven months of the year and a larger payment on the twelfth month.

- **Closing costs are lower**. Sellers do not usually ask for points, loan application fees, origination fees, etc. The seller is not covering advertising costs, overhead, or other costs that a lending institution has to cover.

- **You will complete less paperwork**. Sellers do not answer to a bureaucracy, so the only paperwork you will complete is what is necessary for the transaction to be legal in your locality.

- **The sale can take place much more quickly**. Buyers have been able to close on a second home within a week or two of signing a contract if their financing is already in place.

Some sellers will ask for a balloon note, because they want monthly payments for a certain number of years, and after that, they would like to cash out. Situations like that are common when the owner is nearing retirement age. If the owners are in their early 60s, for instance, they are probably not interested in receiving mortgage payments for the next 30 years. Five or ten years may be long enough.

When the balloon payment is due, you will simply get traditional financing or use another creative financing method. If your goal is to refurbish your second home and re-sell it, make sure you negotiate enough time before the balloon note becomes due for you to complete your repairs and sell the property.

Keep in mind that the loan agreement you reach can have "unusual" requirements. It is not uncommon to buy a home using owner financing and find a clause in the contract stipulating that you cannot sell the property for at least five years. The owner just wants to be sure he receives mortgage payments for at least five years before receiving the balance of the principal. Make sure you are comfortable with whatever agreements you reach.

There is a major advantage to using seller financing if you are trying to accumulate properties. If you have bought a property financed by the seller, the transaction will not show up on your credit report. That can be an advantage if you are trying to buy multiple properties or if your credit is marginal to begin with. Properties purchased through seller financing are "transparent" to lending institutions.

When you are looking for properties, some will be advertised as "owner financing available" or "seller financing available." In many cases, the seller may be willing to offer financing but is not advertising that fact. If you find a property you want to buy, you can always make seller financing a contingency of your offer.

Like most things, you will not know until you ask. If the seller is not interested in carrying financing, that is okay, because he or she does not have to agree.

If the sellers were not originally offering financing, they are unlikely to entertain the idea unless you put the request in writing as a part of your offer to buy the property. Think about it. If you are selling a property, and a person casually asks if you are interested in financing it, you are likely to say no. If their request comes with an attractive offer on the property, and you have not had many offers, you may be more willing to at look at the possibility.

TYPES OF SELLER FINANCING

There are a number of different seller financing techniques. All have different features, and all can be useful depending on your needs and the seller's needs.

Trust Deeds

If you finance your property with a bank, the bank loans you money, and you sign a mortgage. By signing the mortgage, you pledge the property as collateral or security for the loan. If you do not make your payments, the lender institutes legal proceedings to take the property back. If you live in a deed of trust state, a trustee will hold a foreclosure sale. If you live in a mortgage state, the bank can sell the property on its own. In either case, you lose the property, so the distinction between the two is irrelevant.

Under a seller mortgage, the arrangement is the same. The seller deeds the property to you in exchange for your agreement to make monthly payments. If you do not pay as agreed, the seller can foreclose by selling the property at a foreclosure auction, or he or she can simply take the property back and hold it or re-sell it. Because you are not paying PMI, the seller is not made "whole" for any losses, however.

Contract for Deed

Normally when you buy real estate, you receive a deed. With

a contract for deed, you do not receive a deed at the time of sale. Instead, you are buying on an installment plan similar to a "rent-to-own" plan. You pay a small down payment and promise to make monthly payments, and in return, you are given possession of the property. This is similar to renting the property. Unlike a normal sale, however, you do not receive a deed. The deed is promised to you after you have made all of your scheduled payments.

Most sellers expect to deliver the deed after a short period, usually three to five years. Very few sellers are interested in seeing the contract run for ten, twenty, or thirty years.

Contract for deed is also commonly known as a "land contract" or an "installment sale." If you have little cash or poor credit, a contract for deed can be an excellent tool.

Why would a seller offer a contract for deed? If the property is hard to sell, it is an easy way to expand the potential pool of buyers. In addition, it is a lower-risk option than renting the property. Since the buyer's intent is to own the property, he or she is more likely to maintain it properly and take good care of it.

Be aware that some sellers see contract for deed arrangements as a way to make additional profits on their properties. Typically, a seller can ask more for the property, because the average contract for deed buyer is exploring that option. He or she cannot buy a house under a more traditional arrangement, due to credit problems, no cash for closing costs, etc. Therefore, the buyers pay a premium for the privilege of purchasing a property they otherwise could not purchase. The average investor finds he or she can sell properties for 5 to 7 percent more when offering a contract for deed.

GUIDELINES FOR BUYING SELLER FINANCED PROPERTIES

Since seller financing takes place under different terms than traditional financing, it can be hard to evaluate the merits of the arrangements you make. If the property and you qualify for traditional financing, it is a little easier. Find out what the bank or lending institution will offer, and compare it to the best deal you can reach with the seller. Then, choose the arrangement that works best for you.

If the property does not qualify for traditional financing or if you do not, always keep these things in mind as you evaluate the deal:

- **You are still buying the property**. Low down payments, easier credit restrictions, and lower closing costs are great, but they should not make you overpay for the property itself. In the end, the property's value is still critical, no matter how easy it is to buy.

  Of course, you will need to evaluate the entire deal. If you save $3,000 on closing costs but pay $1,000 more for the house than you would have, it is still a great deal overall. The best way to make sure you do not overpay is to get an independent appraisal.

- **Look closely for hidden problems**. Sometimes sellers offer owner financing because they know the property will not pass normal inspections. They are hoping to sell "as is" to avoid making costly repairs themselves. You should always have a professional inspection performed and make the inspection a contingency in your contract.

- **Consult an attorney**. The specifics of contract for deed arrangements can vary from state to state. To make sure you fully understand the agreement you reach, have an experienced real estate attorney review the contract and all arrangements before you sign an agreement.

If you buy a property using seller financing, you will not have to use an attorney for closing. Title companies can draw up appropriate paperwork and handle any necessary escrow accounts or filings. If you are new to real estate investing, however, it makes sense to talk with an attorney and have your first few transactions reviewed by an attorney to make sure you understand the exact nature of your agreements.

ASSUMING A LOAN

"Assuming a loan" simply means that you take over the owner's mortgage. You become officially responsible for repaying the loan.

Why would you assume a loan? You might get a lower interest rate than is currently available, pay lower closing costs, have an easier time qualifying for the loan, and put little or no money down.

Years ago, nearly all mortgages were assumable. Starting in the late 1970s and early 1980s, most lenders inserted a "due on sale" clause into the mortgages, which prohibited assumptions. Many people now believe that all loans are non-assumable, but that is not the case.

In general, most FHA, VA, and adjustable rate mortgages offer assumption privileges to buyers. Many conventional loans will also allow assumptions, but you have to ask.

When interest rates are low, mortgages typically are not assumed, since buyers can qualify for low rates on their own. When interest rates jump, assuming mortgages becomes more popular. It makes sense, because if you can assume a mortgage at 6 percent, that saves a tremendous amount of money over taking out a 9 percent mortgage.

You can also lower your risk by assuming an ARM, if interest rates have climbed. If an ARM has a cap of, say, 10 percent, and interest rates are hovering near 10 percent, you have little risk in assuming the ARM. You could possibly benefit if interest rates fall, since your interest rate will fall as well.

Assuming With Consent

If the loan is a non-FHA or VA loan, it most likely includes language like the following:

"If all or any part of the mortgaged property or an interest therein is sold or transferred by the borrower without the lender's prior written consent, the lender may, at the lender's option, declare all the sums secured by the mortgage to be immediately due and payable."

What does that mean? If you sell or in any way transfer ownership of the property, the lender has the right to expect immediate repayment of the full loan balance, if you have not received prior written consent.

Ask the average real estate agent if the loan is assumable, and he or she will say, "No, it is not, because of the due and payable paragraph." However, the agent is wrong, because it is assumable if the owner gets written consent from the lender.

There are several reasons why the lender would give consent:

- The owner has fallen behind on payments, and you will bring the mortgage current.

- You already do business at the lending institution, and you are a valued client.

- You promise to become a valued client by bringing business to the lending institution.

- The interest rate on the mortgage is higher than the current market rate.

Even if it is a conventional mortgage, it can still be assumed. You just have to ask first and see if the lender will agree.

Assuming "Subject To"

Owners sell properties even if they feel the lender will not give consent. The seller is not required to pay off the loan unless the lender calls the note due. If the seller and buyer do not feel the lending institution will grant the assumption, they complete the sale and never inform the lender that the property has changed hands. The new buyer simply continues to make mortgage payments to the lender under the original owner's contractual agreement.

"Subject to" agreements hold risk for both buyers and sellers. If the buyer does not make the mortgage payments on time, the seller's credit will be affected, as he is the person on record and responsible for payments. If the lender finds out the property has changed hands, the buyer will have either to pay off the note or refinance the property.

"Subject to" purchases may make sense if you plan to buy and quickly re-sell the property after refurbishing it. If you only keep the property for, say, six to twelve months, you will have saved a tremendous amount in closing costs and financing costs by buying the property "subject to."

Many real estate advisers promote the use of "subject to" purchases. Their feeling is that lending institutions, even if they find out the property has changed hands, will not take action as long as the payments are made on time. Many recommend tactics like making sure the return address on your envelope is that of the seller or even having the seller write the mortgage checks after he receives your payment to him. Lender indifference may be the case while interest rates are flat, but if rates spike, lenders will have a greater interest in seeing that the loan is refinanced.

CHAPTER NINE

BUYING A SECOND HOME FOR A RESIDENCE

Many people in the market for a second home look for a house that is similar to their primary residence, especially if they plan to spend roughly equal amounts of time in both places. Others look for a house that is completely different. William Boyce explains how he and his wife went about deciding what type of house they wanted for their second home.

My wife and I live in Virginia in the summer and spend the winter in Florida. Our home in Virginia is in the mountains, so we love the contrast in climate and in the surroundings. We also decided that we wanted the home to be as different on the inside as on the outside. We didn't want to feel we'd found a copy of our Virginia home in Florida. Everything about the house is different: the overall layout, how the rooms feel, and the construction of the house. The two homes couldn't be more different. We weren't sure if we were making the right decision in choosing such a different place, but we're really glad we did. Each summer and winter, we look forward to going back to the other house. I do not think we'd feel that way about each house if they weren't so different from each other. When friends tell us they are looking for a second home, they are surprised when we tell them to try to find the opposite of what they are currently living in, but it sure works for us.

———

I f you are buying a second home to use as a secondary residence, what is most important to you is that you enjoy the home. After all, you are not looking for additional income, but for a place to live.

While you are at it, though, you should make sure to take advantage of the financial opportunities that owning a second home can bring.

You already know the tax benefits of owning your own residence are considerable. The same advantages apply when you buy a second home. When you pay rent, you are not allowed to claim those payments as an itemized deduction. By contrast, any interest payments you make on a home mortgage are tax-deductible, reducing your tax liability. If you rent a residence in another location, the rent payments are not tax-deductible. If you buy a second home, your mortgage payments are.

Here is an example. If your monthly house payment is $800 and approximately $750 of that payment is in the form of interest, you will be able to deduct $9,000 from your adjusted gross income on your income taxes. If you are in the first few years of your mortgage, the amount of interest is likely to be higher, since almost all of your payment in the first few years goes to paying off interest charges rather than paying down principal. If you are making monthly $800 rent payments, none of the $9,600 you pay per year can be deducted from your taxes.

Here is a more specific example. To keep things simple, we will assume a renter and a second homeowner both earn $60,000 per year. The homeowner has already paid off his mortgage on his primary residence and is considering whether to rent a home in the mountains or to purchase a home. Here is how it works out:

- The renter pays $1,000 per month in rent and gets no tax breaks.

- The homeowner has a $140,000 mortgage at 7 percent, with a $1,100 per month payment. Real estate taxes are $1,500, and mortgage interest paid for the year equals $9,756.

- Assume both individuals are in the 25 percent tax bracket. The renter will owe $15,000 in taxes, which is .25 times $60,000. The homeowner will be able to deduct the $9,576 in interest, plus the $1,500 in property taxes, for a total deduction of $11,256. Subtracting that from $60,000 leaves a taxable income of $48,744. Multiplying that income by .25 or 25 percent yields a tax liability of $12,186. The homeowner has saved $235 per month by owning instead of renting. In addition, the homeowner can take advantage of the property's appreciation and could sell it for a considerable profit in later years.

An easy rule of thumb to use is that you will save approximately 20 percent of your monthly payment in taxes. An accountant or tax professional can help you determine exactly what you will save based on your individual financial situation.

If you live in the home for long periods, there is an additional and very important benefit. Under the right conditions, you may be exempt from capital gain taxes when you sell the home.

In general, if you live in the home for two out of five years, you are exempt from paying gains taxes. If you live in the home for two years straight, you are exempt. That means if you buy a fixer-upper for $120,000, live in it for forty percent of the time while you spend $20,000 renovating it, and sell it three years later for $180,000, the $40,000 profit you make is exempt from taxes. You pay no taxes on that gain as long as you purchase another house within six months. If you do not purchase another home, you are exempt from taxes on the first $250,000 in profit you make if you are single and on the first $500,000 in profit you make if you are married.

You can use this exemption repeatedly. The tax savings add up nicely, allowing you to acquire more properties that are desirable. Many real estate investors who own multiple properties continue to move into a new personal residence every two to five years just so they can take advantage of the tax exemption available.

How Much House Should You Buy?

According to the National Association of REALTORS®' 2004 Profile of Home Buyers and Sellers, homebuyers look at an average of ten homes before making an offer. That is a lot of data and floor plans to keep track of, so you will need to develop an effective shopping plan. The first thing you will have to decide is how much house you want to buy.

Most lenders will qualify a buyer for the maximum loan possible. Since decision ratios are becoming more and more credit score driven, you may be able to get a loan with your total debt exceeding 50 percent of your income. Some homeowners can handle these high ratios and do well, while others go bankrupt. Everyone is different in the way they handle their cash flow, and only you can decide on your priorities.

From the lenders' point of view, if you have a high credit score, you are more responsible. You should be able handle debt, so they will be a little more generous with a higher income to debt ratio. However, how much house should you buy?

One school of thought is to buy the most expensive second home you can. If you are like most homebuyers and you put less than 20 percent down, you are using the lender's money to control a much larger amount than you have invested. As the home increases in value, the return on investment is a percentage of the home's value, not a percentage of your low down payment. In addition, with a thirty-year mortgage, your monthly payment remains the same. However, as your income goes up, the mortgage payment takes smaller bites out of your paycheck.

Homebuyers who purchased their homes in the 1970s and 1980s saw the value soar and their incomes go up, but their monthly payments stayed the same. Those who stretched and bought bigger homes in great locations benefited more, because their homes appreciated the most. Under the current federal tax rules, a husband and wife can sell their home and walk away with the first $500,000 tax-free.

Proponents of this house buying approach also point out that by buying to the max now, you will save a future move. Since moving is disruptive, time consuming, and costly, you will save about $30,000 in selling, loan, and moving costs if you stay put longer.

On the flip side, the conservative argument is that you should not become a slave to your mortgage payment, especially on your second home. After all, your second home is intended to provide enjoyment, not additional stress. Moreover, if you plan to invest in other properties, you will need money to invest, make improvements, etc. The conservative argument says you should buy a house you can easily afford and with monthly payments as low as possible. If you are so inclined, staying conservative will keep your payment as low as possible and pay off the mortgage early. This approach certainly has merit if your goal is to be debt-free as quickly as possible.

In the end, only you can decide how big a monthly payment you can comfortably handle. Do not let an agent or lender talk you into going for more than you want to go for.

It is important to remember that a home is more than just roof and hearth. It is also one of your most important investments, and you want it to grow through appreciation as well as paying down the mortgage.

THE PROS AND CONS OF LEVERAGING YOUR PURCHASE

Leveraging your purchase simply means borrowing money to make a purchase. The higher the amount of leverage, the more money you borrow. Lenders will often make a zero-down loan, and in that case, you will be fully leveraged. There is no right or wrong amount of leverage, as it varies from person to person depending on an individual's financial situation and goals. While many lenders expect at least a ten to twenty percent down payment on a second home, some offer terms with extremely low down payment requirements.

A zero-down loan allows a buyer to purchase a home without committing any money as a down payment. Thus, if you buy a house for $400,000, your mortgage will be for $400,000; however, you will still have to pay closing costs. You can also get interest-only loans, meaning you will only make interest payments on the money you borrow. You will never pay down the principal that way, but your monthly cost will be lower.

Lenders will generally require you to have at least a few months' worth of reserves in the form of money in the bank or in certain types of retirement accounts or investments.

Here are the advantages and disadvantages of interest-only and zero-down loans.

Advantages:

- Lower monthly costs than almost any principal-and-interest mortgage. Can be a good choice for people who need or want to reserve cash.

- Allows borrowers to qualify for bigger mortgages. The lender approves your loan based on your ability to afford the monthly payment. So, if you can afford about $2,000 a month, that might get you a traditional fixed-rate mortgage of $335,000 at 6 percent, or an interest-only mortgage of $400,000 at 6 percent.

- Borrowers can pay up to 20 percent of their principal annually without penalty. That is helpful to those whose income fluctuates during the year, for example, people who are paid on commission.

- Potentially a good choice for buyers who plan to sell or refinance before the interest-only period ends and their payments go up steeply.

- Allows a buyer with little savings but sufficient income and credit to purchase a home. When home prices are rising, they often outstrip people's ability to save for a down payment. However, by buying a home for no money down, buyers can start building equity quickly.

Disadvantages:

- Monthly payments will rise dramatically after the interest-only period ends and will depend on prevailing interest rates. If you are unable to refinance the loan and do not plan to sell the home, the resulting payments might not be affordable.

- Poor choice for borrowers who want to know exactly what their payments will be after the initial interest-only period.

- Poor choice for borrowers whose goal is to gain equity by paying down their principal.

- If you put down less than 10 percent toward your home purchase, your lender will require you to pay for private mortgage insurance or PMI. PMI can add thousands of dollars to your homeownership costs over the first few years of your loan.

- Interest rates for zero-down loans are typically higher because of the increased risk that the borrower will default.

- If you unexpectedly need to sell your home soon after you buy, you may have gained little equity in the home and will have to pay closing costs and real estate sales commissions out of your own pocket.

CHAPTER TEN

BUYING A REHAB
OR "FIXER-UPPER"

S ome real estate investors make careers out of finding distressed properties and re-selling them after making repairs and enhancements. For them, a "second home" is a transitory situation, because they own serial second homes, buying and "flipping" those homes for profit.

One seasoned investor's motto is, "Paint the walls, replace the carpet, and replace the front door," because that is what he does to every fixer-upper he buys. In fact, sometimes that is all he does to the houses he buys.

Nothing turns off potential buyers like cosmetic problems, such as peeling paint, rotting deck boards, holes or stains in carpets, etc. Often buyers will overlook the fact that under a little mess is a great deal on a property.

You can use that to your advantage. Buying fixer-uppers to re-sell is a quick way to profit from buying a second home, especially if you know your market.

You have two basic choices when you purchase a fixer-upper.

You can perform the work yourself or you can hire others to do it for you. If you perform the work yourself, you can save money, but you also may spend time that you cannot afford to lose. If your goal is to only buy one property at a time, fixing it and selling it before buying another, then performing most of the work yourself may be a great idea. If you want to have multiple projects going at the same time, you will most likely need to hire help. If your job and family keep you extremely busy, you will most likely need to hire help.

Hiring other people to do the work for you may cost a little more, but it can also save you time and money. If you are making payments on a loan, the longer you keep the house, the longer you are making payments. By hiring help, you may be able to flip the property more quickly and reduce your total expense.

Here is a simple way to break down the financial calculations involved in buying fixer-upper or rehab properties:

Initial price of property	*plus*
Refurbishing costs	*plus*
Loan expenses	*minus*
Closing costs	*equals*
Total Cost	*minus*
New sale price	*minus*
Selling expenses	*minus*
Closing costs	*equals*
Total Profit	$ ____

Do not forget to add expenses for loan payments, closing costs, and selling expenses. Anything that you spend money on during the process of refurbishing a house is an expense that takes away from your total profit.

Many people look at a property and say, "Wow, if I can pay $150,000 for this house and put $10,000 in improvements into it and sell it for $170,000, I will make $10,000."

They are wrong. They also need to add in closing cost expenses, interest payments, and the cost of selling the house and closing on that sale.

Refurbishing houses offers another benefit as well. Each time you do, you are improving the quality of a neighborhood or a town, and there is a tremendous satisfaction that comes from helping to improve your town.

THE INVESTOR'S PERSPECTIVE

Compared to the housing inventory in Europe, the housing inventory in the United States is old. Sixty-one million houses are more than 25 years old, and 24 million are between 16 and 25 years old. Most of these older houses were built to a different set of buyer expectations. Changes in family life, new technologies, and building materials have made upgrading aging houses big business. There is a ton of houses for second homebuyers like you to improve and upgrade.

With careful planning, you can purchase property below market value, make improvements to it that increase its value well above the cost of the improvements, and then sell for a profit. Any house that you may consider a candidate for investment does not exist in a vacuum, though. A particular property located in one neighborhood may represent a real opportunity, but that same property in a different location may not be a great prospect. There are several factors that determine the value of real estate, and each of these factors must be considered when sizing up a potential property.

Besides "buy low, sell high," the next most quoted real estate cliché is "location, location, location." Location is important, but it is not the only factor that determines the value of a property. One of the challenges you face when looking at investment property is not only to assess the current value of the property but also to assess its potential value.

You want to acquire property that you can buy for below its current market potential. The property is worth exactly what a buyer is prepared to pay for it, no more and no less. You are the buyer, so you set the value of the property when you purchase it. The question you have to answer which determines your profit potential is, "Can the property be changed in some way to attract another buyer to pay more for the property than the last buyer?"

COMPARING PROPERTIES

Most professional real estate agents with whom you establish a business relationship will do a "comparative market analysis" for no charge. The analysis is an examination of house sale records in recent weeks or months to determine what houses in a given price range, size, location, and general condition have been listed at and what the actual selling prices were. When you are looking at these comps, do not forget to factor in the effect of the neighborhood.

To understand what buyers expect in a house at the price range in which you want to sell a second home, look at the characteristics of a similar property that has recently sold. For example, if you buy a house for $100,000 and hope to resell it for $150,000, you will have to change the property to meet the expectations of buyers shopping for $150,000 homes. The difference in characteristics of $100,000 houses from the $150,000 houses is made up of the size, features, and condition of the higher-valued properties.

Most real estate companies, as well as national real estate Web sites like **Realtor.com**, have their own Web sites with search tools that allow you to screen properties on a wide variety of criteria. Filter your search to display properties with close to $150,000. You may have to visit several sites to make a comprehensive list, and remember that you will have access only to the asking prices, not the actual selling price.

The decision to purchase is made on the individual property, but again, the decision is not made in a vacuum. Several factors, including location, size of the property, its features and condition, how it compares with similar property, and how many similar properties are available, are taken together to determine the value of the property.

Location

The location of a property is one of the most important factors in determining its value, so you must compare properties that are in the same location. All other factors being the same, similar properties located in different areas can have vastly different values. Differences in location, even in the same general area, will affect value. For example, a property located at the edge of what is considered a good neighborhood may be several thousand dollars less expensive than a property located squarely in the neighborhood.

Size

A major factor in evaluating property is its size, and the larger the property, the more valuable it tends to be. The size of the lot and the number of bedrooms and bathrooms all must be considered when comparing several potential properties.

Condition

The condition of the house is the variable that will probably be hardest to compare. Since you are looking at property that needs work, it will be in less than perfect condition. You really cannot compare the condition of two houses before you actually visit the properties. You can use the Intake Sheet for Residential Properties in the last chapter as a guide to comparing the condition of different properties.

Features

Garages, porches, fireplaces, and other features like these add to the property's value. Carefully list all the features of each property so you can determine the property with the best overall value.

Once you have the data, you can compare the properties that have recently sold or are valued around the target sales price for the property you are analyzing. How are the properties different? How are they the same? What do the higher-valued or higher-priced properties have that the property you may purchase lacks? The answers to these questions will give you direction on the best improvements to make to meet potential buyers' expectations.

PLANNING FOR REPAIRS

Whatever repairs, upgrades, or improvements you plan do to a house, be sure they meet the local building code requirements. Any violations or repairs not fixed that come up while selling a house can easily give the buyer second thoughts about the property, not to mention a legal reason to back out of the contract. A homebuyer who is paying market value expects a house will be in good repair and hires a home inspector to look for deficiencies and report them. With that said, make repairs and improvements that make a difference based on comparable houses in the neighborhood.

For example, if you are considering buying a second home for resale, and one of the improvements needed is a new roof that will cost $10,000 or more if the roof sheeting requires replacement, look at your research about comparable houses. If you find they sell for $115,000, there is no reason to buy the house. You will spend excessively on the roof alone. Most experts say that as long as the roof looks OK and passes an inspection, buyers are satisfied. Given the choice among two or more comparable houses, most buyers are unwilling to pay the full premium for a house with a new roof. No doubt, the new roof will make the house easier to sell, but few buyers choose to pay the full $10,000 extra.

Do Not Plan to Repair the Structure

Costs can easily get out of hand as soon as you start to modify the structure or systems of the house. The easiest fix-ups and the most profitable are those that do not require major structural changes, like moving kitchen and bathroom fixtures or opening up load-bearing walls and adding rooms outside the original footprint of the building.

Certainly it is possible to make major structural changes to a property and increase its value far beyond the cost of the upgrade, but consider it only if you are going to live in the property over a period of years so you will have inflation working for you too.

Kitchens and Bathrooms

Improvements to kitchens and bathrooms will cost and pay back the most. Moreover, they are the two key rooms that buyers look at very seriously. Buyers on a shoestring budget still want the best possible kitchen and bathrooms they can get for their money. Most rehabbers have never bought a house where they did not do a lot of work in both of these rooms, because they are the most used rooms in a house.

The upgrades in a kitchen can range from a basic cosmetic face-lift of paint, flooring, and appliances to expanding the kitchen into an adjoining room and replacing everything from the ceiling to the floor and all the cabinets and appliances.

Even buyers of a two-bedroom home expect at least a full bath and a half bath to solve the traffic jam when everyone is getting ready for work and school in the morning. Therefore, by making a one-bathroom house into a two-bathroom house by using existing space, you will easily recover your investment. In a bathroom, the upgrade can be as basic as scrubbing and wallpapering to gutting it and rebuilding everything with a new bathtub and shower, vanity and countertop, tile, and lighting. In some cases, it involves changing the arrangement of fixtures to make a small space work harder.

Experts estimate that homeowners who invest in a midrange kitchen remodel estimated at $40,000 will recover 67 percent, and an upscale kitchen remodel at $70,000 comes in at 80 percent. A bathroom remodel costing $9,720 recoups 88 percent of that cost. The addition of a bathroom for $15,058 that is built within the existing footprint of the home comes in at 94 percent.

If you are living in the house while making improvements and the neighborhood supports a luxury bathroom or a gourmet kitchen, you may be able to rationalize their expense. Before you jump in, do the research and find out what the selling price is for comparable properties and if they feature high-end upgrades.

Avoid Extremes

Specialized areas like wine cellars, dedicated gyms, tennis courts, and swimming pools seldom give a good return on the investment, unless they are the norm in the neighborhood. Still, the expense is seldom recoverable.

EVALUATING THE FINANCIALS

However you look at the business of real estate investing, unless you are in the rental business, the profit has to come from the difference between the purchase price and the sale price. The difference must be large enough to cover all costs.

This is a simple formula: (sales price) − (purchase price + cost) = profit. If you look carefully at the three variables in this equation you realize that each is made up of many smaller variables. Some you have direct control over, like the purchase price and cost, and others, like the sales price, you have to estimate. Here is a look at the three variables and how they relate to different purchase scenarios.

Purchase Price

The most important variable in the equation is the purchase price. Much of your potential profit in any real estate project is determined the moment you settle on a purchase price. If you overpay for the property, the added value of your improvements cannot be fully realized.

The challenge is that most property with any potential will eventually find a buyer. If you plan to live in the house for a number of years and you overpay, you have time for the property to appreciate. Improvements made during the occupation are made not necessarily to generate a profit, but to improve your enjoyment of the home. Eventually, you may make a profit out of the purchase when you sell.

On the other hand, if you are buying a second home as an investment for quick resale, you must purchase the property at a low enough price to afford the necessary improvements needed for the property to reach its full market value. If you plan to upgrade the property, you still must have a low enough purchase price so it supports the planned improvements. With this in mind, you must establish a purchase price, or a "target purchase price," for the property to ensure you do not overpay.

The target purchase price that you can afford to pay for a particular property may be far from what the seller has in mind. Remember that we defined the value of any property as what a buyer will pay, not what the seller is asking.

Costs

The next variables in the profit equation are the costs of purchasing and holding the property, costs of all planned repairs and improvements, sales costs, and, of course, the profit. Some of the costs are easier to calculate than others. Here is a rundown of the major costs involved in fixing up a property for resale.

- **Closing Costs**. At the closing of any real estate deal, certain costs of the transaction are apportioned to the buyer and seller. The buyer pays for an appraisal, survey, property transfer taxes, and legal fees. If the real estate taxes are paid, then a rebate is given to the seller; if not, the seller pays for his or her share of the tax bill. Of course, you also have to settle with the bank and pay any fees they require to execute the loan.

  These are just a few of the possible closing costs, and they can add up to thousands of dollars. Most of the fees and taxes are set fees or a percentage of the sale price. It is possible to make an accurate estimate of what these costs will be. A real estate broker or the bank that is financing the deal can give you a sample closing statement.

- **Holding Costs**. The holding costs include interest on the loan, taxes, and utilities. The length of time you plan to hold the property affects these costs. Unless the project can be turned around in a month or so and put back on the market, use a year as the standard holding time. A fix-it project that takes three or four months to complete may require several more months to sell.

  It is a great motivator to keep the job on schedule if

you break the holding cost down to a monthly figure. Knowing that a project costs $1,800 per month just to own the property is a great motivator to get the job done. Time is money, and if you take this principle a little further, you will see that in this case every hour you have not sold the property costs you $2.50.

- **Repairs and Improvements**. These can run the gamut from a simple paint and polish to a second-floor expansion, so it is essential that you have a good idea of what these costs will be. The challenge is that you do not have a lot of time to pull these costs together. If the property has potential, other buyers will be looking at it and may be able to act more quickly than you can.

  The repair and improvement costs represent a major portion of the project's overall expense. If after you calculate the total cost you arrive at an unrealistically low purchase price, some adjustments are in order. In some cases, the market will not support the cost of the repairs and improvements and return a decent profit. If that is the case, it is better to find out before you purchase the property.

- **Contingency**. Like any other business, fixing up property for resale has its risks, so this is why there is a contingency allotment. While changing a kitchen faucet seems straightforward, it can get grim if you break a rusted pipe in the wall, because a repair that was budgeted for $100 suddenly costs $400. The contingency is an important part of the budget, because it allows you to anticipate the unexpected and provide sufficient funds if they are needed. Because you include the contingency amount as an expense up front to lower your target purchase price, not having the expense of a broken pipe ends up on the bottom line. The older and more run-down the property, the higher your contingency allotment should be.

- **Sales Costs**. Every real estate transaction has costs to both the seller and purchaser. You will estimate these costs separately from the sales costs, because the value of the property is different. The largest component of the selling costs is the commission paid to the real estate broker, which a steady customer can negotiate. Both seller and buyer get the same closing statement, so you can estimate the selling costs.

- **Profit**. This line is considered an expense, because the difference between the purchase price and selling price must contain the profit. The figure is the actual cash that you hope to realize after the dust settles, the property is sold, and all loans and bills are paid. Because most of the money to buy and improve the property comes from the lender, even a small amount of cash down can represent a hefty return on your investment.

- **Sales Price**. It would be nice if you could add up all the costs, decide on a profit, add the figures to the price paid for the property, and then place it back on the market. You can if you buy the property at the right price. Any of the real estate Web sites on the Internet are a good place to take an initial look for comparable properties. The search results will give you a ballpark idea of the value of the house, or at least the asking prices. As suggested earlier, your real estate broker can also prepare a market analysis of comparable houses that have recently sold. If you have expanded and improved a property, look for comparable properties in the same neighborhood and condition.

- **Time**. One important variable that is not explicitly stated is time. Owning real estate has costs, such as interest on the loan, taxes, utilities, etc. The longer you own the property, the more costs you incur. However, over that same period, most real estate appreciates, and this has historically offset the costs. Unless the local real estate market is very hot, appreciation over a short time will not cover the holding costs. Nevertheless, if you open that horizon to several years or more, the property can appreciate enough to cover these costs. That is the most appealing characteristic of a real estate investment.

  With some exceptions, a fix-up-and-sell second home with a short window of ownership will appreciate very little, and your gains will come from the improvements you make. A fix-up-to-occupy second home with a window of ownership of several years may experience considerable appreciation during the time of renovation and occupancy.

CHAPTER ELEVEN

BUYING RENTAL PROPERTIES

T he vast majority of second homeowners cannot afford to make two mortgage payments without a little help. Unless you can afford to buy or finance your second home outright without it generating any income for you, then you will need to consider renting the property for all or part of the year. If you are buying a second home with the intention of generating income or building wealth, then you will want it to be a classic rental property with a tenant occupying the property and paying monthly rent payments to you. If you are buying a vacation home at a beach or resort with the intention of staying there for two to four weeks or more a year, then you will hope to rent the property for as much of the time as possible that you will not be there. If it is a beachfront property, it is unrealistic to think you will be able to rent the property year-round. Many beach rental properties average one week of rental occupancy per month or less in the winter months and at a dramatically reduced price compared to in-season summer rent levels.

No matter what your intended use for the property, the bottom line consideration is whether you can afford to own a second property. If you can afford to make the payments and handle maintenance, upkeep, etc., without renting the property, great! Any rental income you receive is icing on the cake. If you need rental income to make ownership possible, you will need to consider a few things. Analyzing the financial possibilities starts with understanding gross rent multipliers.

GROSS RENT MULTIPLIER

A gross rent multiplier or GRM gives you a sense of how much rent you can collect based on the value of the property. The lower the ratio, the better the deal may be. The gross rent multiplier is calculated with the following formula:

sale price / rent collected annually = GRM

For instance, if a property is selling for $300,000, and the total rent collected per year is $60,000, then the GRM is 5.0.

As a rule of thumb, a GRM over 8.0 will probably yield a negative cash flow, meaning you will be paying more in expenses than you receive in rent, unless you put twenty or thirty percent down on the property to lower your payments.

If you are looking at a number of different properties and assessing their potential, it is helpful to compare them on an equal basis. It can be tricky to evaluate properties with different purchase prices and different rental incomes, but here is how you can use the GRM calculation to evaluate different properties.

	PRICE	RENT	GRM
Property A	$550,000	$75,000	7.3
Property B	$600,000	$78,000	7.6
Property C	$900,000	$140,000	6.4

All other things being equal, Property C is the best value because of its lower GRM.

If you compare prices and the GRM of one price is relatively high compared to the others, there could be two reasons. Either the price of the property is too high or the rent collected is too low. To determine which, you will need to appraise the property and compare the rent prices to other similar units.

Now let us take your financial review a step further. We will use another simple calculation to determine the profitability of a property.

NET OPERATING INCOME

Your net operating income, or NOI, is how much money you make from the property. To calculate your NOI, simply divide your gross rental receipts by your gross operating expenses.

It is easy to underestimate your expenses when you are evaluating a property. Expenses include the following:

- Mortgage payments

- Property taxes

- Insurance

- Utilities, if applicable

- Maintenance and repairs

- Advertising

- Licenses or permits

- Accounting fees

- Legal fees

- Losses due to vacancy or damage

Do not underestimate your expenses. You are always safer overstating anticipated expenses so you know exactly what you may be getting into. If the expenses turn out to be lower than you estimated, so much the better. However, if they do not, at least you are not surprised, and you have accounted for those expenses in your estimate of the property's value.

It is tempting to assume the property will stay rented twelve months out of the year, but it is also unrealistic. For example, when determining whether to make the loan, many lenders assume the property will be vacant 25 percent of the time. If they determine that you do not have sufficient income to cover a certain percentage of vacancy periods, they will not make the loan. While 25 percent vacancy rates may be pessimistic, they can happen with even the most desirable properties. If you are forced to evict a tenant for non-payment of rent, it can take three to four months in some localities before you regain possession of the property, and you do not generate income during that time. You can hope to collect when you sue for damages, but the odds are poor that you will be successful.

If you want to know what the current owner's expenses on the property have been in the last year, ask to see a copy of the

Schedule E form he filed with his taxes. Schedule E breaks down rental income and expenses for tax purposes. The owner has no reason to underestimate expenses, since those expenses offset any income gains for tax purposes. From the owner's point of view, the more expenses he can claim, the better. The owner does not have to show you the Schedule E form, of course, but most will if it helps make the sale.

Once you have your estimated income and expense figures, subtract expenses from income to determine the property's NOI. For example, if you expect to receive $12,000 per year in rental income and your estimated yearly expenses are $10,400, then your NOI is $1,600, and the property is considered "cash flow positive."

An NOI can and often will be negative. If you expect to receive $12,000 per year in income and your expenses are $15,000, then your NOI is negative $3,000. Your expenses exceed your income, and the property is considered "cash flow negative."

Is a second home with negative cash flow a bad deal? It depends on your goals for owning the home, which is why we talked about determining your goals in the first chapter. If you wish to live in the home for a part of the year, then $3,000 in cost may seem like a great deal. If you wish to generate monthly income from the home, then $3,000 out of pocket is a terrible deal and makes no sense at all.

While GRM and NOI calculations can help you make sense of the financial implications, only you can determine what you are willing to pay or receive in income for the privilege of owning a second home.

CHAPTER TWELVE

FINDING GREAT DEALS FROM OWNERS

T he same "by low, sell high" adage holds true for real estate as it does in the stock market or any investment vehicle. In order to buy low, you have to be able to spot opportunities where the property is undervalued. One of the best ways to find an undervalued property is from an owner, but those properties will take some digging to uncover.

Why would a property be undervalued? There are many reasons, and it is helpful to understand why a property would be properly valued first. Then, you can start to see opportunities to purchase properties at below market value and to make excellent profits. Keep in mind that properties can be overvalued, too, and if you are an investor, your goal is to avoid those properties like the plague.

Here are the main drivers of why a property is properly valued:

- Neither the buyer nor the seller is under any kind of financial duress. The seller wants to sell but has no compelling reason to sell today, and the buyer wants to make a purchase but is not compelled to make this purchase.

- Both the buyer and the seller are knowledgeable about local market conditions and can make educated and informed estimates of value.

- The property has been marketed in a way so that qualified buyers are informed that it is available.

- Financing is "standard," and major concessions are not being offered by the seller or demanded by the buyer.

- No unusual sales concessions are demanded by the buyer or seller.

If you think about it, the above reasons make perfect sense. A property is most likely to sell for market value if the sellers have marketed the property well, can to take their time and accept reasonable offers, and if there is a reasonable pool of qualified buyers interested in the property. If any of these conditions and more are not present, then the property is likely to sell below market value. Your goal is to find those opportunities, because that is how you will maximize your profits.

There are a number of situations where you can find a below-market deal on a property. To be candid, many people buying and selling real estate are not particularly astute. They may be trying the FSBO route, but they have not marketed their property well and are getting very few lookers, much less buyers. On the other hand, they may be facing personal situations that cause them to be in a hurry, and desperate owners are your best source of below market-value deals.

Here are a few situations where sellers create below market-value situations in which you can profit.

The Owners Face Financial Hardship

No matter what shape the economy is in, some segment of the population will be struggling to make ends meet. Whether due to a loss of job, medical problems, or simple financial mismanagement, some people will face financial hardship and will be looking for a way out. Many times, that way out is to raise cash to pay bills, and the property they own may be their biggest asset.

Keep in mind that you are not taking advantage of anyone. The seller is looking for a way out of his or her problems, and you may help this seller if you buy the property. In addition, if the price you offer is too low, the owner does not have to sell. It is that simple. There are always two parties that have to agree to any transaction, and they are the buyer and the seller. If selling the property helps the seller, you have both profited. For many people, selling a property today, even for less than market value, is better than being foreclosed upon tomorrow.

You may not know the owner is in distress, and that is why you make an offer that will yield you a profit. If the owner is in financial trouble, your offer may be accepted. Just be ready to act quickly, because the owner will probably also be in a hurry to close.

The Owners Found a Better Opportunity

Imagine a house is on the market and listed by an executive who has been transferred overseas. He received a huge promotion but had to move within two weeks to take his new position. The last thing the executive wants is a house in another country sitting idle. He will have to take care of maintenance and utilities, and he will be dealing with a real estate agent while he is halfway around the world getting settled into a new job and a new country. The last thing he may feel he needs is his old house sitting on the market.

While he certainly would like to maximize his sales price, he is also motivated to complete the sale as soon as possible, even if he does not make as much as he could. When a seller has found a great opportunity somewhere else, whether in real estate or in their personal life, you may get an opportunity to buy at below-market rates.

Typically, when a house is vacant, it is empty because the owners have found a better opportunity elsewhere, such as a job transfer, another home purchase, or foreclosure on their present home. Vacant houses make for motivated sellers and are a source of potential profit for you. The fact that the owners are in a hurry to take advantage of their new opportunity will often make them accept a lower offer so they can move on.

Vacant houses also do not show as well, and they feel like houses, not homes. People want to buy homes, and they want to buy a property they can see themselves living in. Typically, a vacant house will bring less than a house that is still occupied.

Lifestyle Sellers

Lifestyle sellers are those who no longer wish to live in the type of property they own. They may be an older couple who are ready to retire and move to a property with fewer maintenance or upkeep demands. They can be proprietors who no longer wish to deal with tenants. They can be a young couple whose house no longer meets the demand of a growing family. Sellers whose lives are in transition will often accept a lower price for the property in order to complete that transition.

It is also important to note that lifestyle sellers also make great candidates for seller financing opportunities. If the owners are older, they may have substantial assets built up. They do not have to cash out of the property in order to make a lifestyle transition, and they may be happy to provide financing.

The Less Than Savvy Seller

Some sellers will under-price their properties simply because they do not know better. This situation has become especially true in recent years as real estate prices have escalated sharply. Many owners simply do not realize that prices have experienced double-digit increases in recent years in certain parts of the country.

Alternatively, the seller may not understand that local conditions have changed. Let us say the area you are looking at has recently been reclassified as a historical district. In some states and localities, that type of reclassification allows the properties to quality for tax credits up to fifty percent of the cost of renovation. The values in the neighborhood may jump sharply as a result, but not all the owners may understand the impact of the change. A great opportunity for a below-market purchase might exist. If you have early knowledge of a market condition change, you may be able to put that knowledge to profitable use.

Owner-Landlords

Remember earlier I asked you to assess whether being a hands-on landlord was right for you. Many people do not perform that assessment and end up disliking the role of landlord. Unhappy landlords create great opportunities for bargain shopping.

Owning rental properties does not have to cause headaches, but it is not right for some people. If you find a landlord who is completely fed up with the idea of owning rental real estate, you have found a source of a great deal. An easy way to find a fed up landlord is to find a property that is vacant or in need of repair. Chances are the owner is tired of the hassles of owning rental property.

Here is something to keep in mind, though. Some people's first comments when they look at a property are, "I wonder what's wrong with it. Why do the sellers want to sell it?" They are convinced the only reason an owner would sell is that there is some problem with the property. They are especially convinced there is a problem when a cash flow positive rental property is on the market.

It is a fair question, but there can be a number of answers to that question. The first is that the owner simply does not want to be a landlord anymore. He may have an opportunity elsewhere and needs to free up cash to take advantage of it, or he may be experiencing financial hardship and needs to free up cash. Alternatively, he may simply not know how good a deal he is giving up.

There can be legitimate reasons for concern on your part as well. Possibly the location has become a poor one due to changes in the area, or the property is in need of repair. Remember, the owner is required to disclose issues of which he or she is aware.

Asking yourself, "Why does the owner want to sell?" is always a good question. Just make sure you dig deeply enough for the answers. If you perform a financial analysis, have an inspector look at the property and understand the local market. You can easily determine the suitability of making an offer and owning the property.

The Owners Do Not See Potential

Some owners simply do not realize their property contains potential for gain. They may not understand zoning regulations. They may not see that making simple changes could make the property much more desirable, or they may simply not be particularly imaginative.

Here is a great example. A few years ago, a couple looked at a small brick ranch, and they wanted a second home to use as an income-generating property.

It was located directly across from a local college, had a two-bedroom unit on the main floor, and several rooms, including a bathroom and kitchen, on the top floor. The top floor had a separate entrance and could be ideal for an additional apartment, but the owner was not using it that way. He assumed that since the property was zoned R-1, he could not have two separate tenants in the property.

He was wrong, because the R-1 zoning allowed for a family and one unrelated party to occupy a dwelling. The zoning would not allow three or four unrelated parties, but it certainly allowed for two unrelated parties.

The couple bought the house, because the income statement they developed showed that renting the downstairs to a family would yield enough rent to more than cover monthly expenses, making it a cash flow positive purchase. However, there were other reasons as well.

They spent about $2,000 refurbishing the upstairs of the house. They were able to rent the one bedroom apartment upstairs for an additional $375 per month, and this made the rental property extremely cash flow positive. They also rented a small, detached garage on the property to a local motorcyclist who wanted a place to keep his bikes safe and out of the weather. In all, they increased the rental income by 60 percent by making a few small changes to the property and by seeing an opportunity that the previous owner did not.

ACT QUICKLY, BUT PRUDENTLY

When you see a great deal, you will be tempted to dive in immediately, so you do not lose the deal. You do want to act quickly, but you also need to make sure the property is truly underpriced. If you act too quickly, you may miss issues or problems that cause the property to be fairly priced as is. In effect, you might buy someone else's problem and maybe one without a ready or inexpensive solution.

Always do a thorough financial analysis, have the property inspected, and make sure a title search is completed. Have your attorney look at the contract before you submit it, especially if the seller has requested unusual terms or arrangements.

Remember, a great deal is one where you can sell the property for more than you paid for it and have to put into it. If unexpected problems exist and your repair expenses are too high, you could even lose money on the deal.

HOW TO FIND BELOW-MARKET SELLERS

To find bargains, you will have to look. Rarely will a bargain simply fall into your lap. However, as you gain experience and local contacts, you will find that more and more often, bargains will find you instead of your finding them.

The best way to find great deals is to network. Most of us network in our business and personal lives, and that is how we find jobs, opportunities, day care providers, good auto mechanics, etc. However, very few real estate investors put the power of networking to work for them, but if you do, you will quickly gain an advantage.

How do you network? Tell everyone you know what you are doing and that you are looking for a second home. Tell them what you are looking for, whether it is a vacation home, a fixer-upper, a potential rental property, or a larger investment property. Real estate is a topic that almost everyone is interested in, because everyone has to live somewhere. Many people will find it fascinating that you are looking for a second home, and they will tell friends and family.

If your second home will be a rental property, you can also find potential tenants by networking. In addition, you can find skilled craftsmen that way, too. If you treat real estate investing like a job and you network as if you would in your job or profession, you can uncover a number of leads that would otherwise be unavailable to you.

Real Estate Agents

Real estate agents are not paid unless they find buyers or sellers for properties. As a result, a good real estate agent is always looking for a qualified buyer, and an agent loves a repeat buyer.

Explain your goals and your situation. Let the agent know what types of properties you are interested in and what your price parameters are. Tell the agent if he or she finds a property that meets your criteria, you would love to hear about it.

Use other means to find properties; after all, the real estate agent expects to be paid, and the commission comes from the seller's proceeds of the sale. This puts more pressure on the seller to get a higher price to offset some of the real estate agent's expense. However, occasionally a good agent will find a property you have missed or may have the inside track on a property just coming to market.

The agent can also help you do some homework by running an initial operating income statement for you. Let us say you want the property you buy to be cash-flow positive. Simply tell the agent you are interested in looking at any property where the rent is, say, $200 more than the monthly payment would be. The agent can do the initial screening for you, so whatever your target is, let the agent know, and he or she will screen properties for you.

Internet Prospecting

In the past, only real estate agents and other real estate professionals had easy access to the REALTOR® Multiple Listing Service. Now, thousands of Web sites list properties for sale, and you can access virtually all properties listed through a real estate agent on sites like **www.realtor.com**.

You can also visit sites listing foreclosure and FSBO properties. Keep in mind, however, that most of them charge a fee for information you can receive free elsewhere.

The beauty of Internet prospecting is that you can view multiple properties quickly and comfortably, narrowing your list to the few properties that meet your criteria. You can stay in constant touch with the local market or the market in which you are interested and can stay abreast of any changes or trends.

Expired Listings

When a seller signs an agreement with a real estate agent to list a house, the agreement is for a fixed period, typically sixty to ninety days. At the end of that period, the homeowner is under no obligation to continue the agreement. Many properties do not sell by the end of the listing period, and the owner renews the agreement, looks for another agent, or decides to sell the house himself. Many times other agents will also call the seller soliciting the listing.

If you are not in a hurry and are looking for a great deal, you do not have to work through the agent, and there is nothing unethical about it if you proceed in this way.

Do not call the agent listing the house; instead, contact the owners by mail. Simply write a brief letter explaining that you are interested in their house. Briefly describe your tentative price and terms. Mention that you know they are currently selling their house through an agent, and if they sell the house, you wish them well. If the house does not sell, ask them to contact you.

At no time should you create an agreement to buy the house, because if the seller reaches a separate agreement during the listing period, the agent is still entitled to a commission. In order to maintain ethical business standards, you should be clear that the owner should only contact you if the property does not sell during the listing period and if he or she decides not to renew the listing agreement.

Why would the owners accept your offer, especially if it is lower than the price at which they listed the house? The typical agent commission is 6 percent, so if the house sells for $100,000, the owners net $94,000. If you offer $94,000 after the listing period has expired, the owners are still netting the same amount they hoped to receive.

There is a risk to this type of transaction. If the sellers find a buyer during the listing period, you will not be able to buy the house. This strategy is only appropriate if you are in no hurry and are willing to let the house in question get away. As a smart buyer, you should be willing to let the house get away, because you will only want to make deals where you have an excellent chance of making a profit. If the house in question is your "dream" second home, you may not want to let it get away. The choice is yours. If the house is a great deal even with an agent involved, it may make sense to purchase the house for a higher price than you may have been able to get it for a month or two later, if no one else buys the house in the meantime, of course. That is the risk you will have to be willing to take.

CHAPTER THIRTEEN

HOLDING PROPERTY

A s a property owner, you can certainly hold title to your properties in your name as an individual or as a couple. If you own more than one property, or own rental properties, you may decide that you would like to create a separate legal entity responsible for holding the properties. You can form a corporation or a corporate entity to do so on your behalf. In effect you still own the property since you own the corporation, but you will be afforded some legal and financial protection and qualify for certain business and tax advantages.

There are several corporate entities you can create, and the following is an overview of corporate structures and their advantages. Please note that you should always consult an accountant for advice specific to your situation.

SOLE PROPRIETORSHIP

Most people who work out of their homes or who run small service oriented companies are classified as sole proprietors. As a sole proprietor, you are the only principal involved in the ownership and management of your business, and you are the only one responsible for the outcome. You solely reap the benefits, pay the bills, and suffer the consequences of any liability.

Even if you now have or eventually will have other people working for or with you, you will probably remain the sole proprietor of your business. If someone else works for you, that in no way changes the status of your business. As sole proprietor, you will still be the owner and manager of your business, which has certain advantages and disadvantages.

Advantages of a Sole Proprietorship

On the plus side is simplicity. There is little involved in setting up a sole proprietorship. You are not stuck with endless paperwork, and you do not need a lawyer to advise you or to create documents for the operation of your business. You pay taxes through your personal tax return, and your tax rates will usually be lower than corporate rates.

Disadvantages of a Sole Proprietorship

Among the disadvantages of a sole proprietorship is that it is difficult to obtain outside financing. You will be entirely responsible for any legal and financial problems your business encounters. If you get sued then it is you personally who gets sued, not your company.

The vast majority of home based entrepreneurs are sole proprietors. Be aware, however, that you are not bound to that status forever. However, even if you eventually find partnership or incorporation advantageous, you will probably want to start out as a sole proprietor. It is a simple and easy way to start.

PARTNERSHIP

When two or more persons go into business together, they usually form some sort of partnership. Partners share profits, expenses, responsibilities, and liabilities. They might own equal divisions of the business or have some other arrangement.

Partners enjoy the same tax breaks as sole proprietors. Each reports business profit and loss on his or her personal tax return. It is fairly easy to set up a partnership and does not cost much in the way of attorney's fees. Many people purchase their second home as a partnership. That way two parties share in the expenses and in the burdens of upkeep, property maintenance, etc. If you find a partner with the same goals, you may be able to afford a property you otherwise could not.

Advantages of a Partnership

Among the advantages of partnership is the division of equipment, supplies, and labor. The main advantage is that the expenses and headaches will be shared between you and another party. Of course, any profits down the road will be shared as well.

Disadvantages of a Partnership

Partnerships face the same financial difficulties and liabilities as sole proprietorships. Division of management responsibilities can lead to disagreements. For example, if you are handling the bulk of the queries from prospective renters, you may quickly become frustrated with your partner's lack of involvement. In addition, there are always potential problems when a partner leaves the business. What if your partner wants to sell and you do not?

Persons considering partnership have to overcome numerous obstacles and work out many potential problems. Will the partners carry equal workloads? How will they measure work? Will investments be equal? Will expenses be shared equally?

Partnership Agreement

Because of the possibilities for misunderstanding or disagreement, any partnership requires a good written agreement. The more complete the agreement, the fewer the hassles in the future. Partners should spend time, individually and together, considering, discussing, and writing down everything pertaining to the partnership. Put everything you can think of in writing. Do not go into a partnership assuming you will be able to work out any problems if they come up, because it is unlikely you will be able to do that.

Give an attorney a copy of the document you and your partner or partners have created and schedule a meeting. Your attorney should draft an agreement for approval by all parties. After the parties have reviewed the document and submitted revisions, the attorney will draft the final agreement for the partners' signatures.

The agreement should make provisions for division of expenditures, profits, losses, responsibilities, and liabilities as well as prolonged illness, disability, or death of a partner. You must also consider the disposition of the share of a partner who wishes to end the partnership for any other reason. Include a buyout clause and have your attorney give you advice on restrictions pertaining to buying and selling of the business or any partner's share.

No matter how well you think you will get along, assume in

your partnership agreement that the worst might happen and plan for what will take place if it does occur. If your prospective partner objects to putting together a detailed agreement, you may want to consider another partner.

The partnership agreement can be revised or amended at any time and should be whenever the partners make major changes in the way the business is operated. If you own a second home together, you are running a business. Put it in writing, and keep it current.

LIMITED LIABILITY COMPANY

A limited liability company is similar to a partnership, but enjoys some of the advantages usually restricted to a corporation. If you are thinking about forming a partnership, ask your attorney about the possibility and advantages of forming a limited liability company.

The main advantage is that income passes through to the principals of the company. If your LLC makes $15,000 in profit, those profits can pass straight to the principals without being taxed. The disadvantage of an LLC is that the owners are liable for any debt incurred. In a corporation, the owners are not personally liable.

COMPANIES AND CORPORATIONS

It is unlikely that you will want to consider incorporating when you buy a second home. In fact, you may never wish to incorporate. In the event your circumstances change however, you should know something about the pros and cons. A good attorney and accountant will be able to advise you on this major step.

Incorporation can be expensive. You will certainly need an attorney's help and you will have to pay your state a fee that might amount to $1,000 or more.

In a sole proprietorship or partnership, the principals are the business and vice versa. Everything that affects the business affects the owners. A corporation is an entity in and of itself.

Advantages of Incorporation

In a corporation, shareholders' assets are protected, and corporate assets are initially protected by current bankruptcy laws. Depending on the type of business, corporations generally find financing more readily available than sole proprietorships and partnerships.

Disadvantages of Incorporation

On the downside, corporations are much more complicated and expensive to set up. Most pay high corporate tax rates. In general, a corporation faces more complications with requirements for bylaws, a board of directors, corporate officers, annual meetings, and a greater need for attorneys and accountants.

There are two types of corporations: S-Corps and C-Corps. Most major corporations are C-Corps. The S-Corp operates in ways similar to an LLC where the income flows to the owners and is taxed as personal income. If there are multiple owners, the income is shared proportionately among them.

Limited liability companies are a relatively new corporate entity. In the past few years, most ventures considering forming an S-Corp have instead chosen to become an LLC. The main difference between an S-Corp and an LLC is that the S-Corp protects owners from personal debt liability. On the other hand, when you first form the corporation, it will have no credit history, so owners will have to sign personally for debt. In effect, there is no protection. Years later the corporation may have built a credit history and assets that allow it to qualify for financing on its own, and then the owners will be protected from debt liability.

You may be tempted to form a corporation so you will be protected from any financial liabilities if your investment fails or if a tenant sues you. That is not technically correct. As mentioned, when you first form a company, whether it is a corporation or a limited liability company, the entity will have no credit history. Because of that, it is your credit history lenders will use to determine whether or not to approve a loan. You will have to sign personally for that loan. Therefore, while you may have formed a corporation, you will still be liable for the corporation's debt.

What you will be protected from are losses due to injury or other liability. For example, if a tenant is injured and you are found to be at fault, you will be protected from liability by your corporate structure. Note that if you have been negligent, the tenant may be able to take civil action, which is another issue entirely.

See your accountant and attorney for advice. In some cases, incorporating may make great sense, or may give you tremendous piece of mind. Some investors never form corporations. The choice is yours. Seek out advice from a competent professional for your specific situation.

Basic Advantages of Incorporating

- **Asset Protection**: If you operate as a sole proprietor or partnership there is virtually unlimited personal liability for business debts or lawsuits. In other words, should you be a defendant in a lawsuit, your personal assets such as homes, jewelry, vehicles, savings, etc. are up for grabs. This is generally not the case when you incorporate. When you incorporate, you are only responsible for your investment in the corporation. The limited liability feature of a corporation, while not a guarantee, is definitely one of the most attractive reasons for incorporating.

- **Tax Savings**: When you incorporate, there are numerous tax advantages at your disposal that are virtually impossible to accomplish with other business entities. When you incorporate, you create a separate and distinct legal entity. Because of this, there are many transactions that you can structure between you and your corporation to save money on taxes.

- **Privacy and Confidentiality**: The corporate form of business is a great way to keep your identity and business affairs private and confidential. Do you not want other people to know you own a second home? If you want to start a business, but would like to remain anonymous, a corporation is the best way to accomplish this. States like Nevada offer even more privacy protection for corporations and their shareholders.

- **Perpetuity**: When you incorporate, you create a separate and distinct legal entity. This separate and distinct entity, the corporation, can endure almost forever, irrespective of what happens to the shareholders, directors, or officers. This is not the case with sole proprietorships, partnerships, or even limited liability companies. For example, if an owner, partner, or member dies, the business automatically ends or finds itself in a legal tangle. Corporations, on the other hand, have unlimited life.

TRUSTS

Forming a trust is similar to forming a corporation in that you gain some anonymity and protection from liability. For example, if you form a trust and the trust owns a particular property, the property is titled to ABC Housing Trust or even to the property address, 1234 High Street Trust.

You can take your home and property out of the public domain and transfer it into a land trust or an irrevocable trust. This is not a fail-safe method of protecting yourself from liability, however.

In a typical land trust, you control all the decisions and you and your family are the beneficiaries of the trust. If you are taken to court, a good lawyer will argue that you have too much control over the trust. Asset protection lawyers argue that land trusts work in theory, but be aware that they may not hold up in court.

A real trust is one where you do not control the trustee. The trustee is a lawyer or accountant or even a bank. You cannot change a real trust; it is truly irrevocable, because you do not control it. Real trusts cannot be broken. For that reason, many wealthy families create trusts. Once they are set up they cannot be broken and the family protects whatever assets are in the trust.

The main advantage of setting up a trust is to avoid estate taxes. Say you own three houses. If you bring your heirs into the trust, the ownership of the trust stays with them upon your passing. They will not incur estate taxes because they were already owners of the trust.

Use life insurance as an example. Say you buy a $1 million life insurance policy. If your life insurance is in your name and is included in your estate, your heirs could face a tax liability if your estate hits the $2 million mark. If you put the $1 million in an irrevocable trust, it is out of your name and therefore out of your estate.

See a competent real estate or tax lawyer to set up a trust. Trusts are a popular way to protect assets and avoid estate taxes, but they must be set up properly in order to be valid. A good attorney can advise you whether to set up an LLC, a corporation, or a trust to hold your properties and run your business.

CHAPTER FOURTEEN

PROPERTY MANAGEMENT

L ook forward and pretend you have already purchased your second home. Congratulations!

Now you need to manage the property. If you will be the only tenant of your second home, management is simple because you are in charge. You can hire someone to look after the property when you are away, but you will not have to worry about tenant problems, collecting rent, etc.

If you plan to rent the property, for either the entire year or part of the year, you will need to be active in managing the property. Getting a great deal on your second home is only half the battle. Managing the property successfully is extremely important, too.

If you will be renting your property, there is an important legal consideration to keep in mind. You may be tempted to skim over this section, but do not. Be sure you understand your legal responsibilities as a landlord even if you will only be renting your second home on a short-term basis for a few months each year.

FAIR HOUSING ACT

The Fair Housing Act is government legislation that affects landlords and tenants. For instance, withholding an apartment available for rent, segregating certain persons in separate sections of an apartment complex or parts of a building, and charging persons in a protected class a different amount for rent or security deposits are all violations of the law.

The Fair Housing Act goes even farther. A landlord cannot charge a different amount of rent or a higher security deposit because one of the tenants is a child. Landlords have historically argued that children are noisy and destructive, but it is unlawful to charge a different amount due to the presence of a child.

If you are renting or selling a property, you cannot take any of the following actions on the basis of race, color, creed, religion, sex, handicap, or family status:

- Refuse to negotiate, rent, or sell housing.

- Make housing unavailable.

- Deny someone a dwelling.

- Set different terms, conditions, or privileges for different groups of people.

- Provide different services or facilities to different groups of people.

- Falsely claim that housing is unavailable for sale or rent.

- Profit by persuading owners to sell or rent based on news of changes to neighborhood demographics or the overall makeup of people who live in the neighborhood.

If the Department of Housing and Urban Development (HUD) finds that you have discriminated in any way, you can be sued if a pattern of discriminatory behavior can be proven.

What does all this mean? Be fair and equitable to all parties and you have nothing to worry about.

There are exemptions. For instance, if you own three or less single-family residential properties, you are exempt from the Fair Housing Act. Rooms for rent are exempt in an owner occupied dwelling of four or fewer units.

There are other exemptions, but the bottom line is that treating all people fairly will ensure you do not run afoul of government regulations. Discriminate and you run the chance of legal proceedings or lawsuits.

Also, be sure to consider the language you use in any notices that advertise your property. To ensure you do not make discriminatory statements when you write classified ads for your rental properties, focus on the features of the property, not on the type of tenants you are trying to attract.

For instance, do not say "Perfect for older couples." Say, "Low maintenance, single floor living." Do not say, "Perfect for college student." Say, "Next to the university." Simply highlight the features of the unit, not the person you are trying to attract.

TYPES OF LEASES

There are a number of different types of leases. In most cases, you will only be likely to use one or two of them, but it is helpful to understand the basic types of leases you can utilize.

- **Gross Lease**: In a gross lease, the tenant pays a fixed rental and the landlord pays all taxes, insurance, repairs, utilities, etc. In effect, the landlord pays all operating charges.

- **Net Lease**: In a net lease, the tenant pays all or some of the property charges in addition to the rent. The monthly rental is net income for the landlord after operating costs have been paid. Leases for commercial or industrial buildings and long-term leases are usually net leases. In a net lease, the tenant pays all operating and other expenses related to the property.

- **Percentage Lease**: Gross leases and net leases can also be percentage leases. The rent is based on a minimum fixed rental plus a percentage of the gross income received by the tenant doing business on the leased property. The percentage charged is of course negotiable. These leases are typically used for commercial leases for retail properties.

- **Variable Lease**: A variable lease allows for increases in rental charges. A graduated lease allows for periodic rental increases based on set time periods. An index lease allows rent to be increased or decreased based on changes in some economic indicator.

- **Ground Lease**: When a landowner leases unimproved land to a tenant who agrees to erect a building on the land, the lease is usually referred to as a ground lease. The term of lease is usually long enough to make the transaction desirable for the tenant. Ground leases of fifty years or more are common. Ground leases are generally net leases where the tenant must pay rent on the ground as well as all real estate taxes, insurance, upkeep, and repairs.

- **Lease Purchase**: A lease purchase covers when a tenant eventually wants to purchase the property, but is unable to do so at the time. The purchase agreement is the primary consideration and the lease is secondary. Part of the periodic rent is applied toward the purchase price of the property until it is reduced to an amount at which the tenant can obtain financing or purchase the property outright.

In most cases, residential leases, like ones for second homes, are either gross leases, net leases, or a combination of the two. For instance, you could agree to a gross lease. In that case, you will be responsible for all utilities, taxes, repairs, etc. More common is a gross lease arrangement where the tenant is responsible for utilities and you are responsible for upkeep, taxes, insurance, and other operating expenses.

Keep in mind that your lease can contain any provisions you see fit. You can require the tenants to clean the property to a certain set of standards before they leave, such as mow the grass, maintain the landscaping, or perform other duties. Alternatively, you can retain responsibility for those duties.

Also, keep in mind that a lease is a binding contract between both parties. You will want to make sure the lease you construct is appropriate for your needs.

Laws and regulations vary from state to state and locality to locality. Your best bet is to find an experienced real estate attorney in the location where you are buying the home. Make an appointment to sit down and discuss your plans. Ask the following questions:

- Are there any special considerations I need to consider as a landlord? Are there special codes or area laws of which I need to be aware? For example, in some localities landlords are responsible for dealing with excessively noisy tenants. Failure to do so can result in fines to the landlord even though the landlord is not the person making the noise.

- Are there any special zoning considerations of which I should be aware?

- As a new rental property owner, is there any general advice you can give me?

- Can you provide me with copies of an effective lease agreement and any other documents I may need?

The last question is important. General lease agreements are readily available and can be purchased at just about any office supply store. They cover the majority of basic issues that may arise. Specific areas or localities may have specific laws that are not covered under a general lease.

In the example of the locality that makes landlords responsible for tenant noise, many landlords include provisions in their leases that state something like this: "If a complaint is made by a neighbor or other party regarding noise levels and the complaints are repeated subsequent times, the landlord may terminate the lease agreement and immediately begin eviction proceedings." Standard leases will not include locality specific language such as this.

An hour's consultation with a lawyer may cost you $75 to $125, but you will find it to be money well spent. See that consultation as an insurance policy against future problems, costs, and headaches, and you will not mind the expense.

TYPICAL LEASE PROVISIONS

While lease forms and provisions may vary, some provisions are common and should appear on any lease.

- **Intention to vacate**: Typically, you will require tenants to give you thirty days notice if they plan to vacate. If they do not provide such notice, you can withhold their security deposit based on the terms of your agreement. If it is difficult to find new tenants in your area, you may want to consider increasing the intention to vacate period to forty-five or sixty days.

- **Use of property**: Your lease can state how the property will be used. In most cases, it will be used for residential purposes, but if the area is zoned appropriately, a tenant may decide to operate a business out of the home. You are allowed to determine what types of businesses or use you will allow.

- **Property description**: Your lease should describe the state of repair of the property when the tenant moves in. The easiest way to do so is with a checklist you develop that is specific to the property. You and the tenant can perform the inspection together and then both sign off that the condition is as stated on the form. If you have removable items on the property, such as dishwashers, appliances, window treatments, or furniture, your lease should also describe those items. Many landlords take photographs of the property and require the tenant to date and sign them. Such photos make great evidence if there is a later dispute about the condition of the property.

- **Rent specifics**: Your lease should state the rent amount, the due dates, and how the payment will be delivered to you. It should also specify charges for late fees and the security deposit amount. Many states regulate the amount you can charge for a security deposit, so check with your local government office for details.

- **Pets**: Your lease should include provisions for tenants having pets. Whether you allow pets is up to you. Many landlords who allow pets collect additional security deposit amounts in case of damage to the property.

- **Laws**: Even though your tenants are bound to observe all laws and regulations, it is a good idea to have a provision in the lease requiring them to observe all laws and government regulations. See your attorney for effective language to use in your lease.

- **Cleanliness and damage**: Your lease should include provisions for how you want the property maintained. You should not have to pay for repairs caused by tenant abuse. Your lease should include language defining what can and cannot be considered tenant abuse.

- **Inspections**: Your lease should include provisions for when, and under what conditions, you are allowed to inspect the property. Many leases require the landlord to give reasonable notice, while others allow inspections at any time. Twenty-four hour notice periods are common, but your lease should include language allowing you to have immediate access to the property in case of emergency or if you think the property has been damaged.

- **Eviction proceedings**: Evictions are covered by local laws, but your lease should still include language about when and why you are allowed to initiate eviction proceedings. If a tenant agrees, your lease could include language that allows you to evict him or her without cause. Just because you initiate eviction proceedings does not mean the tenant will instantly leave. In most areas, it can take from thirty to sixty days or longer before a tenant is compelled to leave. You can also include heavy penalties if tenants are evicted. You may not ever collect them, but the fact they exist may scare some tenants into behaving responsibly.

- **End of lease provisions**: Once the initial period of the lease is up, your lease should include language about what happens. Does the lease continue on a month-to-month basis or is a new lease required? You could also include language that allows you to require the tenant to leave the property after the lease period is over. If your lease allows a month-to-month arrangement, you may have to give the tenant notice that you will be terminating the lease.

- **Co-tenant provisions**: If you rent to co-tenants, you will want to include a statement called a joint and several liability clause. The result of this statement is that all parties are responsible both collectively and individually for rent, damages, etc. If you do not have this clause included, tenants can and will argue that they are not responsible for monies owed or for damages because it is the other person's fault. This clause is also important in case the co-tenants are married and file for divorce.

- **Guests**: Some tenants will allow others to move in without notifying you that they have new co-tenants. You may or may not care, especially if the tenants are responsible for all utilities. Additional tenants may cause zoning issues for you. If you are concerned, you can include language in your lease restricting the number of guests and restricting the length of time they can stay on the property.

- **Limits to property changes**: Many tenants will make changes to the property without asking permission. For instance, they may paint, install new built in furniture, or remove the doors or windows. To keep tenants from making unwanted changes, you can require that any changes to the property, including paint, wallpaper, carpet, paneling, wall materials, or any other types of renovations or removals, be granted by you in writing. Failure to obtain written permission can result in eviction or forfeiture of security deposits.

- **Subletting**: Subletting is common in college towns where students move home for the summer and want someone else to take over their apartment. Whether you allow subletting is up to you, but in general, you should not allow it. If you have carefully screened the original tenant, you at least have some assurance that he or she may be a good tenant, but you will have no ability to screen the subleasing party. Some courts have ruled that unless you specifically prohibit subletting, subletting is permissible. If you do not want subletting on your properties, include prohibitive language.

As you can see, there are a number of legal issues involved in crafting a good lease. Do not use one of the generic leases you can purchase at office supply stores. Consult a lawyer to get a well-crafted lease that is appropriate for your particular locality.

If you buy a property with existing tenants whose leases are still in force, you will be bound by the terms of those leases. Make sure you review all the leases before you buy the property so you will know what you are getting into. Once those leases expire you can transition tenants to your own lease agreement, but in the meantime you will be bound by the provisions of the lease signed by the previous owner.

SCREENING TENANTS

Good tenants will not simply appear at your doorstep. You will have to find them. Keep in mind that you cannot discriminate, but you can screen, as long as you subject all candidates to the same screening process. If you are screening everyone the same way, you are not discriminating. If you decide to check references for one tenant and not for another, and if you subsequently deny one of them housing, you could be facing a discrimination lawsuit.

Here are some basic tenant screening provisions you can implement:

- **Reference check**: Require all prospective tenants to give you the names and numbers of previous landlords. Most previous landlords will gladly let you know if a tenant had payment problems or behavior problems.

- **Minimum income**: You can require all prospective tenants to meet a minimum income standard to ensure they can afford to rent from you. In order to verify their income you can request pay stubs or W-2 forms. You must of course treat all such information as confidential.

- **Credit history**: You can check the credit reports of prospective tenants to see if they have a history of late payments, judgments, bankruptcy, etc. Keep in mind that credit checks will probably not show rent related problems. Most landlords do not report credit events to the credit bureaus. You will also have to find a local source for processing your credit report requests.

- **Employment status**: You can require prospective tenants to be currently employed, and to have a minimum employment history.

You should make employment status, income, and reference checks a part of your standard screening process. While it is true that references can be faked, employment generally cannot, and neither can pay stubs or W-2 forms. If you check all three, you have a greater likelihood of getting a sense of the prospective tenant's financial stability and willingness to be a good tenant.

When you perform the checks, make notes and save copies of any documents you receive, whether you eventually rent to the person or not. Those notes are your documentation proving that you consistently apply your screening tools to all applicants.

DAY-TO-DAY MANAGEMENT

Once you have purchased a rental property, someone will have to manage it. Either you can manage the property yourself or you can hire someone to do it for you. There are pros and cons to either approach. We will look at both.

Managing Your Own Properties

Most experts suggest you should start out managing your own properties. You will learn a lot from the experience, and you will save money that you can use to invest in other properties.

Managing your own properties keeps you close to the action. Managing properties and making successful real estate investments are both an art and a science and you learn the art from doing, not from watching others do the work.

If your second home will be hundreds of miles away in a beach or resort area, you should consider hiring a property management firm. The distance will be a problem you will find hard to overcome. If the second home is close by or is intended to generate income, most second homeowners manage their own properties for the following reasons:

- **It costs less**. A property management firm will charge a fee for their services, typically 10 to 15 percent of the gross lease rental amount. Property management firms will not provide services that you cannot provide yourself.

- **You will learn about local market conditions**. You will be talking to prospective renters yourself, talking to local tradespersons, and talking to local government officials, and you will learn a lot about conditions in your area. You will also find that you are building a network that will help you later on.

- **You will understand how to manage the business of owning a second home**. You need the ground floor experience. There is no substitute for hands on experience. Understanding the business issues will help you spot good deals, problems to avoid, and talented individuals who you would like to work with or partner with in the future. If you do not understand the business, you cannot evaluate the services that others provide you.

Whether you manage your own properties or hire someone to do it for you, you will still need the occasional advice of an attorney and an accountant. The attorney can help you avoid any legal problems or issues, while the accountant can make sure you take full advantage of any business or tax provisions that help you maximize your income and your return.

Managing your properties is straightforward. You advertise for tenants, you screen candidates based on criteria you establish, you keep an eye on your property, and you make repairs when necessary. It is not complicated, although it will require effort.

If you decide to manage your own properties, here are some tips:

- Unless the property is already immaculate, clean and paint all units before you allow tenants to move in. It is much easier to clean and paint when the units are empty, and you are more likely to attract good tenants to a clean and pleasant property.

- Make sure all appliances, windows, doors, etc. are in good working order. The last thing you want to face is the awkward moment of surprise when you are showing the property and one of the appliances does not work properly.

- When you meet prospective tenants, you should not act like the owner of the property. Act like a customer service specialist. After all, you are providing a service, not allowing them to rent your property. Try to sell the property. Point out its attractive features and make sure they get the impression that you will be a good landlord. Most renters have had bad landlords. They will jump at the chance to rent from a good one.

- Target your prospective renters and advertise to them. If you are seeking young professionals as tenants, do not say so in an ad. Advertise where young professionals are likely to see your ads. If you want students as tenants, place flyers at the local college or college hangouts. If you seek young families as tenants, place flyers at churches, community centers, or recreation facilities.

- Make sure you receive security deposits and rent payments before you allow tenants to move in. If they pay by check, leave enough time for the checks to clear. If that is not possible, insist on cash or a cashier's check.

- Screen your tenants consistently. Follow the criteria you set up. If a tenant makes an excuse for why he cannot provide references or an employment history, simply thank him for his or her time and move on. Why? You cannot complete your screening consistently, and excuses are typically just that - excuses.

- Network for tenants even when you do not have vacancies. Renters are always looking for a better apartment, a better lease, or a better landlord. Some will leap at the chance to rent your property when it becomes available. If you have a list of prospective tenants, you may avoid advertising costs and it will limit your vacancy time.

- When your tenants move in, take the time to explain all of your rules one more time. Also, perform the walk-through inspection together so you both can sign off on the condition of the property.

- Make contacts with plumbers, electricians, heating and air conditioning specialists, and other tradesmen now rather than when you actually need them. Call a reputable firm and set up an account now. Then if you need them on an emergency basis, they will respond. If they do not already know you, they may not be as responsive as you need them to be.

TENANT EVICTIONS

No matter how tightly you screen potential tenants, the day will eventually come when eviction proceedings are necessary. Your tenants may experience financial hardship or they may simply refuse to pay the rent, maintain the property correctly, or follow the rules established in your lease.

Eviction proceedings must take place according to state and local laws. The process is simple, but it can be time consuming.

Your first protection against bad tenants is a well-constructed lease. I cannot stress strongly enough the need to consult with an attorney to ensure you have a solidly crafted lease to offer maximum protection to you as a landlord.

When a tenant breaches a lease, the landlord may regain possession through a legal process known as an actual eviction. In effect, you are suing to regain access to your property. Some states require a ten-day notice period from the landlord to the tenant that eviction proceedings will commence if conditions are not met. In other states, the notification period is five days. For instance, if the tenant is late paying rent, you can notify him or her that you will proceed with eviction processes if you do not receive the rent within five days. The notice must be in writing.

If the tenant does not comply, you will go to the local courthouse to initiate eviction proceedings. The court will issue an eviction notice, for a fee, to the tenant, alerting him or her of impending proceedings. The court will set a court date for a hearing if the tenant has not complied with the terms of the lease. Typically the court date can be anywhere from two weeks to a month from the date of your visit to the courthouse. During this time, the tenant maintains possession of the property.

At the court hearing, the judge will hear both sides of the case. If you have a well-constructed lease, have given notice of your intention to evict, and the tenant cannot prove payment has been made, the judge will set a date by which the tenant must vacate the property. He will also assess damages that you can try to collect.

If the tenant does not vacate by the set date, the county will either physically evict the tenant or will make the property safe for you to do so.

Here is an example of how the process can work in real terms:

Your lease specifies that tenants must pay the rent on the first of each month. Your lease also specifies that if the tenant is more than five days late you can assess a $75 late charge, and if the tenant is more than eight days late you can begin eviction proceedings.

On the fifth day, you send the tenant a notice that his rent is late. On the eighth day, you send a notice that you will begin eviction proceedings, and you go to the courthouse to do so on the thirteenth day, which is five days after the notice.

At the courthouse, you pay the eviction-filing fee and fill out the appropriate paperwork. The clerk will keep a copy of your lease agreement and your written notice to the tenant that you plan to evict. At that time, you will specify the damages you are seeking such as late payments, late payment fees, and any other reasonable costs you have incurred.

Court officials, typically personnel from the local sheriff's department, will deliver the eviction notice to the tenant, either in person or by affixing it to the front door of the property. On the notice is the court date when you both must appear.

At the day of the hearing, the judge will quickly review the documents you provided and then ask if the tenant has made payment. If the tenant shows up for court, but has not paid, the judge will set a date by which the tenant must vacate the property. Until that date, the tenant is allowed to remain in the property.

If the tenant does not show up for the hearing, oftentimes the judge will allow you to regain possession of the property within twenty four to seventy two hours. A notice will be delivered to the tenant stating such. At that time, you are granted possession of the property. The judge may also grant you possession of the tenant's personal property to satisfy any unpaid debts you are owed.

If the tenant has not vacated, in some localities the sheriff's department will move his property to the curb. In other localities, and this is a more likely situation, the sheriff's department will send a deputy to keep the peace while you move his possessions to the curb. In either case, if the tenant is still physically on the premises, you can expect the situation to be awkward, to say the least. It is a good idea to ask the deputy to require the tenants to remove themselves from your property entirely.

The eviction process probably does not sound like much fun, and it is not, but it is a necessary part of being a landlord. Again, the more tightly your lease is constructed, the better job you do of screening potential tenants, and the more in touch you stay with your tenants and your property, the less likely you are to find yourself initiating eviction proceedings.

HIRING OTHERS TO MANAGE YOUR PROPERTIES

If you would prefer not to manage your second home, you will need to hire someone to manage it for you.

There are two basic ways you can hire management help. You can hire an individual, or you can hire a property management firm that specializes in rental management.

Typically, an individual you hire is called a superintendent or a caretaker. Some caretakers live on the premises and manage the property in exchange for free rent, pay, or other concessions. Others live off-site and manage the property for a fee.

If you hire a caretaker that lives on the premises, you will have to create a very specific agreement about expectations and pay. For instance, if you offer free rent in exchange for the caretaker collecting rent checks from other tenants and performing basic maintenance on the property, you will want to spell out exactly what those maintenance duties are. You will also want to set up firm guidelines about how and when the caretaker can call in outside professionals to perform repairs or maintenance. You may also set up a fee schedule where you pay the caretaker an hourly rate for tasks that fall outside your standard agreement.

If you hire an off-site caretaker, you will simply agree to an hourly rate or to a monthly fee. Hourly rates are preferable because that way both parties can feel they are treated fairly.

You will also want to create an agreement that covers termination of the agreement. If your caretaker lives off the premises, it is easy. You simply inform him or her that services are no longer required. If the caretaker lives on-site, you will want to specify rental amounts and terms in the event that you return to a standard landlord-tenant business relationship.

A more common way to hire others to manage your properties is to hire a property management firm. Most property management firms operate on a percentage basis. They charge a percentage of gross rent in exchange for providing certain services. They may charge additional fees for providing special services like evictions.

Property management fees vary depending on locality and the services offered. Fees can range from five percent to twenty percent or more. Ten to fifteen percent is typical. You will want to be sure you understand exactly what the management company is responsible for and what duties they will carry out.

Keep in mind that even though the property managers are managing your home, you are still ultimately responsible for the home. If there are tenant problems, ultimately those problems are your problems. If tenants fall behind on rent, that problem is ultimately your problem. If tenants damage the property, that problem is your problem. The management company will simply help facilitate the remedies to those problems.

Property management companies will typically do the following:

- Screen tenants per your criteria, including performing reference checks, credit checks, and employment checks.

- Advertise and solicit tenants for vacant properties.

- Perform periodic property inspections.

- Coordinate repairs and maintenance tasks.

- Serve as the main point of contact for tenants.

- Collect rent payments, forwarding your portion to you after they deduct for their fees.

- Maintain files and records.

- Coordinate eviction notices and eviction proceedings.

- Perform other duties as negotiated.

Keep in mind that agreements can and do vary. You will need to discuss thoroughly the responsibilities and services the property management company will perform.

If you are renting a beach or resort home, you will in all likelihood choose a property manager, otherwise you will need to find twelve to sixteen or more different renters just to cover the summer months and someone to clean the home after each renter vacates, and someone to check on its condition as the renters leave. Make sure you understand exactly what services the property managers will provide and that you understand the fee structure they propose. If you purchase a property in a prime spot, do not be afraid to shop around for the best combination of services and price. Property managers will actively bid to represent the best properties.

CHAPTER FIFTEEN

BASIC IMPROVEMENTS FOR QUICK PROFITS

I f you have purchased your second home with the intention of making a quick profit by reselling it, you will want to make sure you do at least a few things to maximize its selling price. If your intention is to rent the home, you will want to make sure you can charge an optimum amount of rent. In either case, the home will need to stand out from competing properties. If you bought the house for less than market value, you are off to a great start. Now we are going to make sure you can sell it or rent it for a great price with as little additional investment as possible. How do you accomplish that?

It is a simple formula. You will repair or replace only what shows, because your customers are not likely to be impressed by what they cannot see. What a prospective buyer or renter will notice is faulty or incomplete workmanship or things that do not work, so spend your time making basic repairs and replacing inexpensive things that are visible and eye-catching. These improvements tell a buyer that care was given to making the house ready to occupy in move-in condition, which is just the impression you want to make. Here is a rundown of fast fixes, cleanup chores, and repairs that are easy to do and are not too expensive. They add value to the house and make it more saleable or rentable.

Decorating

These quick fixes and decorating ideas go a long way to making a house clean, fresh, and inviting. The small investment required for these finishing details makes a house livable and appealing.

- **Paint**: If you do nothing else to the home, at least paint the rooms. You will get the best bang for your buck with a $25 gallon of paint because nothing else will make such a dramatic improvement to a dingy home. Use off-white flat latex paint on walls and an eggshell or satin finish on woodwork and trim. By choosing a neutral shade of paint, you give prospective buyers a blank canvas to make decorating easy. To keep it simple, paint ceilings and walls the same color. Another benefit of painting is the inviting aroma of a freshly painted house.

- **Window blinds**: For a finished appearance and to eliminate the fishbowl appearance of an empty house, install mini-blinds on the windows. For as little as $10 a window, you can buy one-inch vinyl mini-blinds. The aluminum ones start at around $20 each. An inexpensive vertical blind for a patio door costs about $70. Installing these window treatments is easy, especially because you learn by doing and repeating the process and the more windows there are, the more learning you will face.

- **Decorative window film**: If a window is open to the street and a sense of privacy is needed without blocking the daylight, apply a decorative window film that looks like etched glass. It is as simple as cleaning the glass, measuring and cutting the film, and then positioning it on the glass using a squeegee to smooth it in place. You will find the film sold at home and decorating centers in several designs and patterns.

- **Floor registers and heat grates**: Replace any old units that have rusted or have bent louvers that no longer operate. New registers and grates cost $5 to $10 and are available in a wide range of sizes and shapes. They go a long way toward updating the look and appeal of a room.

- **Dark knotty pine paneling**: Remove the dark finish on old paneling with gel-type paint and varnish remover. Apply it with a paintbrush and scrape off the finish with a wide putty knife when the remover bubbles and softens. Then clean the paneling with a rubdown of mineral spirits and let it dry. Use an electric finish sander, vacuum away the dust, and apply water based polyurethane with a brush or tung oil with a rag.

Electrical Projects

Here are some inexpensive electrical repairs and replacements that give an old house an updated look. These basic and easy projects require a minimum of tools and talents. Learn how to do them yourself so you will be confident and can do them later on other investment properties.

- **Electrical switches and receptacles**: To create a sense of newness and uniformity throughout all the rooms in a house, replace the electrical light switches, receptacles, and plate covers. At around $5 each, it is a small investment in an improvement that updates the house. It is a particularly noticeable upgrade if the existing ones have layers of paint or if they are the old push button type found in many older homes.

To comply with the National Electrical Code, replace each electrical outlet in the kitchen and bathroom with a ground fault circuit interrupter (GFCI). The device reduces the danger of a deadly shock from a faulty plug-in cord or appliance. It measures outgoing and returning current and shuts off the power if it detects a possible dangerous current imbalance. It has a test button that switches off the power to the outlet and any receptacles connected to it when it is pushed in. In addition to the kitchen and bathroom, GFCIs are required in all the wet areas of a house, such as the laundry room, unfinished basement, garage, outdoor areas, or wherever there is construction activity. It is not difficult to replace a standard receptacle with a GFCI (under $15) or you can hire an electrical contractor to do it.

- **Dimmer switches**: Another easy electrical upgrade is to replace a standard light switch in the dining room with a dimmer switch. It is a nice touch that costs about $15 and creates a cozy feeling in a room. The job involves turning off the power at the main circuit panel, removing the old device by disconnecting and cutting the wires, installing the new switch, reattaching the wires to the terminals, testing the device, and finally turning the power back on.

- **Test the switches and receptacles**: If the existing switches and receptacles are okay, check to see that they work. Turn on the switches and plug in a small lamp or radio in the receptacles. Make a note of any switches or receptacles that do not work and replace them.

- **Light fixtures**: In many homes, there is a hodgepodge of ceiling light fixtures that are distractions instead of attractions. Assess the style and condition of all light fixtures in the ceilings and replace those that are dated and worn. Do not go overboard with expensive new ones. For the bedrooms choose a basic $10 ceiling fixture with two bulbs that hugs the ceiling. For a dining room or kitchen, choose a traditional style. There is a great selection of fixtures in the $50 range at home centers. The same is true for hall lights. Coordinate the hall, dining room, and kitchen fixtures so they are similar in style and finish.

- **Thermostat**: Replace an old thermostat with a new one, especially if it has years of paint around its edges. You will find a standard round device for about $30 to $40 and a programmable unit for $50 to $100. Either one is a noticeable upgrade.

Walls, Doors, and Windows

When you enter a room, your eyes immediately go to a hole in the wall or a broken windowpane. Any eyesore usually draws attention, which is not the impression you want to make to prospective buyers. These repairs cost next to nothing and can be completed in little time. They are all worth well more than the expense.

- **Wall repairs**: The holes in walls left from pictures and decorations look like nasty pockmarks when the house is emptied out. Before painting walls, spend the time to repair the holes so the finished surface will be flat and smooth. Look for holes in the walls behind doorknobs with no doorstop and on walls in eating areas behind where a chair was often pushed back and made a dent. Repair the hole in the wallboard and then install a new doorstop.

- **Closet doors**: Tune up closet sliding doors so they open and close easily. Lift the door up so its glide wheel comes off the track. Then inspect the rollers along the top and apply a few drops of household oil if they do not turn freely. If the ball bearings do not move and the glide wheels are frozen, replace the tracks or glides, which are $2 items.

  Add lighting to a closet without wiring with battery operated closet lights. Some of these $6 push on/off fixtures have a hanger for a clothes rack. Others are installed on the wall with a backing of a self-stick adhesive.

- **Exterior door**: Replace an old lock and add a sense of security with a new deadbolt lock for about $40. If you are giving your entry door a facelift, replace the threshold, too, especially if you have plans to change the carpeting or flooring material. In case you discover uneven surfaces after removing layers of old flooring, choose a threshold that is self-adjusting so that you can even out the surface. The best time to make these improvements is after you paint or finish the door.

- **Storm/Screen door**: Make an old storm door feel new

with a $15 screen door handle. The job involves removing the old handle and checking out the holes to see if they can be used for the new handle. If not, use the paper template that comes packaged with the handle as a guide for drilling new mounting holes.

- **Sliding patio door**: A patio door may be difficult to open and close because of a buildup of dirt or debris in the track that clogs the lubrication in the rollers. Clean out the track with cotton swabs, and if that does not help, replace the old rollers with new track hardware, which costs about $10. You have to remove the door panels, so schedule the job during temperate weather.

- **Double hung windows**: If an old window sash is difficult to slide up and down, lubricate the pulley shafts with a squirt of lubricating oil like WD-40. The pulleys are located at the top of the window jamb where the rope enters the jamb. The lower sash must be closed to expose the pulleys, but the upper sash has to be open to get to them. Use the extension straw of the can to direct the oil into the center of the pulley. The oil helps the wheels turn freely so the window sash can open and close.

- **Window glass**: You can replace a windowpane in a double hung window for about $15, which covers the materials. The job involves removing the broken pane and putty and then using new glazing putty and glazier points to secure the replacement glass.

- **Screens**: Anyone can replace old or torn screening with new fiberglass screening fabric. First, remove the spline in the groove of the frame, which holds the screening in place. Then replace the screening and secure it with the old spline. If it is brittle, you will need a roll of new spline. Fifteen dollars will buy the material and tools you need.

- **Window sills**: Two part epoxy wood filler does a good job of rebuilding damaged wood and lets you shape and sand the surface so it conforms to its original appearance. It is a good choice for fixing a rotten windowsill. The filler system has two parts: a liquid that is squeezed into the damaged sill to stabilize the wood, and a paste-like filler applied with a putty knife that hardens and conforms to the shape. When the filler is dry, you sand it smooth and paint it.

Bathroom

Although it is a small room, a bathroom can be dirty with buildup of scum and mildew. It takes time and patience to scrub and scour, but your work will pay off because a dirty bathroom is a definite negative to homebuyers.

- **Clean all surfaces**: To remove the buildup of soap scum and watermarks on chrome bathtub fixtures, use a 50-50 solution of household vinegar and water. Soak a rag in the solution and wrap it around the fixture for a few minutes. Then use the rag to scrub the fixture. You may have to make more than one application for tough stains.

  Use a spray cleaner that attacks mildew on all surfaces in the bathroom where mildew has grown. Increase the ventilation in the room to prevent it from returning.

- **Tile grout**: Apply a new coat of grout around a ceramic tile bathtub surround for a fast face-lift. It is a good idea to protect the tub floor with a heavy drop cloth or cardboard, and remove the tub spout and handle faucets first. The job involves removing the old grout with an inexpensive grout saw, cleaning out the seams with the crevice tool of a vacuum, and then applying the new grout. Smooth the joints, wipe away the grout haze, caulk the joints, and then reinstall the fixtures.

- **Bathtub caulk**: Remove old caulk with a putty knife and clean the joint between the wall and tub and the wall around the sink. Scrub the joint with an old toothbrush to remove dirt and grit. Let the joint dry completely before applying a new silicone sealant or tub caulk, which are easy to apply.

Kitchen

No matter how much of a neat freak the previous owner was, go through the cabinets and appliances, and scrub and scour them clean. This grunt work will pay off because no prospective buyer wants to think about moving into a less-than-sparkling kitchen. Troubleshoot the appliances to make sure they are in working order.

- **Cabinets**: Wash the insides of cabinets with a household cleaner. If cabinet pulls or hardware are worn and outdated, replace them with new hardware. To avoid having to drill new holes for new hardware and filling the old holes, bring a sample of the old hardware to the store. Limit your selection of new hardware to ones with installation holes spaced like the old ones.

- **Cabinet hinges**: Stuffing a wooden matchstick or

toothpick with wood glue into the screw hole is one way to repair ill-fitting hinges, but that is a temporary fix. For a permanent repair, remove the loose screws and hinges and fill the holes with an epoxy or polyester wood filler mixed with its catalyst. After it has hardened, sand the filler and drill new screw holes to reinstall the hinge.

- **Range hood**: Turn off the power to the range hood or range if the hood is part of the appliance. Look for the grease filter, which is usually under the hood in front of the blower air intake. Remove the filter and wash it in soapy water. You may need to use grease cutting cleaner if the filter has not been cleaned recently. Use a scrub brush to remove grease and dirt between the grill louvers, and clean the inside of the fan housing and the exterior and interior of the hood. When dry, reassemble the filter and resume power.

- **Dishwasher**: Check to see that the pump screen and the spray armholes are free of small food particles and mineral deposits. The pump screen is usually located in the well at the base of the unit. Scrub the screen with a stuff brush and soapy water. Use a straight pin or thin wire to unclog any holes you cannot see through in the spray arm. Clean the exterior of the dishwasher.

- **Refrigerator**: Clean the interior and exterior of the unit with soapy water and then pull it away from the wall so you have access to the condenser coils located on the bottom or back. A buildup of dust and lint prevents the flow of air from inside the unit to the air outside. Use a long handled snowbrush to dust off the coils. If the refrigerator has a drain pan at the bottom, clean it thoroughly to remove odors.

- **Butcher block**: To renew a stained or knife-scarred butcher block, use a hook-type paint scraper with a sharpened blade and an electric palm sander. Protect the surface around the butcher block with a strip of masking tape. Then, following the grain of the wood, press down as you pull the scraper toward you. Use a palm sander with a heavy sandpaper to work on dark stains or burn marks. Then use lightweight sandpaper to finish-sand the surface. Brighten the surface with a sponge and a 50-50 solution of household bleach and water. Then neutralize the bleach with a rag soaked in white vinegar and wash the surface with soap and water. Final-sand the surface with lightweight sandpaper and apply a top finish of a clean rag soaked in mineral oil.

Safe and Efficient Systems

The safety of a house and the efficiency of its systems are important features noted by appraisers, home inspectors, and prospective buyers. Take the time to install the necessary safety equipment and service the systems so the house makes a good impression.

- **Smoke and CO detectors**: This $30 device measures the concentration of CO (carbon monoxide) and smoke and sounds an alarm when a potentially harmful level is reached. Because the unit is battery operated, there is no electrical outlet needed. Install one alarm on each level of the house and outside the bedrooms. These detectors are on the list of requirements for insurance, so make sure they are installed when the house is inspected. Home inspectors look for them, too.

- **Heat pump or central air**: Trim back any overgrown plants or shrubbery around the unit. While the foliage can shield it from the hot sun and make it more efficient, overgrown bushes can get sucked against the air intake grill and block the flow of air through the coils.

- **Furnace**: Use the crevice tool of a shop vacuum to clean the area around the blower of the furnace. Measure the size of the furnace filter, buy a new one, and replace it.

- **Radiators**: Before the heating season begins, slowly empty or bleed the air from the system. Get a small can or bucket to catch the water runoff and use a radiator key or screwdriver to turn the bleed valve stem counterclockwise about a half turn or until you hear air hiss out. The bleed valve is located at the top end of the radiator and at one end of the baseboard convector. You may have to remove a cover or open the panel at the end of a baseboard unit to find the valve.

Home Exterior

It is easy to forget about the exterior of a house unless you inspect it regularly. Make a favorable impression on everyone who drives by with these basic maintenance chores for the outside of the house.

- **Gutters and downspouts**: Clean out gutters so rainwater can drain through them and not pool around the foundation of the house. Position a diverter, also called a splash block (about $6 to $10), at the base of each downspout to direct the water away from the house.

Seal any leaking joints with silicone caulk. Refasten any hangers and gutters that sag or have pulled away from where they are attached to the house.

- **Exterior light and house numbers**: Drive up to the house in the evening when it is dark and see if you can read the address and if the front entry is well lit. If not, replace the light and get larger house numbers.

- **Dirty or discolored deck**: Sweep the deck and hose it down with the spray nozzle of a garden hose. Then use a scrub brush broom to remove a buildup of dirt. Alternatively, rent a power washer to spray wash the dirty deck. When clean and dry, apply a coat of sealer and repair any loose or broken boards, railing, or stairs. Rake out debris that accumulates beneath the deck.

- **Garage**: Clean out the garage and organize anything that is stored there. If the previous owner left behind lawn tools, leave only the ones in good condition, and get rid of everything else in the garage. Sweep and scrub the floor with a heavy-duty degreaser. If there is a garage door opener, get fresh batteries for the remote opener and change the light bulb in the garage.

- **Blacktop driveway**: If the driveway shows signs of wear, a new topcoat of sealer will improve its appearance and maintain it for longer use. Pull the weeds growing alongside the driveway and rake the area so it is neatly edged. Before applying the sealer, sweep the surface and fill in any holes with an asphalt-patching compound. Apply the sealer with an old push broom or applicator, spreading it from the garage door and working your way out toward the street. Do not forget to barricade the wet surface and park your car elsewhere while the coating dries.

Landscaping

Second only to putting a new coat of paint on the siding, trimming overgrown and neglected landscaping is an improvement that will not go unnoticed. With a few basic pruning and grooming lawn tools and a lawn mower, you can transform an eyesore into a nicely manicured landscape.

- **Lawn, trees, and shrubs**: Maintain the lawn by cutting it on a regular basis. Prune and groom trees and shrubbery by cutting away the excess foliage, dried ends, and heavy branches with pruning shears and loppers. Get advice from a local lawn and garden center about the best time to prune specific trees and shrubbery in your area.

- **Edging lawn and garden beds**: A $20 edging tool will pay off when you have a neatly manicured lawn and garden beds. This is a no-brainer spruce up that keeps the lawn from invading garden beds. Dig the edger down about six inches into the soil and create a V-shaped trench between the lawn and garden. As you work, remove any weeds and loosen the soil so that it is easy to work with.

- **Worn lawn**: Reviving a lawn involves removing the weeds, raking and leveling the soil, and adding amendments such as organic matter, fertilizer, lime, or sulfur. Then apply a starter fertilizer and seed and nurture the new seedlings with a steady watering routine.

CHAPTER SIXTEEN

INCREASING RENTAL PROPERTY PROFITS

If you are buying a second home to generate income, look carefully for additional opportunities to generate increased rent. Almost every property has the potential to provide increased services to a renter and increased rent payments to you. Andy Carrier purchased a small, three-bedroom ranch in an older neighborhood, and he took a few steps to make sure he maximized the property's income potential.

I bought my second home for $110,000. Here is how I decided it was a good deal. The price was a bargain. The neighborhood was well established and most of the owners kept their homes in good repair. The house was also in a good school district. The roof had been replaced a few years before and so had the heating system. I expected little in the way of maintenance costs for at least the first few years.

The ideal renter I had in mind is a small family eager to live in a house instead of an apartment, possibly a couple with one child or a single parent with two children. Fortunately, that target market is pretty broad in my area since a reasonable percentage of local families do not have enough money or the right credit to buy a home, so I expected I would have no trouble finding tenants.

I estimated my expenses, including the mortgage, to be $675. After looking at similar rental homes in the area, I calculated I could easily rent the home for $775. A net of $1,200 per year may not sound like a lot, but to me it is enough to take on the risk of buying the property. I also saw more potential in the home. It is located a few minutes walk from a local college where parking space is hard to come by. The back of the lot had street access, so I could make a parking area for three cars and rent each space for $40 per month to college students. I also decided I could rent a small garage at the back of the lot as a storage building or place to keep a vehicle for $60 per month. Those two changes increased my anticipated net to $2,400, and in my mind made the house a great deal.

———————

S ay the second home you buy is will be rented to others for at least part of the year. Say you have found a great property, you have done your homework, run the numbers, completed your inspections, and completed the purchase. Now we will look at ways you can increase your income or reduce the amount of negative cash flow, if that is the case.

It is easier than you think. You will apply the same principles to your investments that business owners and retailers apply to their businesses. You will look for a competitive advantage and you will use your intelligence and creativity to find opportunities that other people have missed. Those opportunities are out there, you just need to find them.

Take a look at ways to increase the value of your properties in terms of income and in overall worth.

DIFFERENTIATION

Differentiation is a word marketers and advertisers use to describe a situation where a business finds a way to stand out from its competition. In its early years, Domino's Pizza created a point of differentiation by guaranteeing pizza deliveries within thirty minutes or less. Later they realized they no longer needed or could afford the legal repercussions of this point of differentiation, so they dropped it. Nevertheless, it certainly got them started on the road to success.

Domino's succeeded not by seeing themselves as just pizza makers, but as a company that delivered value to its customers by providing fresh pizza conveniently and reliably. Your goal will be to differentiate yourself from others. If you do so, the value of your properties will rise substantially.

To create a point of differentiation, first you need to know the local market. If you own a rental property, then the people owning other rental properties are your competition. You will need to know what they offer and what their units are like so you can determine how to position your home effectively.

How do you learn what they offer? Go look. Make appointments to look at available units. Check out nearby apartment complexes, residential units, and rooms for rent. Look closely at each and notice what you like and do not like about them. Keep in mind you are searching for a way to stand out from the crowd, not fit in.

Provide a Service, Not Just Housing

If you own a rental property, the first thing you should remember is that your tenants are your customers. They are not doing you a favor by renting your property. Your job is to keep them satisfied and happy. If you do, you will have lower turnover, higher rents, and fewer problems to deal with. If you see your tenants as a necessary evil, they will become one. If you see your tenants as customers, you will naturally be quicker to identify other opportunities to differentiate yourself and raise the value of your properties.

Here is the key. You can read a number of how to books about being a landlord, and many of them will be helpful. You can learn about leases, regulations, and legal issues, all of which you need to know. What you will not learn about is customer service, and your tenants are your customers. The first thing you will need to do is see yourself as a customer service person, not an owner or a landlord. Treat your tenants like customers and they will reward you because very few landlords do.

BEFORE YOU BUY A RENTAL PROPERTY...

In previous chapters, we talked about thoroughly analyzing a property's value and profit potential. If you are considering buying a home that is currently used as a rental property, you can take the process one step further by actually talking to the tenants. It is easy to do. Simply stop by and tell them you are thinking of buying the home. You will quickly get their attention.

You will be looking for as much information as you can get in four specific areas:

- **Ideas for improving service**: Every property has opportunities for improvement, whether it is additional parking, better outside lighting, or problems with utilities. If you ask, the tenants will tell you. If they have been frustrated in the past by the owner's lack interest in making necessary repairs or improvements, they will quickly fill you in. Your job will be to sift through the information you get to find things that you can improve and charge a premium for, and things that may need repair that affect the amount you are willing to pay for the property.

- **Lease accuracy**: Some owners simply will not be honest with you. They will over estimate rental income, under estimate expenses, and in some cases neglect to tell you about special arrangements they have made with tenants. You may inspect a potential apartment building purchase and learn that one of the tenants no longer pays rent because he does handyman work around the property. The tenant may even have a written agreement with the landlord stating that fact and the agreement is not provided to the potential buyers. Ask about rent amounts, how much time the tenants have left on the leases, and about whether they are interested in staying after the term is over. If they are not interested in staying, ask why. You will learn more about the current state of the property.

- **Property problems**: If you ask, the tenants will tell you. If they exist, you will hear about pest problems, parking problems, building repair issues, and leaky faucets. All you have to do is ask. It is a guarantee that you will hear things from tenants that the owner would never say.

- **Tenant problems**: Current tenants will also tell you about problem neighbors. As a landlord, you have a responsibility to maintain a safe and positive environment. For instance, in some localities, if the tenants are too noisy, the owner of the property is eventually responsible for remedying the situation. You may find out about tenant problems that are causing high turnover rates that may cause you to pass on the purchase, or it may cause you to decide that if you solve the tenant problems you may be able to profit more from the property.

ESTABLISH OPTIMUM RENT AMOUNTS

If you do not know the local market, you are unlikely to set your rent levels accurately. The average new landlord sets prices too low rather than too high out of fear that the property will sit vacant. While that certainly can happen, if you create a point of differentiation in your property, you will be able to charge premium rates. Best of all you will know that the price you are charging is fair.

The best way to set your rent is to compare your property to other comparable homes. Find out what other properties are renting for, and adjust the rent of your home accordingly. If your property is similar in most regards to another, but your property also has a deck and a large yard suitable for children to play in, you can probably charge a premium for those services. If your property has deficiencies, you may have to charge less.

When you look at a rental property, you may only be seeing the basics like number of bedrooms, number of bathrooms, etc., and the items that typically are found in the average classified ad for an apartment for rent.

Your potential renters, on the other hand, are looking at a lot more variables. They are in all likelihood comparison shopping, so you need to make sure you understand how your property stacks up. Detail oriented renters are looking at:

- Square footage

- Parking

- Level of noise

- Cleanliness

- How fresh the paint is

- How new the carpet is

- Number of windows

- Landscaping

- Electrical outlets

- Storage space

- Closets

- Kitchen features

- Security

- Lighting

- Laundry facilities

- Age of the property

- Heating and air conditioning

- Energy efficiency

- Convenience

- Decks or other outdoor features

- Types of tenants in the building, if applicable

- Neighborhood

- Quality of schools

As you can see, your potential tenants are evaluating a whole list of items, so in order to properly set your rent amount, you need to compare your property in all these aspects to other properties in which you are competing.

Keep in mind that setting your rent accurately is an evolving process. As you make changes to the property, your rent prices may change, although you will not be able to change that price until the current lease you have with a tenant expires. Look at some ways you can increase the value of your investment properties. If you do, not only will they be worth more, but they will also provide you with higher rent amounts and increase your yearly net operating income.

INCREASING YOUR VALUE INSIDE

Walk into the average rental unit and here is what you will see: dingy and stained carpets, marks on the walls, cracked linoleum, stained bathtubs, and faded paint. Depressing, right? It does not have to be. If you have found a unit like this, you have found an easy way to boost the value of an investment.

Cosmetic conditions make a huge difference in property values. Prospective buyers and renters discount the price more heavily than necessary. On the flip side, if you correct those problems, you can raise your sales or rental prices dramatically.

Here are a few ideas.

- **Overhaul kitchens and bathrooms**. Kitchens and bathrooms are typically feature rooms. People pay more attention to the condition of kitchens and bathrooms than any other rooms in a house. If you spend some time and effort on those rooms, you can change the impression the property makes.

In bathrooms, consider replacing the sink, shower, and toilet with new ones. The replacements do not have to be expensive or ornate; they simply need to be clean and solid. You can also replace the linoleum, eliminating any stains or cracks in the old floor. By replacing those items and painting the walls, you will have completely remade the bathroom, all for less than $3,000.

The same can be true in the kitchen. Replacing the floor, repainting the walls and replacing or cleaning appliances will make a dramatic difference. Remember, prospective tenants have to picture themselves living in that kitchen. If you make it appealing, they will reward you for it.

- **Clean the home thoroughly**. If you cannot afford to replace fixtures, then perform a thorough cleaning. Clean everything. Remember that prospective tenants are looking for a place to live, not a rental property.

  There is an added bonus. Typically, tenants who appreciate the cleanliness of the unit will keep it clean and will probably be less likely to cause any damage to the property. A tenant who moves into a dirty apartment is unlikely to take steps to clean it on his or her own. That may sound odd, but it is true.

- **Improve natural lighting**. A brighter, more open unit is more attractive. Consider different window treatments, removing bushes or trees that block light outside the windows, or even adding a few windows if you can afford it. Also, take time to see if there are ways to improve the view. If the only view a unit has is of the trash can area, try moving the cans to somewhere less conspicuous.

- **Create gasp opportunities**. Make your property stand out without spending too much. Find inexpensive touches that cause your property to stand out like lining a closet with cedar or installing new lighting or ceiling fans. Remember you are running a business so do not spend too much on wow items, but installing a few can greatly improve the perception potential tenants have of your property. Your goal is to make prospective tenants gasp or say, "Wow," when they notice a few of the features your rental home has to offer.

- **Create more storage space**. No one feels that they have enough storage space. Rental properties are notorious for having limited storage space since most owners want to maximize the available rental space, not the available storage space.

  You can create storage by opening up unused space. Look for dead space in places like:

  - Kitchen cabinets.

  - Walls where cabinets or shelves could go.

  - Hanging racks in kitchens.

  - Areas under stairs.

  - Cabinet ends.

  - High closets with no shelves above the clothes rack.

You can also increase the capacity of current storage space by using storage organizers. Many companies now make closet and cabinet organizers that free up dead space.

Lastly, you can add storage space by utilizing an attic or basement or by adding outdoor units to which tenants have access. If the property has a garage, consider dividing it into separate spaces the tenants can use.

- **Add safety features**. By adding dead bolt locks, better outside lighting, fire extinguishers, and other home safety features, you can make your property stand out from your competition. Safety conscious tenants will appreciate your attention to this detail. Make sure all entry doors are adequately lit, and that all windows and doors have effective locks.

CURB APPEAL

Potential tenants or buyers pass your home all the time. Even if they are not in the market now, they will still notice your property. In addition, if they later enter the market, you want them to remember you favorably.

Your property's first impression is even more important when prospective renters or buyers visit. Make sure your property looks great from the outside and you have a better chance of wowing potential tenants on the inside.

Here is how to improve the curb appeal of your properties:

- **Clean up**. Pick up trash, leaves, debris, sticks... everything. Thoroughly clean up the yard. Make sure the tenants use the parking areas provided. Get rid of any clutter or junk, and ensure that your tenants throw their trash away properly.

- **Give the yard a makeover**. You do not have to make it a landscaper's dream. Your goal is clean, neat, and attractive. Plant a few flowers, plant bushes or shrubs to hide unattractive items or views, and put trash containers or other outside items in a convenient, but out of the way place. Consider building a small fenced area for them if you cannot find a suitable spot. Maintain the yard as if you owned the property, not just like it is a rental.

- **Repair sidewalks and parking areas**. Repair cracks, get the weeds out of the sidewalk, and make sure the walkways are safe.

- **Replace old or rusty mailboxes and outside light fixtures**. For some reason, mailboxes at rental properties take a lot of abuse. We have no idea why, but invariably the mailbox at a rental property will be in horrible shape. The same is true with outside light fixtures. Replace or paint old fixtures, make the property inviting to drive up to if it is dark out.

- **Look closely at the building's exterior**. If wood trim is rotting, replace it and repaint it. You will have to eventually anyway so by replacing problems now, you may be able to maximize your rent. Think of simple ways to improve the appearance like shutters, a new front door, and a small porch. Think of ways to make the property feel more like a home. After all, to your tenants it is home, so make it feel that way and the value of your property will increase.

MAKE IMPROVEMENTS TO GENERATE MORE INCOME

Once you have overhauled the property itself, you are ready to consider improvements that can pay for themselves over time and instantly add value to your property. Remember, you are providing a service, not just housing, so we will look for ways to add services to your rental home.

- **Parking**: If you have the space, consider renting spaces to non-tenants or rent to tenants if they have a number of cars. In most cases, your property will have room for a certain number of vehicles per tenant or per unit. If the tenant needs more space, you are well within your rights to charge for it. If your unit is near an area with severe parking shortages, you may be able to rent a spot or two to a non-tenant. Some property owners located near civic arenas or stadiums even rent parking space on their properties for events or games.

- **Laundry facilities**: Study your competition first. If the average rental property has laundry facilities, you will need them in order to compete. In some cases, you may be able to furnish the hookups alone and require tenants to provide their own washer and dryer. In others, especially if your target market is young people just starting to live on their own, providing the units themselves can be a competitive advantage. If you own a large complex, you may want to consider adding coin-operated machines in a common area.

- **Storage space**: Most people have storage needs. If you have the space, you can solve those needs for them. Most tenants will appreciate and pay more for the ability to store items on the property instead of at a storage unit located elsewhere. Consider converting a garage, other building, or even building units. You can even rent units to non-tenants if you like.

- **Offer other services**: Depending on your market, your tenants may need other services. In college towns, many large apartment complexes offer shuttle services or short trip transportation. You may offer a dry cleaning pickup and delivery service that you coordinate with a local dry cleaner. Alternatively, it could be as simple as adding a small playground. Think about things your tenants would appreciate, and that would give you a competitive advantage.

Add More Rentable Space

Properly executed, adding more rental space to an existing unit offers a tremendous increase in property value. If you can convert an attic or basement into a suitable unit, you can rent that unit and increase your monthly income.

Keep in mind that you will want the new space you create to fit within the overall style and attractiveness of your existing units. Do not simply slap a few walls up, add a sink and a bathroom, and call an attic a studio apartment. Doing so may allow you to charge more rent, but it also lowers the perceived value of your property. Make sure any changes you undertake will add value to the property as well as adding income potential.

Before you convert a space, consider who your target market is and what point of differentiation you can create.

If you are converting an attic into a studio apartment, consider who a potential renter might be and what that person's needs are. Is it a student who needs a space to study? Then create an area for a desk and bookshelves and make sure there is plenty of light for reading or studying. Is it a young person who will be living at the beach during the summer while working? Make sure it is safe and has room to store items like bicycles, surfboards, or other beach gear.

If you are converting a basement into a small apartment for one person, consider safety. Make sure doors and windows have secure locks, and that outside entry areas will be well lit.

By considering your target market, you will make sure you create a space that is optimal for their needs and you will increase your income potential.

Change the Use of a Property

Imagine you own a house that is currently being used as a single-family residential rental. It is possible you could change the use of the property from residential to office space and greatly increase your rental income.

First, check the zoning. It will need to be zoned commercial or you will need to get the zoning changed. You can find out about zoning and zoning changes by visiting your local government office.

If zoning is not a problem, then make sure the demand for office space exists. Check local listings or call a commercial REALTOR® and ask about office space supply. If there is a glut of open space on the market, you may not want to change the use of your property unless you can serve a need that is not already being met.

Then make sure you have adequate parking. Local governments have parking regulations requiring a certain number of spaces per occupant or per building square footage, so make sure you can accommodate those regulations.

Finally, run a cost analysis to find out how much it will cost you to convert the property and what your anticipated rent amounts will be. You will do the same calculations you would do for any other property you were considering purchasing.

Not all properties are suitable for conversion to office space, but opportunities do exist. If you want to own a second home is in a college town, the college may continue to expand and office space will be at a premium. You could buy a large residential property directly across the street from the main administration area and convert it to office space. You could lease all the units to the college for a multiple of what you could get for a residential property. Even if office space supply is high in your area, you may be able to find a niche where converting your property makes great economic sense.

LOWER YOUR EXPENSES TO INCREASE YOUR VALUE

There are two sides to increasing your value and your operating income. You can charge more, of course, but if you spend less then your operating income also increases. You should look just as closely at ways to decrease your expenses as you do at ways to increase your revenue.

- **Maintenance**. Your biggest expense other than mortgage payments, of course, will be maintenance and repair related. When you are selecting properties, look for brick or vinyl siding, aluminum or vinyl windows, and solid, but basic construction. You want a property that is built to last, but that does not have too many frills or expensive features.

  Once you have found a property like that, keep it well maintained. Do not let small problems become bigger and more expensive ones.

- **Insist on high security deposits**. If a tenant damages your property to an extent greater than the security deposit, you can try to collect, but expect to face time consuming small claims court proceedings. In many cases, the effort of collecting simply will not be worth it. You can avoid that problem by requiring high security deposits. One month's rent is typical, but feel free to ask for at least two. You may narrow the field of prospective renters, but the ones you get will likely be more responsible. That carries two benefits: they are less likely to harm your property, and if they do, you have a greater chance of the damages being covered by the security deposit.

- **Select your tenants with care**. Ask for references. Find out how they treated their last rentals. Most owners will gladly let you know if the tenant caused damage.

- **Add a repair clause to the lease**. Many owners now require their tenants to pay the first $75 or $100 of property repairs. In effect, it is like a deductible on an insurance policy.

- **Determine the accuracy of the property assessment**. If you can find comparable properties that sold for a value lower than the current assessment of your property, you may be able to have the assessment amount reduced. On the other hand, if you paid less for the property than its assessed value, you can argue that the market value is what you paid, not what the assessor calculated.

- **Find part-time skilled help**. If you only own one additional home, hopefully your repair needs will be infrequent. Try to find local tradespersons who are willing to work part time on your property. Many are happy to make a little extra money and you can feel confident your properties are being kept in good condition. Having a good handyman on call will save you tremendous amounts of time and money.

- **Refinance your property when appropriate**. If you can reduce your monthly payments, you will increase your net operating income.

CHAPTER SEVENTEEN

MAXIMIZE YOUR RESALE PRICE

Windy Crutchfield is an agent with Realty Consultants in Virginia Beach, VA, specializing in residential listings in an area where vacation properties make up a significant segment of the real estate market. As she describes, marketing a vacation property requires a different level of expertise. Standard marketing techniques simply are not enough if you want to maximize your sales price.

An agent's ability to effectively market a vacation home and to target the marketing to the right audience is key. The average beachfront home, for example, is not purchased by a local resident. It is purchased by someone from outside the area, sometimes hundreds of miles away. While standard marketing techniques are sometimes effective, an aggressive agent will market your house outside the immediate area to attract the right buyers. Since they are likely to view the home as an investment, a local buyer will tend to be a bargain shopper and as a result extremely price conscious. A vacation homebuyer is more concerned about the location, the amenities, and the livability of the home. A good agent will aggressively market to a regional and national audience, making it more likely you will receive top dollar for your home. Require prospective agents to describe, in detail, their marketing plans before you list your second home so you can be sure they will cast as wide a net as possible.

E ven if you bought your second home with the intention of living in it or using it for a vacation home, chances are someday you will decide to sell it. Should you not try to get the best price you can when you sell the home? Absolutely! Look at ways you can maximize the sales price of your second home. Who knows, the sale of your first vacation home may finance the purchase of your next one!

Mental Preparation – Do Your Homework

To prepare your house for sale, start by thinking about how a buyer will look at your house. Buyers should never see your house before you are ready. You want to get it ready to make a splash on the local market.

A major asset to acquire is seeing your house the way potential buyers will see it. You will need to be able to ask yourselves questions such as, "Is this what I want buyers to see?" and "Is this how I want buyers to feel?" You cannot view the home the way you see it, and you will have to try to put yourself in the place of a potential buyer instead. What is important to you may be meaningless to someone else.

Your first step is to recognize that the way you want your house to look and feel on the market may be completely at odds with how you tend to live in the house. If it is always been a rental property, this is not a problem. If you have lived in the home, it can be a major hurdle you will need to overcome.

Many people get defensive about their homes, but do not take it personally. This is not a suggestion that your house is a mess or that your decorating sensibility is awful. To position your house for the eyes of buyers, you will need to look at it differently while it is on the market. It is a product for sale and not a place in which you live. There is a big difference.

No one can prepare your house for sale as well as you can because you know exactly what your house has to offer. This knowledge can also be a huge handicap because your emotional attachment and associations with a house can actually prevent you from seeing it objectively from a potential buyer's point of view.

Remember, your home is where you live. Almost as soon as you move into a house, you become less objective about it. You have mental images of the home, like memories of family occasions and milestones, of raising children, entertaining friends, and sharing holidays. It takes on a life of its own, for you, anyway. Because of that, you may not notice the crack in the ceiling anymore. You may not notice the missing tile in the closet. You do not care much about the window that will not open smoothly. To maximize your sales price, you will need to be able to see your house the way potential buyers see it.

Develop Objectivity

To develop the ability to look at your house objectively, you will need to act like a buyer.

The easiest first step to take is to go to open houses. You will not have to feel bad about taking up agents' time when you are not interested, because they have to be at the open house anyway. They will also be glad you came if for no other reason than they want to impress the seller with how many potential buyers they were able to attract. Your goal is to become accustomed to looking at houses critically, and you will need some practice on other houses before you take on your own house.

While you are there, watch how other buyers go through a house. Notice what they look at and how they talk about what they see. Listen for their emotional statements, both positive and negative. Emotional statements are critical because your goal in preparing your house for sale is to create emotional appeal as well as rational appeal.

Also, think about your reactions to the house. Evaluate your first impressions:

- As you drive up to the house.

- As you walk to the front door.

- Of the entryway.

- Of the kitchen.

- Of the bathrooms.

- Of the closet space.

Do you feel comfortable in the house? Think about why you do or do not.

You can also look at model homes. Model homes are professionally staged to appeal to buyers. Pay attention to how a carefully staged house makes you feel. In particular, notice the difference a thoroughly clean house makes. Notice how uncluttered rooms and closets feel. Most importantly, notice the impression a house that needs no work can make on you. That is the feeling you will want your house to project, and when you get home you will notice that your house is not ready to make that impression yet. However, it will be when you are done with it.

As you look at houses, look for little touches or specific rooms that you like and take notes about ideas you can use in your house. If a little touch appeals to you or creates a sense of home for you, it will also work for someone like you. After all, chances are good that someone with tastes similar to yours will purchase your home.

No matter how great your home may be, a potential buyer's eyes are drawn to negative features first. Buyers are inspecting your house and are looking for clues to uncover hidden problems. They will tend to exaggerate the amount of work and cost required to overcome any negative features they come across.

Look at a number of houses. Try to do it in one day over the course of a few hours. Get used to looking critically at houses. It will be easy, because the ones you are looking at are not your house.

Next, go home. Walk through your house as if it is just another house you are inspecting. You will be amazed how things you never notice will suddenly jump out at you, such as cluttered closets, a messy entryway, or dusty ceiling fans. These are things you may have never noticed, but will now be easy to spot.

If you had trouble coming home and seeing your house critically, you probably did not spend enough time looking at other houses.

If you cannot seem to get the objectivity and distance you need to look critically at your house, call in reinforcements. Ask trusted friends or relatives to do it for you.

I have used the word trusted for a reason, because nothing is harder than walking through someone else's house to critique it. Most homeowners, no matter how much they say they want to hear about all the problems in their house, do not really want to hear about any problems. If you think you want to ask someone to give you feedback, be prepared to hear it or do not ask at all.

ELIMINATE CLUTTER

Now you are prepared to get the house ready for sale.

The first step you should take is to eliminate all the clutter from the house. It will make a huge difference to potential buyers, and it makes your house easier to clean thoroughly, paint, or perform minor repairs. Cluttered rooms make your house feel smaller, and no one wants to buy smaller. You want your house to feel large even if it is not particularly large.

Clutter is not just your everyday possessions. It includes your decorating touches or hobbies. Having many pillows on couches or beds and your end tables and shelves filled with knickknacks, candles, figures, etc., will be distracting and make rooms feel cluttered and small.

In addition, your goal is to somewhat depersonalize your home. When prospective buyers come in, you want them to be able to pictures themselves living in your house. That is hard to do when signs of your presence, your decorating taste, or your hobbies fill each room. You want your house to feel like a home, but not to the extent buyers cannot picture themselves living there.

If you have kids, and you have a playroom, it is probably filled with toys. To a visitor this will feel cramped and messy. If your kitchen counters are full of appliances, cookbooks, cooking utensils, or other odds and ends, your kitchen will appear messy and crowded. That may be the way you live, and it may be a great way to live, but it is a terrible way to show your house to its best advantage.

To unclutter your house, you will need to go through every room, every closet, every drawer, and every cubbyhole. Doing so may feel excessive, but you would be surprised at how closely some buyers will look at your house.

It is important to note that you do not have to worry about clearing out or organizing dresser drawers or similar furniture that you will not be leaving in the house. Anything that is part of the house and that is staying needs to be uncluttered. Therefore, you will need to unclutter kitchen cabinets and drawers, closets, and bathroom cabinets, because they stay with the house, and a buyer has every right to look inside. Buyers do not have a right to look in, for instance, your dresser drawers.

Look at some of the basics of uncluttering.

Rent a Storage Unit

Rent a storage unit for items you will take out of your house during the uncluttering stage. You may think you will not need one, but there are two good reasons to do so, and it is fairly inexpensive. In most areas, you can rent an adequate size unit for less than $60 per month.

As you are uncluttering, there is a simple rule to follow: if in doubt, throw it out or give it away. That is great advice, but it is also hard to follow. Most of us have trouble getting rid of things, even if we will never use them or need them again. What we tend to do is err on the side of keeping things that we really should throw out. After all, we can always throw it away later, but if we throw it away now it is gone forever.

Renting a storage unit eliminates the temptation to keep things you should not. If you are in doubt, put it in the storage unit. That way you will be more aggressive about uncluttering your house, and the better job you do, the greater the possibility you will maximize your home's sale price. A storage unit also comes in handy for items you know you want to keep, but that do not belong in your home during the sales process.

Organize as You Unclutter

Your ultimate goal is to show potential buyers that everything in your home has a place and that there is a perfect spot for everything.

Most of us do not live that way, so we think it feels unnatural and cold, but this impression is what you must show potential buyers. Give buyers the impression that if they live in your house, they will be organized, too. Of course they probably will not, but if they have always wanted to be more organized, your house will make them feel like this time they can if they buy your house.

As you go through your house, decide where items will go. If you do not have a place, put them in the storage unit. It is that simple.

Clean as You Go

When you are unclutter drawers or cabinets, you will probably take everything out, sift through what you absolutely must keep, and then put those items back in. Before you put things back, clean the drawer or cabinet thoroughly. It is a time saving move, and it makes it less likely you will later stash items in those cabinets or drawers that do not belong there. Giving yourself a sense of completion as you go through your house will make the job seem less overwhelming, and will also ensure you do not have to handle items multiple times.

Now we will look at specific areas you will want to focus on as you unclutter.

Closets and Cabinets

Closets and cabinets are typically cluttered and small, but are key items on most prospective buyers' lists of household features to focus on. If you do nothing else, you have to make your closet and cabinet space seem as roomy as possible. Buyers will want to see whether their stuff will fit. If your closets are packed tightly, they will have a hard time imagining their possessions fitting.

Remember, you are uncluttering your house temporarily just for the sale period. Store closet items you do not need to use every day. If it is in the closet to begin with, you probably do not use it often anyway. If it is summertime, take out all the winter coats, hats, gloves, and boots and put them in the storage unit. If it is wintertime, keep one heavy coat for everyone and store the rest. The emptier your closets are, the more appealing they will be to potential buyers.

The same thing is true for cabinets. If you have a number of pots and pans, keep a few and store the rest. If you have dozens of sets of towels, keep enough for a two-week period and store the rest.

When your closets and cabinets are uncluttered, clean them thoroughly, and then do what retail and grocery stores do: face your items. If items have labels, place them so the label faces forward. Line shoes up facing forward. Stack boxes with the largest on the bottom. Line up your spices with all the labels facing forward. If bookshelves are full, remove half of the books, especially the paperbacks, so the shelves seem roomier.

Furniture

Too much furniture or too many accessories in a room will make it feel small and confining. If a piece of furniture obstructs your view of a room, move it so it does not block a buyer's eyes from seeing the entire room. If you have a large four-poster bed and it is close to the doorway, it will overwhelm the room and make it feel small even if it is not. If you cannot find a place for a particular piece of furniture, put it in storage. Obviously, you need your bed, but do you need all your couches, chairs, end tables, etc.?

Remove as much excess furniture as possible, but do not make your rooms look bare. You do not want your rooms to feel empty; you want them to feel spacious and roomy.

Plants

Plants add life and fill empty spaces, but they can also overwhelm a room. If you have dozens of plants, consider removing at least half of them. Open up your rooms. Most buyers will not see the beauty of your plants. They will see small rooms filled with plants.

If you have plants you are nursing back to health, remove them. The last thing you want is a dead or dying tree to catch buyers' eyes. They will have no idea you are nursing it back to health, they will just think you do not take care of it.

Doors

If you have doors that stand open most of the time, like in entrances to kitchens, dining rooms, playrooms, or even basements, consider taking the door off completely and storing it. Open doors make rooms feel smaller and can sometimes block a buyer's view, and anything that blocks a view creates an impression of smaller. If the buyers want to put the door back on, fine. If they buy the house, it is their door. However, for now, removing unneeded doors will make your house feel more open and spacious.

Your goal in uncluttering is to give the perception that your house is large, spacious, and has plenty of storage space. There is an additional bonus. Your move will be easier when your house sells. The more you throw away now, the less you have to move later. In addition, since what remains in your house is well organized, it will be easier to pack and then to unpack and put away in your new house.

CLEANING

Most of us clean up when friends are coming over. We vacuum, dust, and straighten up a little, all of which is fine for our guests.

If you are going to maximizing your home's sale price, that kind of cleaning is not good enough for potential buyers. Buyers hold your house to a different standard of cleanliness than they hold their own. If you are thinking to yourself, "Oh, people do not expect my house to be spotless, because people live here," you are wrong. It may be unfair, but they do.

They will also see things you do not pay attention to. When you went to open houses, model homes, etc, you developed skill at looking at houses objectively. You probably also noticed it was much easier to spot problems in other houses than in your own. That is natural because we get used to our own homes. We start to overlook things because we are accustomed to seeing them. You probably do not even notice the stain made in your hallway carpet a month ago, because you have walked over it so often it does not even register. Nevertheless, a prospective buyer will notice it instantly.

The good news is that if you put the work into cleaning your house properly it will stand out from the crowd of other houses for sale. Most people do not do thorough cleanings when they list their homes. They should, but they do not. If you do, you will gain an advantage that will definitely show up in your sales price.

Clean Everything

You may think I am kidding with the headline "Clean Everything," but I am not. Clean everything. Clean every room, every bathroom, every baseboard, all your blinds, all your utility rooms…everything. Pay special attention to kitchens, bathrooms, and the master bedroom, since those are areas in which prospective buyers look most closely.

Pay attention to odors, too. If your basement smells musty, clean it thoroughly and then take steps to do something about the odor.

Have you ever noticed that everyone's house has a smell except yours? The truth is that yours does too, but you do not notice it since you live there. Normal smells are okay, but musty smells or pet odors are instant warning signs for prospective buyers. A thorough cleaning will help eliminate many odors.

Some agents recommend that you bake cookies before buyers are coming to visit. Even though it is a hassle, baking cookies ensures your house has an inviting smell.

If you smoke, start smoking outside. Start smoking outside today. Smoke odors are tough to eliminate, and they will not go away if you smoke inside your house.

Clean All Woodwork

Inspect all the woodwork or paneling in your home. Wood does not tend to look dirty, but it will become dull looking over time. By cleaning and polishing all woodwork, your house will take on a glow that will make it seem more inviting.

Pay special attention to kitchen cabinets. A thin film quickly builds up in the kitchen from microscopic particles of grease or other cooking by-products. That layer dulls the finish of your cabinets. Use a wood soap, fill small scratches with a scratch cover, and polish the woodwork. You will be surprised how your woodwork will look brighter and richer in color.

Clean Every Window and Light Fixture

Windows let in light and create a bright and warm feeling in your house. Sunlight pouring through a window, highlighting the finish on a floor or piece of furniture, cannot possibly happen with streaked or dirty windows.

Lighting is an important part of showing your house and buyers respond much more positively to houses filled with light. Well-lit houses are warm and inviting. Clean your windows and remove plants or other objects that block the sun. Clean all your light bulbs and lampshades. Consider higher wattage bulbs if the fixtures you have do not properly light a room.

Consider Professional Cleaning

If you do not think you have the time to clean your house on your own, you can hire someone to do it. However, it is easy to argue that you do have the time after all, because if your house sells for more because it is cleaner, you will have paid yourself a very nice wage to do the work.

Professional cleaners cost between $100 and $400 per day. The average three-bedroom, two-bathroom house can be professionally cleaned for approximately $200.

Of course, that is a basic cleaning, and you will want something more extensive when you are preparing your house to sell. If you decide to engage a cleaning service, first describe in detail exactly what you are looking for. In most cases, they will need to come to your house to evaluate the extent of the job. Ask for a detailed description of the services they will provide. Make sure they understand that you want everything cleaned.

Thoroughly and extensively cleaning the same three-bedroom house is likely to cost between $300 and $400. That is a fair amount of money, but if you do not have the time or inclination to do it yourself, it is money well spent.

If you have pets or smokers in the house, consider having all carpets professionally cleaned. The average house can be done for approximately $200 and your house will smell and look a lot better.

Curb Appeal

Curb appeal can be defined as how your house looks when a prospective buyer first drives up. It is the first impression a buyer has of your house, so it is hugely important. You would be surprised how many buyers will pause, glance at a house, and then tell the REALTOR®, "No, we will look at another house," simply because they did not have a good first impression of a particular house.

Buyers will form an attitude about your house in the first 15 seconds or so. Curb appeal can make or break you. After all, you want buyers to come inside and see how wonderful your house is, and how well you have done uncluttering and cleaning it. If they do not walk inside, you cannot impress them and you cannot sell your house.

Front Door

Your front door is the focal point of your home. Try this experiment: take a drive, and when you see a house for sale sign, look at the house. Within seconds, you will find yourself looking at the front door. Your eyes will quickly slide to other parts of the house, but almost everyone looks at the front door within the first few moments. It is natural, and we all do it.

The front door is also the entryway to your home, so it sets the stage for the inside of the house.

Think about what happens when an agent shows you a house. You get out of the car, gaze around the yard for a second, and then head to the front door. Unless the agent arrived at the house first, he or she now has to unlock the door to let you in, which usually involves opening a lockbox and struggling with a key so you spend a minute or two standing at the front door. At no other time while looking at the house are you such a captive audience, and at no other time will you likely stare so long at what is around you.

Some real estate investors purchase older or poorly maintained homes, renovate them, and then sell them, usually for very nice profits. If you ask, the advice many will give is, "Paint the walls white, replace the carpet, and install a new and very nice front door." Even if it is a lower end house, a nice front door makes a world of difference.

You may not need a new front door. At the very least, though, paint or refinish the one you have, replace the knob if it is old or weathered, and make sure the front door sparkles. Add a wreath, and consider replacing an older light fixture with an up to date one. Replace your doormat. Buyers will naturally look down to wipe their feet before entering and a clean doormat will create the impression that your entire house is probably clean.

Landscaping

Add fresh mulch around flowerbeds and bushes. If you have bare spots in the yard, find creative ways to hide them by planting inexpensive shrubs or flowers. Place potted plants at the front door or annuals along a walkway. Feel free to over plant. It will make your yard look lush and thriving.

If it is summertime, rake up your grass trimmings after mowing. Kill any dandelions you see. Those little spots of yellow ruin the impression your yard makes. Your yard will look much bigger if it is consistently green instead of broken up by small yellow dots everywhere.

Put away all tools, toys, bikes, etc. Make your yard as uncluttered and inviting as the inside of your house. Everyone wants a larger yard, so make sure yours looks as large as it can.

REPAIRS

Your house will not sell for top dollar unless everything is as close to perfect as possible. Even small maintenance problems like leaky faucets, one cracked floor tile, or a small area of peeling paint on the exterior creates a warning signal in a buyer's mind, and warning signals reduce the price you will get. Buyers perceive house repairs, no matter how small, as things that take away from what they would rather be doing.

If your house is perceived as a fixer-upper, the number of potential buyers you will see and the price they will pay will be greatly reduced. Buyers quickly factor the cost of repairs into their offers and they usually estimate that repairs will cost a lot more than they actually will.

Do not underestimate the importance of repairing absolutely everything, no matter how small. If you think something is too much trouble to fix, buyers will too, and they will not make offers.

If you do not have the time or money to make all repairs, lower the price of your house to take into account the state of your house.

Remember, repairing is not remodeling. If your kitchen cabinets are dated, replacing them is remodeling, not repairing. If you make sure your cabinets are as clean and well maintained as possible, that is repairing. Major improvements, like adding new rooms, renovating kitchens, or replacing bathroom fixtures, are all remodeling jobs. Repainting your kitchen cabinets is a repair while replacing them is remodeling.

As you go through your house looking for problems, watch out for the tendency to say, "Oh, it is not that bad," because if you noticed something, it is a problem. Anything you notice should be repaired, painted, or replaced. If you do not, it should be factored into your home's sale price.

DEPERSONALIZE YOUR HOUSE

By creating a neutral environment that appears to accommodate any buyer's furniture, lifestyle, or personal tastes, you will broaden your potential buyer base. A house with neutral paint colors, décor, and carpeting will accommodate anyone's style, and allow potential buyers to see themselves living in your house.

Any strong decorating element, no matter how attractive, shifts a buyer's attention away from the house and onto you. You do not want buyers to think of it as your house; they need to feel it could be their home.

If your house is too tailored to a specific taste, buyers have trouble imagining their own things in the same environment. Even large groups of family photographs can be intimidating. A few nicely framed pictures can make your house feel comfortable and homelike, but a large collection of personal photos will make buyers feel like intruders.

Unnerving artwork, loud paint colors, or roaming pets can cause a buyer to focus on those negatives instead of all the positives your house has to offer. Most people are not very good at visualizing furniture arrangements, so they will latch on to the idea that what they see is what they will get.

In short, depersonalizing your house increases the number of potential buyers by appealing to as many different people as possible.

Paint

Paint is number one on the list of things you can do to improve the sales price of your home, and provides the biggest return for the expense. Light, neutral color paint not only makes a room feel larger, it enhances the feeling of clean, fresh, and new. Paint rooms that flow together the same color to heighten the feeling of space such as the living room, dining room, and hallways.

When in doubt, paint it white. Okay, that one did not rhyme, but you get the drift. If nothing else, white is an easy color to paint over if the buyer chooses. You may find a slightly more dramatic color like gray green or gray blue, works better for bathrooms, bedrooms, or dens. Depersonalizing or neutralizing does not have to mean boring, but it should never mean striking.

Floors

If the existing carpeting is extremely worn or stained, new carpeting is worth the investment. In all likelihood, the buyer will force you to discount the price of the house to take into account new carpeting and at an estimated cost that is double what it will cost you. If you have wood floors under the carpeting, tear out the carpet and refinish the floors. Wood floors usually yield a higher value than carpeted floors.

Personal Items

Most people personalize their homes by displaying photographs on walls, tables, refrigerators, and bookshelves, as it reinforces a feeling of family and togetherness. Family photos are too personal to display if you are selling your house because they distract buyers. Remove and store photographs while your house is on the market. An occasional photo in an interesting frame or on an end table suggests a warm and inviting atmosphere. Anything more than that is too personal.

Remove Personal Fixtures

You can avoid potential conflicts by removing personal fixtures before putting your house on the market. In the overall scope of things, one light fixture should not kill a deal, but that often happens. Remove anything you absolutely want to keep before listing the house and save yourself potential aggravation later.

Stage Your Home for Maximum Appeal

If you decide to hold an open house, you need to make sure your house will show at its best. First, perform all the steps we have already discussed, like cleaning, uncluttering, repairing, etc.

Staging goes way beyond common sense things like cleaning the house until it sparkles. It involves more than removing all the clutter and painting the walls.

For instance, pay attention to buyers' senses of smell. Some agents say, "If you cannot smell it, you cannot sell it." The sense of smell is one of the strongest of all of the senses. A smelly house turns off buyers tremendously. If they have looked at several houses, they will even refer to one as, "The one that smelled like a wet dog." Incidentally, a colleague automatically advises owners to take 10% off the price of a house if a smoker owns it.

If bad smells do not sell, does that mean pleasant smells do? Yes. Anything you can do to enhance how the home shows is important. Some simple techniques you can use are making chocolate chip cookies or baking bread. Making chocolate chip cookies is even better because not only does the house smell great, but also prospective buyers get to eat the cookies. This further adds to a positive impression and might move the house up a notch in a buyer's mind.

Another trick is potpourri cooking on the stove. Alternatively, place a drop of vanilla extract on several light bulbs strategically arranged throughout the house. As the bulb heats up, the fragrance of the vanilla is released. If there is a fireplace, there should always be a fire going, unless it is summertime, of course. Seeing a fire burning in a fireplace creates a sense of home and hearth.

ADDITIONAL HOME SALE TIPS

- Always work with a good real estate attorney. Buyers should too, but it is even more crucial for the seller because you are the one conveying the property. There is more to mess up or go wrong on the sell side of the equation.

- When negotiations bog down, always reduce it to a dollars and cents issue. If a buyer argues over whether the fireplace set conveys, reduce it to a dollar amount and ask yourself, "Do I really want to let this deal go for $100 to $200?" Negotiating can become emotional, but you should stay as rational as possible. Most things just are not worth arguing over. You want the best price you can get, but you also could be left waiting months to sell your home all because you let a buyer get away for a few hundred dollars.

- If buyers ask for a home inspection, never argue. Let them do it. However, you should never pay for the inspection. Also, have the buyers do their home inspection before they put in their offer. Many buyers and their agents will balk at this. They are probably thinking, "…but I want to tie the property up while I am deciding whether or not I should buy." Your response should be, "No. If you want an inspection, that is fine. It will make both of us feel better that you are getting just the house you want. I think that is great, but I am not going to tie the house up in the process."

  In addition, if the buyer puts in a contract that is subject to a house inspection, in effect they will be negotiating twice. You will have already negotiated once before you agreed to the contract. It is guaranteed the house inspector will find something wrong with your house. They all do. Cynics would say that is because they have to justify their fee for inspecting the house. The buyer will then come back and want to negotiate a lower price based on the problems the inspector found. If the house is inspected before the offer is finalized, you will only have to negotiate once.

- Keep contingencies under control. You have the right to accept any contingencies you want. However, if you do elect to sell your house subject to the sale of another house, make sure the house is on the market with a reputable broker and that it is priced right.

In addition, offers with contingencies frequently have call provisions in them. If the first buyers receive notice that an acceptable offer is received from a third party, they have three to seven business days to make their offer non-contingent. Make it seventy-two hours, not three business days. Business days can sometimes run you into a whole week with holidays and weekends thrown in. Moreover, make sure notice to the buyer's agent is deemed adequate. Buyers themselves are sometimes hard to find, but agents usually are not. Make sure that giving notice to the agent is sufficient to satisfy the contingency.

- Insist on nonrefundable earnest money unless the financing falls through. Earnest money is the money buyers put down as a part of the contract. It is money they pledge so you will hold the house for them.

  In most cases, the buyer will say no. However, good contracts are structured that way. Try to get one. If you cannot, ask that if for any reason, if the buyer cannot perform, the earnest money is nonrefundable. If he flatly refuses, ask why. What possible reason could there be outside of the ability to get a mortgage? Find out what reservations exist. If there is too much wiggling up front, you may have an insincere buyer who will cost you time and aggravation. You might be better off letting that contract go.

- Keep an eye on closing costs and use them as a negotiating tool. In general, there are standard practices for which party pays which portion of closing costs. In reality, anything goes. You as a seller could pay all closing costs, or the buyer could pay all closing costs. It depends on how you structure the deal.

When interest rates are low many potential first time buyers can afford the monthly payment for a new home, but they do not have adequate cash to cover a down payment and closing costs. Some sellers will offer to pay closing costs as a way to help the buyer close the deal. That is a great negotiating tool to use because often the buyer will pay more for the house.

Closing costs can be used in negotiations two ways: as a last minute deal sweetener, or as an up front positioning strategy to attract a wider variety of potential buyers. Do not be surprised if a buyer asks you to assume closing costs not normally consider a seller's cost. Simply reduce the offer to a dollars and cents issue, and decide if it makes sense to you.

GLOSSARY

401(k)/403(b) An investment plan sponsored by an employer that enables individuals to set aside pre-tax income for retirement or emergency purposes. 401(k) plans are provided by private corporations. 403(b) plans are provided by non-profit organizations.

401(k)/403(b) Loan A type of financing using a loan against the money accumulated in a 401(k)/403(b) plan.

Abatement Sometimes referred to as free rent or early occupancy. A condition that could happen in addition to the primary term of the lease.

Above Building Standard Finishes and specialized designs that have been upgraded in order to accommodate a tenant's requirements.

Absorption Rate The speed and amount of time at which rentable space, in square feet, is filled.

Abstract or Title Search The process of reviewing all transactions that have been recorded publicly in order to determine whether any defects in the title exist that could interfere with a clear property ownership transfer.

Accelerated Cost Recovery System A calculation for taxes to provide more depreciation for the first few years of ownership.

Accelerated Depreciation A method of depreciation where the value of a property depreciates faster in the first few years after purchasing it.

Acceleration Clause A clause in a contract that gives the lender the right to demand immediate payment of the balance of the loan if the borrower defaults on the loan.

Acceptance The seller's written approval of a buyer's offer.

Ad Valorem A Latin phrase that translates as "according to value." Refers to a tax that is imposed on a property's value that is typically based on the local government's evaluation of the property.

Addendum An addition or update for an existing contract between parties.

Additional Principal Payment Additional money paid to the lender, apart from the scheduled loan payments, to pay more of the principal balance, shortening the length of the loan.

Adjustable-Rate Mortgage (ARM) A home loan with an interest rate that is adjusted periodically in order to reflect changes in a specific financial resource.

Adjusted Funds From Operations (AFFO) The rate of REIT performance or ability to pay dividends that is used by many analysts who have concerns about the quality of earnings as measured by Funds From Operations (FFO).

Adjustment Date The date at which the interest rate is adjusted for an adjustable-rate mortgage (ARM).

Adjustment Period The amount of time between adjustments for an interest rate in an ARM.

Administrative Fee A percentage of the value of the assets under management, or a fixed annual dollar amount charged to manage an account.

Advances The payments the servicer makes when the borrower fails to send a payment.

Adviser A broker or investment banker who represents an owner in a transaction and is paid a retainer and/or a performance fee once a financing or sales transaction has closed.

Agency Closing A type of closing in which a lender uses a title company or other firm as an agent to finish a loan.

Agency Disclosure A requirement in most states that agents who act for both buyers or sellers must disclose who they are working for in the transaction.

Aggregation Risk The risk that is associated with warehousing mortgages during the process of pooling them for future security.

Agreement of Sale A legal document the buyer and seller must approve and sign that details the price and terms in the transaction.

Alienation Clause The provision in a loan that requires the borrower to pay the total balance of the loan at once if the property is sold or the ownership transferred.

Alternative Mortgage A home loan that does not match the standard terms of a fixed-rate mortgage.

Alternative or Specialty Investments Types of property that are not considered to be conventional real estate investments, such as self-storage facilities, mobile homes, timber, agriculture, or parking lots.

Amortization The usual process of paying a loan's interest and principal via scheduled monthly payments.

Amortization Schedule A chart or table that shows the percentage of each payment that will be applied toward principal and interest over the life of the mortgage and how the loan balance decreases until it reaches zero.

Amortization Tables The mathematical tables that are used to calculate what a borrower's monthly payment will be.

Amortization Term The number of months it will take to amortize the loan.

Anchor The business or individual who is serving as the primary draw to a commercial property.

Annual Mortgagor Statement A yearly statement to borrowers which details the remaining principal balance and amounts paid throughout the year for taxes and interest.

Annual Percentage Rate (APR) The interest rate that states the actual cost of borrowing money over the course of a year.

Annuity The regular payments of a fixed sum.

Application The form a borrower must complete in order to apply for a mortgage loan, including information such as income, savings, assets, and debts.

Application Fee A fee some lenders charge that may include charges for items such as property appraisal or

a credit report unless those fees are included elsewhere.

Appraisal The estimate of the value of a property on a particular date given by a professional appraiser, usually presented in a written document.

Appraisal Fee The fee charged by a professional appraiser for his estimate of the market value of a property.

Appraisal Report The written report presented by an appraiser regarding the value of a property.

Appraised Value The dollar amount a professional appraiser assigned to the value of a property in his report.

Appraiser A certified individual who is qualified by education, training, and experience to estimate the value of real and personal property.

Appreciation An increase in the home's or property's value.

Appreciation Return The amount gained when the value of the real estate assets increases during the current quarter.

Arbitrage The act of buying securities in one market and selling them immediately in another market in order to profit from the difference in price.

ARM Index A number that is

publicly published and used as the basis for interest rate adjustments on an ARM.

As-Is Condition A phrase in a purchase or lease contract in which the new tenant accepts the existing condition of the premises as well as any physical defects.

Assessed Value The value placed on a home that is determined by a tax assessor in order to calculate a tax base.

Assessment (1) The approximate value of a property. (2) A fee charged in addition to taxes in order to help pay for items such as water, sewer, street improvements, etc.

Assessor A public officer who estimates the value of a property for the purpose of taxation.

Asset A property or item of value owned by an individual or company.

Asset Management Fee A fee that is charged to investors based on the amount of money they have invested into real estate assets for the particular fund or account.

Asset Management The various tasks and areas around managing real estate assets from the initial investment until the time it is sold.

Asset Turnover The rate of total revenues for the previous 12 months divided by the average total assets.

Assets Under Management The

amount of the current market value of real estate assets that a manager is responsible to manage and invest.

Assignee Name The individual or business to whom the lease, mortgage, or other contract has been re-assigned.

Assignment The transfer of rights and responsibilities from one party to another for paying a debt. The original party remains liable for the debt should the second party default.

Assignor The person who transfers the rights and interests of a property to another.

Assumable Mortgage A mortgage that is capable of being transferred to a different borrower.

Assumption The act of assuming the mortgage of the seller.

Assumption Clause A contractual provision that enables the buyer to take responsibility for the mortgage loan from the seller.

Assumption Fee A fee charged to the buyer for processing new records when they are assuming an existing loan.

Attorn To agree to recognize a new owner of a property and to pay rent to the new landlord.

Average Common Equity The sum of the common equity for the last five quarters divided by five.

Average Downtime The number of months that are expected between a lease's expiration and the beginning of a replacement lease under the current market conditions.

Average Free Rent The number of months the rent abatement concession is expected to be granted to a tenant as part of an incentive to lease under current market conditions.

Average Occupancy The average rate of each of the previous 12 months that a property was occupied.

Average Total Assets The sum of the total assets of a company for the previous five quarters divided by five.

Back Title Letter A letter that an attorney receives from a title insurance company before examining the title for insurance purposes.

Back-End Ratio The calculation lenders use to compare a borrower's gross monthly income to their total debt.

Balance Sheet A statement that lists an individual's assets, liabilities, and net worth.

Balloon Loan A type of mortgage in which the monthly payments are not large enough to repay the loan by the end of the term, and the final payment is one large payment of the remaining balance.

Balloon Payment The final huge payment due at the end of a balloon mortgage.

Balloon Risk The risk that a borrower may not be able to come up with the funds for the balloon payment at maturity.

Bankrupt The state an individual or business is in if they are unable to repay their debt when it is due.

Bankruptcy A legal proceeding where a debtor can obtain relief from payment of certain obligations through restructuring their finances.

Base Loan Amount The amount that forms the basis for the loan payments.

Base Principal Balance The original loan amount once adjustments for subsequent fundings and principal payments have been made without including accrued interest or other unpaid debts.

Base Rent A certain amount that is used as a minimum rent, providing for rent increases over the term of the lease agreement.

Base Year The sum of actual taxes and operating expenses during a given year, often that in which a lease begins.

Basis Point A term for 1/100 of one percentage point.

Before-Tax Income An individual's income before taxes have been deducted.

Below-Grade Any structure or part of a structure that is below the surface of the ground that surrounds it.

Beneficiary An employee who is covered by the benefit plan his or her company provides.

Beta The measurement of common stock price volatility for a company in comparison to the market.

Bid The price or range an investor is willing to spend on whole loans or securities.

Bill of Sale A written legal document that transfers the ownership of personal property to another party.

Binder (1) A report describing the conditions of a property's title. (2) An early agreement between seller and buyer.

Biweekly Mortgage A mortgage repayment plan that requires payments every two weeks to help repay the loan over a shorter amount of time.

Blanket Mortgage A rare type of mortgage that covers more than one of the borrower's properties.

Blind Pool A mixed fund that accepts capital from investors without specifying property assets.

Bond Market The daily buying and selling of thirty-year treasury bonds that also affects fixed rate mortgages.

Book Value The value of a property based on its purchase amount plus upgrades or other additions with depreciation subtracted.

Break-Even Point The point at which a landlord's income from rent matches expenses and debt.

Bridge Loan A short-term loan for individuals or companies that are still seeking more permanent financing.

Broker A person who serves as a go-between for a buyer and seller.

Brokerage The process of bringing two or more parties together in exchange for a fee, commission, or other compensation.

Buildable Acres The portion of land that can be built on after allowances for roads, setbacks, anticipated open spaces, and unsuitable areas have been made.

Building Code The laws set forth by the local government regarding end use of a given piece of property. These law codes may dictate the design, materials used, and/or types of improvements that will be allowed.

Building Standard Plus Allowance A detailed list provided by the landlord stating the standard building materials and costs necessary to make the premises inhabitable.

Build-Out Improvements to a property's space that have been implemented according to the tenant's specifications.

Build-to-Suit A way of leasing property, usually for commercial purposes, in which the developer or landlord builds to a tenant's specifications.

Buydown A term that usually refers to a fixed-rate mortgage for which additional payments can be applied to the interest rate for a temporary period, lowering payments for a period of one to three years.

Buydown Mortgage A style of home loan in which the lender receives a higher payment in order to convince them to reduce the interest rate during the initial years of the mortgage.

Buyer's Remorse A nervousness that first-time homebuyers tend to feel after signing a sales contract or closing the purchase of a house.

Call Date The periodic or continuous right a lender has to call for payment of the total remaining balance prior to the date of maturity.

Call Option A clause in a loan agreement that allows a lender to demand repayment of the entire

principal balance at any time.

Cap A limit on how much the monthly payment or interest rate is allowed to increase in an adjustable-rate mortgage.

Capital Appreciation The change in a property's or portfolio's market value after it has been adjusted for capital improvements and partial sales.

Capital Expenditures The purchase of long-term assets, or the expansion of existing ones, that prolongs the life or efficiency of those assets.

Capital Gain The amount of excess when the net proceeds from the sale of an asset are higher than its book value.

Capital Improvements Expenses that prolong the life of a property or add new improvements to it.

Capital Markets Public and private markets where individuals or businesses can raise or borrow capital.

Capitalization The mathematical process that investors use to derive the value of a property using the rate of return on investments.

Capitalization Rate The percentage of return as it is estimated from the net income of a property.

Carryback Financing A type of funding in which a seller agrees to hold back a note for a specified portion of the sales price.

Carrying Charges Costs incurred to the landlord when initially leasing out a property and then during the periods of vacancy.

Cash Flow The amount of income an investor receives on a rental property after operating expenses and loan payments have been deducted.

Cashier's Check A check the bank draws on its own resources instead of a depositor's account.

Cash-on-Cash Yield The percentage of a property's net cash flow and the average amount of invested capital during the specified operating year.

Cash-Out Refinance The act of refinancing a mortgage for an amount that is higher than the original amount for the purpose of using the leftover cash for personal use.

Certificate of Deposit A type of deposit that is held in a bank for a limited time and pays a certain amount of interest to the depositor.

Certificate of Deposit Index (CODI) A rate that is based on interest rates of six-month CDs and is often used to determine interest rates for some ARMs.

Certificate of Eligibility A type of document that the Department of

Veterans Affairs issues to verify the eligibility of a veteran for a VA loan.

Certificate of Occupancy (CO) A written document issued by a local government or building agency that states that a home or other building is inhabitable after meeting all building codes.

Certificate of Reasonable Value (CRV) An appraisal presented by the Department of Veterans Affairs that shows the current market value of a property.

Certificate of Veteran Status A document veterans or reservists receive if they have served 90 days of continuous active duty (including training time).

Chain of Title The official record of all transfers of ownership over the history of a piece of property.

Chapter 11 The part of the federal bankruptcy code that deals with reorganizations of businesses.

Chapter 7 The part of the federal bankruptcy code that deals with liquidations of businesses.

Circulation Factor The interior space that is required for internal office circulation and is not included in the net square footage.

Class A A property rating that is usually assigned to those that will generate the maximum rent per square foot, due to superior quality and/or location.

Class B A good property that most potential tenants would find desirable but lacks certain attributes that would bring in the top dollar.

Class C A building that is physically acceptable but offers few amenities, thereby becoming cost-effective space for tenants who are seeking a particular image.

Clear Title A property title that is free of liens, defects, or other legal encumbrances.

Clear-Span Facility A type of building, usually a warehouse or parking garage, consisting of vertical columns on the outer edges of the structure and clear spaces between the columns.

Closed-End Fund A mixed fund with a planned range of investor capital and a limited life.

Closing The final act of procuring a loan and title in which documents are signed between the buyer and seller and/or their respective representation and all money concerned in the contract changes hands.

Closing Costs The expenses that are related to the sale of real estate including loan, title, and appraisal fees and are beyond the price of the property itself.

Closing Statement See: Settlement Statement.

Cloud on Title Certain conditions uncovered in a title search that present a negative impact to the title for the property.

Commercial Mortgage-Backed Securities (CMBS) A type of securities that is backed by loans on commercial real estate.

Collateralized Mortgage Obligation (CMO) Debt that is fully based on a pool of mortgages.

Co-Borrower Another individual who is jointly responsible for the loan and is on the title to the property.

Cost of Funds Index (COFI) An index used to determine changes in the interest rates for certain ARMs.

Co-Investment Program A separate account for an insurance company or investment partnership in which two or more pension funds may co-invest their capital in an individual property or a portfolio of properties.

Co-Investment The condition that occurs when two or more pension funds or groups of funds are sharing ownership of a real estate investment.

Collateral The property for which a borrower has obtained a loan, thereby assuming the risk of losing the property if the loan is not repaid according to the terms of the loan agreement.

Collection The effort on the part of a lender, due to a borrower defaulting on a loan, which involves mailing and recording certain documents in the event that the foreclosure procedure must be implemented.

Commercial Mortgage A loan used to purchase a piece of commercial property or building.

Commercial Mortgage Broker A broker specialized in commercial mortgage applications.

Commercial Mortgage Lender A lender specialized in funding commercial mortgage loans.

Commingled Fund A pooled fund that enables qualified employee benefit plans to mix their capital in order to achieve professional management, greater diversification, or investment positions in larger properties.

Commission A compensation to salespeople that is paid out of the total amount of the purchase transaction.

Commitment The agreement of a lender to make a loan with given terms for a specific period.

Commitment Fee The fee a lender charges for the guarantee of specified loan terms, to be honored at some point in the future.

Common Area Assessments Sometimes called Homeowners' Association Fees. Charges paid to the homeowners' association by the individual unit owners, in a condominium or planned unit development (PUD), that are usually used to maintain the property and common areas.

Common Area Maintenance The additional charges the tenant must pay in addition to the base rent to pay for the maintenance of common areas.

Common Areas The portions of a building, land, and amenities, owned or managed by a planned unit development (PUD) or condominium's homeowners' association, that are used by all of the unit owners who share in the common expense of operation and maintenance.

Common Law A set of unofficial laws that were originally based on English customs and used to some extent in several states.

Community Property Property that is acquired by a married couple during the course of their marriage and is considered in many states to be owned jointly, unless certain circumstances are in play.

Comparable Sales Also called Comps or Comparables. The recent selling prices of similar properties in the area that are used to help determine the market value of a property.

Compound Interest The amount of interest paid on the principal balance of a mortgage in addition to accrued interest.

Concessions Cash, or the equivalent, that the landlord pays or allows in the form of rental abatement, additional tenant finish allowance, moving expenses, or other costs expended in order to persuade a tenant to sign a lease.

Condemnation A government agency's act of taking private property, without the owner's consent, for public use through the power of eminent domain.

Conditional Commitment A lender's agreement to make a loan providing the borrower meets certain conditions.

Conditional Sale A contract to sell a property that states that the seller will retain the title until all contractual conditions have been fulfilled.

Condominium A type of ownership in which all of the unit owners own the property, common areas, and buildings jointly, and have sole ownership in the unit to which they hold the title.

Condominium Conversion Changing an existing rental property's ownership to the condominium form of ownership.

Condominium Hotel A condominium project that involves registration desks, short-term occupancy, food and telephone services, and daily cleaning services, and is generally operated as a commercial hotel even though the units are individually owned.

Conduit A strategic alliance between lenders and unaffiliated organizations that acts as a source of funding by regularly purchasing loans, usually with a goal of pooling and securitizing them.

Conforming Loan A type of mortgage that meets the conditions to be purchased by Fannie Mae or Freddie Mac.

Construction Documents The drawings and specifications an architect and/or engineer provides to describe construction requirements for a project.

Construction Loan A short-term loan to finance the cost of construction, usually dispensed in stages throughout the construction project.

Construction Management The process of ensuring that the stages of the construction project are completed in a timely and seamless manner.

Construction-to-Permanent

Loan A construction loan that can be converted to a longer-term traditional mortgage after construction is complete.

Consultant Any individual or company that provides the services to institutional investors, such as defining real estate investment policies, making recommendations to advisers or managers, analyzing existing real estate portfolios, monitoring and reporting on portfolio performance, and/or reviewing specified investment opportunities.

Consumer Price Index (CPI) A measurement of inflation, relating to the change in the prices of goods and services that are regularly purchased by a specific population during a certain period of time.

Contiguous Space Refers to several suites or spaces on a floor (or connected floors) in a given building that can be combined and rented to a single tenant.

Contingency A specific condition that must be met before either party in a contract can be legally bound.

Contract An agreement, either verbal or written, to perform or not to perform a certain thing.

Contract Documents See: Construction Documents.

Contract Rent Also known as Face Rent. The dollar amount of the rental obligation specified in a lease.

Conventional Loan A long-term loan from a non-governmental lender that a borrower obtains for the purchase of a home.

Convertible Adjustable-Rate Mortgage A type of mortgage that begins as a traditional ARM but contains a provision to enable the borrower to change to a fixed-rate mortgage during a certain period of time.

Convertible Debt The point in a mortgage at which the lender has the option to convert to a partially or fully owned property within a certain period of time.

Convertible Preferred Stock Preferred stock that can be converted to common stock under certain conditions that have been specified by the issuer.

Conveyance The act of transferring a property title between parties by deed.

Cooperative Also called a Co-op. A type of ownership by multiple residents of a multi-unit housing complex in which they all own shares in the cooperative corporation that owns the property, thereby having the right to occupy a particular apartment or unit.

Cooperative Mortgage Any loan that is related to a cooperative residential project.

Core Properties The main types of property, specifically office, retail, industrial, and multi-family.

Co-Signer A second individual or party who also signs a promissory note or loan agreement, thereby taking responsibility for the debt in the event that the primary borrower cannot pay.

Cost-Approach Improvement Value The current expenses for constructing a copy or replacement for an existing structure, but subtracting an estimate of the accrued depreciation.

Cost-Approach Land Value The estimated value of the basic interest in the land, as if it were available for development to its highest and best use.

Cost-of-Sale Percentage An estimate of the expenses of selling an investment that represents brokerage commissions, closing costs, fees, and other necessary sales costs.

Coupon The token or expected interest rate the borrower is charged on a promissory note or mortgage.

Courier Fee The fee that is charged at closing for the delivery of documents between all parties concerned in a real estate transaction.

Covenant A written agreement, included in deeds or other legal documents, that defines the requirements for certain acts or use of a property.

Credit An agreement in which a borrower promises to repay the lender at a later date and receives something of value in exchange.

Credit Enhancement The necessary credit support, in addition to mortgage collateral, in order to achieve the desired credit rating on mortgage-backed securities.

Credit History An individual's record which details his current and past financial obligations and performance.

Credit Life Insurance A type of insurance that pays the balance of a mortgage if the borrower dies.

Credit Rating The degree of creditworthiness a person is assigned based on his credit history and current financial status.

Credit Report A record detailing an individual's credit, employment, and residence history used to determine the individual's creditworthiness.

Credit Repository A company that records and updates credit applicants' financial and credit information from various sources.

Credit Score Sometimes called a Credit Risk Score. The number contained in a consumer's credit report that represents a statistical summary of the information.

Creditor A party to whom other parties owe money.

Cross-Collateralization A group of mortgages or properties that jointly secures one debt obligation.

Cross-Defaulting A provision that allows a trustee or lender to require full payment on all loans in a group, if any single loan in the group is in default.

Cumulative Discount Rate A percentage of the current value of base rent with all landlord lease concessions taken into account.

Current Occupancy The current percentage of units in a building or property that is leased.

Current Yield The annual rate of return on an investment, expressed as a percentage.

Deal Structure The type of agreement in financing an acquisition. The deal can be un-leveraged, leveraged, traditional debt, participating debt, participating/convertible debt, or joint ventures.

Debt Any amount one party owes to another party.

Debt Service Coverage Ratio (DSCR) A property's yearly net operating income divided by the yearly cost of debt service.

Debt Service The amount of money that is necessary to meet all interest and principal payments during a specific period.

Debt-to-Income Ratio The percentage of a borrower's monthly payment on long-term debts divided by his gross monthly income.

Dedicate To change a private property to public ownership for a particular public use.

Deed A legal document that conveys property ownership to the buyer.

Deed in Lieu of Foreclosure A situation in which a deed is given to a lender in order to satisfy a mortgage debt and to avoid the foreclosure process.

Deed of Trust A provision that allows a lender to foreclose on a property in the event that the borrower defaults on the loan.

Default The state that occurs when a borrow fails to fulfill a duty or take care of an obligation, such as making monthly mortgage payments.

Deferred Maintenance Account A type of account that a borrower must fund to provide for maintenance of a property.

Deficiency Judgment The legal assignment of personal liability to a borrower for the unpaid balance of a mortgage, after foreclosing on the property has failed to yield the full amount of the debt.

Defined-Benefit Plan A type of benefit provided by an employer that defines an employee's benefits either as a fixed amount or a percentage of the beneficiary's salary when he retires.

Defined-Contribution Plan A type of benefit plan provided by an employer in which an employee's retirement benefits are determined by the amount that has been contributed by the employer and/or employee during the time of employment, and by the actual investment earnings on those contributions over the life of the fund.

Delinquency A state that occurs when the borrower fails to make mortgage payments on time, eventually resulting in foreclosure, if severe enough.

Delinquent Mortgage A mortgage in which the borrower is behind on payments.

Demising Wall The physical partition between the spaces of two tenants or from the building's common areas.

Deposit Also referred to as Earnest Money. The funds that the buyer provides when offering to purchase property.

Depreciation A decline in the value of property or an asset, often used as a tax-deductible item.

Derivative Securities A type of securities that has been created from other financial instruments.

Design/Build An approach in which a single individual or business is responsible for both the design and construction.

Disclosure A written statement, presented to a potential buyer, that lists information relevant to a piece of property, whether positive or negative.

Discount Points Fees that a lender charges in order to provide a lower interest rate.

Discount Rate A figure used to translate present value from future payments or receipts.

Discretion The amount of authority an adviser or manager is granted for investing and managing a client's capital.

Distraint The act of seizing a tenant's personal property when the tenant is in default, based on the right the landlord has in satisfying the debt.

Diversification The act of spreading individual investments out to insulate a portfolio against the risk of reduced yield or capital loss.

Dividend Yield The percentage of a security's market price that represents the annual dividend rate.

Dividend Distributions of cash or stock that stockholders receive.

Dividend-Ex Date The initial date on which a person purchasing the stock can no longer receive the most recently announced dividend.

Document Needs List The list of documents a lender requires from a potential borrower who is submitting a loan application.

Documentation Preparation Fee A fee that lenders, brokers, and/or settlement agents charge for the preparation of the necessary closing documents.

Dollar Stop An agreed amount of taxes and operating expenses each tenant must pay out on a prorated basis.

Down Payment The variance between the purchase price and the portion that the mortgage lender financed.

DOWNREIT A structure of organization that makes it possible for REITs to purchase properties using partnership units.

Draw A payment from the construction loan proceeds made to contractors, subcontractors, home builders, or suppliers.

Due Diligence The activities of a prospective purchaser or mortgager of real property for the purpose of confirming that the property is as represented by the seller and is not subject to environmental or other problems.

Due on Sale Clause The standard mortgage language that states the loan must still be repaid if the property is resold.

Earnest Money See: Deposit.

Earthquake Insurance A type of insurance policy that provides coverage against earthquake damage to a home.

Easement The right given to a non-ownership party to use a certain part of the property for specified purposes, such as servicing power lines or cable lines.

Economic Feasibility The viability of a building or project in terms of costs and revenue where the degree of viability is established by extra revenue.

Economic Rent The market rental value of a property at a particular point in time.

Effective Age An estimate of the physical condition of a building presented by an appraiser.

Effective Date The date on which the sale of securities can commence once a registration statement becomes effective.

Effective Gross Income (EGI)
The total property income that rents and other sources generate after subtracting a vacancy factor estimated to be appropriate for the property.

Effective Gross Rent (EGR) The net rent that is generated after adjusting for tenant improvements and other capital costs, lease commissions, and other sales expenses.

Effective Rent The actual rental rate that the landlord achieves after deducting the concession value from the base rental rate a tenant pays.

Electronic Authentication A way of providing proof that a particular electronic document is genuine, has arrived unaltered, and came from the indicated source.

Eminent Domain The power of the government to pay the fair market value for a property, appropriating it for public use.

Encroachment Any improvement or upgrade that illegally intrudes onto another party's property.

Encumbrance Any right or interest in a property that interferes with using it or transferring ownership.

End Loan The result of converting to permanent financing from a construction loan.

Entitlement A benefit of a VA home loan. Often referred to as eligibility.

Environmental Impact Statement Legally required documents that must accompany major project proposals where there will likely be an impact on the surrounding environment.

Equal Credit Opportunity Act (ECOA) A federal law that requires a lender or other creditor to make credit available for applicants regardless of sex, marital status, race, religion, or age.

Equifax One of the three primary credit-reporting bureaus.

Equity The value of a property after existing liabilities have been deducted.

Employee Retirement Income Security Act (ERISA) A legislation that controls the investment activities, mainly of corporate and union pension plans.

Errors and Omissions Insurance A type of policy that insures against the mistakes of a builder or architect.

Escalation Clause The clause in a lease that provides for the rent to be increased to account for increases in the expenses the landlord must pay.

Escrow A valuable item, money, or documents deposited with a third party for delivery upon the fulfillment of a condition.

Escrow Account Also referred to as an Impound Account. An account established by a mortgage lender or servicing company for the purpose of holding funds for the payment of items, such as homeowner's insurance and property taxes.

Escrow Agent A neutral third party who makes sure that all conditions of a real estate transaction have been met before any funds are transferred or property is recorded.

Escrow Agreement A written agreement between an escrow agent and the contractual parties that defines the basic obligations of each party, the money (or other valuables) to be deposited in escrow, and how the escrow agent is to dispose of the money on deposit.

Escrow Analysis An annual investigation a lender performs to make sure they are collecting the appropriate amount of money for anticipated expenditures.

Escrow Closing The event in which all conditions of a real estate transaction have been met, and the property title is transferred to the buyer.

Escrow Company A neutral company that serves as a third party to ensure that all conditions of a real estate transaction are met.

Escrow Disbursements The dispensing of escrow funds for the payment of real estate taxes, hazard insurance, mortgage insurance, and other property expenses as they are due.

Escrow Payment The funds that are withdrawn by a mortgage servicer from a borrower's escrow account to pay property taxes and insurance.

Estate The total assets, including property, of an individual after he has died.

Estimated Closing Costs An estimation of the expenses relating to the sale of real estate.

Estimated Hazard Insurance An estimation of hazard insurance, or homeowner's insurance, that will cover physical risks.

Estimated Property Taxes An estimation of the property taxes that must be paid on the property, according to state and county tax rates.

Estoppel Certificate A signed statement that certifies that certain factual statements are correct as of the date of the statement and can be relied upon by a third party, such as a prospective lender or purchaser.

Eviction The legal removal of an occupant from a piece of property.

Examination of Title A title company's inspection and report of public records and other documents for the purpose of determining the chain of ownership of a property.

Exclusive Agency Listing A written agreement between a property owner and a real estate broker in which the owner promises to pay the broker a commission if certain property is leased during the listing period.

Exclusive Listing A contract that allows a licensed real estate agent to be the only agent who can sell a property for a given time.

Executed Contract An agreement in which all parties involved have fulfilled their duties.

Executor The individual who is named in a will to administer an estate. Executrix is the feminine form.

Exit Strategy An approach investors may use when they wish to liquidate all or part of their investment.

Experian One of the three primary credit-reporting bureaus.

Face Rental Rate The rental rate that the landlord publishes.

Facility Space The floor area in a hospitality property that is dedicated to activities, such as restaurants, health clubs, and gift shops, that interactively service multiple people and is not directly related to room occupancy.

Funds Available for Distribution (FAD) The income from operations, with cash expenditures subtracted, that may be used for leasing commissions and tenant improvement costs.

FAD Multiple The price per share of a REIT divided by its funds available for distribution.

Fair Credit Reporting Act (FCRA) The federal legislation that governs the processes credit reporting agencies must follow.

Fair Housing Act The federal legislation that prohibits the refusal to rent or sell to anyone based on race, color, religion, sex, family status, or disability.

Fair Market Value The highest price that a buyer would be willing to pay, and the lowest a seller would be willing to accept.

Fannie Mae See: Federal National Mortgage Association.

Fannie Mae's Community Home Buyer's Program A community lending model based on borrower income in which mortgage insurers and Fannie Mae offer flexible underwriting guidelines in order to increase the buying power for a low- or moderate-income family and to decrease the total amount of cash needed to purchase a home.

Farmer's Home Administration (FMHA) An agency within the U.S. Department of Agriculture that provides credit to farmers and other rural residents.

Federal Home Loan Mortgage Corporation (FHLMC) Also known as Freddie Mac. The company that buys mortgages from lending institutions, combines them with other loans, and sells shares to investors.

Federal Housing Administration (FHA) A government agency that provides low-rate mortgages to buyers who are able to make a down payment as low as 3 percent.

Federal National Mortgage Association (FNMA) Also known as Fannie Mae. A congressionally chartered, shareholder-owned company that is the nation's largest supplier of home mortgage funds. The company buys mortgages from lenders and resells them as securities on the secondary mortgage market.

Fee Simple The highest possible interest a person can have in a piece of real estate.

Fee Simple Estate An unconditional, unlimited inheritance estate in which the owner may dispose of or use the property as desired.

Fee Simple Interest The state of owning all the rights in a real estate parcel.

Funds From Operations (FFO) A ratio that is meant to highlight the amount of cash a company's real estate portfolio generates relative to its total operating cash flow.

FFO Multiple The price of a REIT share divided by its funds from operations.

FHA Loans Mortgages that the Federal Housing Administration (FHA) insures.

FHA Mortgage Insurance A type of insurance that requires a fee to be paid at closing in order to insure the loan with the Federal Housing Administration (FHA).

Fiduciary Any individual who holds authority over a plan's asset management, administration or disposition, or renders paid investment advice regarding a plan's assets.

Finance Charge The amount of interest to be paid on a loan or credit card balance.

Firm Commitment A written agreement a lender makes to loan money for the purchase of property.

First Mortgage The main mortgage on a property.

First Refusal Right/ Right of First Refusal A lease clause that gives a tenant the first opportunity to buy a property or to lease additional space in a property at the same price and terms as those contained in an offer from a third party that the owner has expressed a willingness to accept.

First-Generation Space A new space that has never before been occupied by a tenant and is currently available for lease.

First-Loss Position A security's position that will suffer the first economic loss if the assets below it lose value or are foreclosed on.

Fixed Costs Expenses that remain the same despite the level of sales or production.

Fixed Rate An interest rate that does not change over the life of the loan.

Fixed Time The particular weeks of a year that the owner of a timeshare arrangement can access his or her accommodations.

Fixed-Rate Mortgage A loan with an unchanging interest rate over the life of the loan.

Fixture Items that become a part of the property when they are permanently attached to the property.

Flat Fee An amount of money that an adviser or manager receives for managing a portfolio of real estate assets.

Flex Space A building that provides a flexible configuration of office or showroom space combined with manufacturing, laboratory,

warehouse, distribution, etc.

Float The number of freely traded shares owned by the public.

Flood Certification The process of analyzing whether a property is located in a known flood zone.

Flood Insurance A policy that is required in designated flood zones to protect against loss due to flood damage.

Floor Area Ratio (FAR) A measurement of a building's gross square footage compared to the square footage of the land on which it is located.

For Sale By Owner (FSBO) A method of selling property in which the property owner serves as the selling agent and directly handles the sales process with the buyer or buyer's agent.

Force Majeure An external force that is not controlled by the contractual parties and prevents them from complying with the provisions of the contract.

Foreclosure The legal process in which a lender takes over ownership of a property once the borrower is in default in a mortgage arrangement.

Forward Commitments Contractual agreements to perform certain financing duties according to any stated conditions.

Four Quadrants of the Real Estate Capital Markets The four market types that consist of Private Equity, Public Equity, Private Debt, and Public Debt.

Freddie Mac See: Federal Home Loan Mortgage Corporation.

Front-End Ratio The measurement a lender uses to compare a borrower's monthly housing expense to gross monthly income.

Full Recourse A loan on which the responsibility of a loan is transferred to an endorser or guarantor in the event of default by the borrower.

Full-Service Rent A rental rate that includes all operating expenses and real estate taxes for the first year.

Fully Amortized ARM An ARM with a monthly payment that is sufficient to amortize the remaining balance at the current interest accrual rate over the amortization term.

Fully Diluted Shares The number of outstanding common stock shares if all convertible securities were converted to common shares.

Future Proposed Space The space in a commercial development that has been proposed but is not yet under construction, or the future phases of a multi-phase project that has not yet been built.

General Contractor The main person or business that contracts for the construction of an entire building or project, rather than individual duties.

General Partner The member in a partnership who holds the authority to bind the partnership and shares in its profits and losses.

Gift Money a buyer has received from a relative or other source that will not have to be repaid.

Ginnie Mae See: Government National Mortgage Association.

Going-In Capitalization Rate The rate that is computed by dividing the expected net operating income for the first year by the value of the property.

Good Faith Estimate A lender's or broker's estimate that shows all costs associated with obtaining a home loan including loan processing, title, and inspection fees.

Government Loan A mortgage that is insured or guaranteed by the FHA, the Department of Veterans Affairs (VA), or the Rural Housing Service (RHS).

Government National Mortgage Association (GNMA) Also known as Ginnie Mae. A government-owned corporation under the U.S. Department of Housing and Urban Development (HUD) that performs the same role as Fannie Mae and Freddie Mac in providing funds to lenders for making home loans, but only purchases loans that are backed by the federal government.

Grace Period A defined time period in which a borrower may make a loan payment after its due date without incurring a penalty.

Graduated Lease A lease, usually long-term, in which rent payments vary in accordance with future contingencies.

Graduated Payment Mortgage A mortgage that requires low payments during the first years of the loan, but eventually requires larger monthly payments over the term of the loan that become fixed later in the term.

Grant To give or transfer an interest in a property by deed or other documented method.

Grantee The party to whom an interest in a property is given.

Grantor The party who is transferring an interest in a property.

Gross Building Area The sum of areas at all floor levels, including the basement, mezzanine, and penthouses included in the principal outside faces of the exterior walls without allowing for architectural setbacks or projections.

Gross Income The total income of a household before taxes or expenses

have been subtracted.

Gross Investment in Real Estate (Historic Cost) The total amount of equity and debt that is invested in a piece of real estate minus proceeds from sales or partial sales.

Gross Leasable Area The amount of floor space that is designed for tenants' occupancy and exclusive use.

Gross Lease A rental arrangement in which the tenant pays a flat sum for rent, and the landlord must pay all building expenses out of that amount.

Gross Real Estate Asset Value The total market value of the real estate investments under management in a fund or individual accounts, usually including the total value of all equity positions, debt positions, and joint venture ownership positions.

Gross Real Estate Investment Value The market value of real estate investments that are held in a portfolio without including debt.

Gross Returns The investment returns generated from operating a property without adjusting for adviser or manager fees.

Ground Lease Land being leased to an individual that has absolutely no residential dwelling on the property; or if it does, the ground (or land) is the only portion of the property being leased.

Ground Rent A long-term lease in which rent is paid to the land owner, normally to build something on that land.

Growing-Equity Mortgage A fixed-rate mortgage in which payments increase over a specified amount of time with the extra funds being applied to the principal.

Guarantor The part who makes a guaranty.

Guaranty An agreement in which the guarantor promises to satisfy the debt or obligations of another, if and when the debtor fails to do so.

Hard Cost The expenses attributed to actually constructing property improvements.

Hazard Insurance Also known as Homeowner's Insurance or Fire Insurance. A policy that provides coverage for damage from forces such as fire and wind.

Highest and Best Use The most reasonable, expected, legal use of a piece of vacant land or improved property that is physically possible, supported appropriately, financially feasible, and that results in the highest value.

High-Rise In a suburban district, any building taller than six stories. In a business district, any building taller than 25 stories.

Holdbacks A portion of a loan funding that is not dispersed until an additional condition is met, such as the completion of construction.

Holding Period The expected length of time, from purchase to sale, that an investor will own a property.

Hold-Over Tenant A tenant who retains possession of the leased premises after the lease has expired.

Home Equity Conversion Mortgage (HECM) Also referred to as a Reverse Annuity Mortgage. A type of mortgage in which the lender makes payments to the owner, thereby enabling older homeowners to convert equity in their homes into cash in the form of monthly payments.

Home Equity Line An open-ended amount of credit based on the equity a homeowner has accumulated.

Home Equity Loan A type of loan that allows owners to borrow against the equity in their homes up to a limited amount.

Home Inspection A pre-purchase examination of the condition a home is in by a certified inspector.

Home Inspector A certified professional who determines the structural soundness and operating systems of a property.

Home Price The price that a buyer and seller agree upon, generally based on the home's appraised market value.

Homeowners' Association (HOA) A group that governs a community, condominium building, or neighborhood and enforces the covenants, conditions, and restrictions set by the developer.

Homeowners' Association Dues The monthly payments that are paid to the homeowners' association for maintenance and communal expenses.

Homeowner's Insurance A policy that includes coverage for all damages that may affect the value of a house as defined in the terms of the insurance policy.

Homeowner's Warranty A type of policy homebuyers often purchase to cover repairs, such as heating or air-conditioning, should they stop working within the coverage period.

Homestead The property an owner uses as his primary residence.

Housing Expense Ratio The percentage of gross income that is devoted to housing costs each month.

HUD (Housing and Urban Development) A federal agency that oversees a variety of housing and community development programs, including the FHA.

HUD Median Income The average income for families in a particular area, which is estimated by HUD.

HUD-1 Settlement Statement Also known as the Closing Statement or Settlement Sheet. An itemized listing of the funds paid at closing.

HUD-1 Uniform Settlement Statement A closing statement for the buyer and seller that describes all closing costs for a real estate transaction or refinancing.

HVAC Heating, ventilating, and air-conditioning.

Hybrid Debt A position in a mortgage that has equity-like features of participation in both cash flow and the appreciation of the property at the point of sale or refinance.

Implied Cap Rate The net operating income divided by the sum of a REIT's equity market capitalization and its total outstanding debt.

Impounds The part of the monthly mortgage payment that is reserved in an account in order to pay for hazard insurance, property taxes, and private mortgage insurance.

Improvements The upgrades or changes made to a building to improve its value or usefulness.

Incentive Fee A structure in which the fee amount charged is based on the performance of the real estate assets under management.

Income Capitalization Value
The figure derived for an income-producing property by converting its expected benefits into property value.

Income Property A particular property that is used to generate income but is not occupied by the owner.

Income Return The percentage of the total return generated by the income from property, fund, or account operations.

Index A financial table that lenders use for calculating interest rates on ARMs.

Indexed Rate The sum of the published index with a margin added.

Indirect Costs Expenses of development other than the costs of direct material and labor that are related directly to the construction of improvements.

Individual Account Management The process of maintaining accounts that have been established for individual plan sponsors or other investors for investment in real estate, where a firm acts as an adviser in obtaining and/or managing a real estate portfolio.

Inflation Hedge An investment whose value tends to increase

at a greater rate than inflation, contributing to the preservation of the purchasing power of a portfolio.

Inflation The rate at which consumer prices increase each year.

Initial Interest Rate The original interest rate on an ARM which is sometimes subject to a variety of adjustments throughout the mortgage.

Initial Public Offering (IPO) The first time a previously private company offers securities for public sale.

Initial Rate Cap The limit specified by some ARMs as the maximum amount the interest rate may increase when the initial interest rate expires.

Initial Rate Duration The date specified by most ARMs at which the initial rate expires.

Inspection Fee The fee that a licensed property inspector charges for determining the current physical condition of the property.

Inspection Report A written report of the property's condition presented by a licensed inspection professional.

Institutional-Grade Property A variety of types of real estate properties usually owned or financed by tax-exempt institutional investors.

Insurance Binder A temporary insurance policy that is implemented while a permanent policy is drawn up or obtained.

Insurance Company Separate Account A real estate investment vehicle only offered by life insurance companies, which enables an ERISA-governed fund to avoid creating unrelated taxable income for certain types of property investments and investment structures.

Insured Mortgage A mortgage that is guaranteed by the FHA or by private mortgage insurance (PMI).

Interest Accrual Rate The rate at which a mortgage accrues interest.

Interest-Only Loan A mortgage for which the borrower pays only the interest that accrues on the loan balance each month.

Interest Paid over Life of Loan The total amount that has been paid to the lender during the time the money was borrowed.

Interest Rate The percentage that is charged for a loan.

Interest Rate Buy-Down Plans A plan in which a seller uses funds from the sale of the home to buy down the interest rate and reduce the buyer's monthly payments.

Interest Rate Cap The highest interest rate charge allowed on the monthly payment of an ARM during an adjustment period.

Interest Rate Ceiling The maximum interest rate a lender can charge for an ARM.

Interest Rate Floor The minimum possible interest rate a lender can charge for an ARM.

Interest The price that is paid for the use of capital.

Interest-Only Strip A derivative security that consists of all or part of the portion of interest in the underlying loan or security.

Interim Financing Also known as Bridge or Swing Loans. Short-term financing a seller uses to bridge the gap between the sale of one house and the purchase of another.

Internal Rate of Return (IRR) The calculation of a discounted cash flow analysis that is used to determine the potential total return of a real estate asset during a particular holding period.

Inventory The entire space of a certain proscribed market without concern for its availability or condition.

Investment Committee The governing body that is charged with overseeing corporate pension investments and developing investment policies for board approval.

Investment Manager An individual or company that assumes authority over a specified amount of real estate capital, invests that capital in assets using a separate account, and provides asset management.

Investment Policy A document that formalizes an institution's goals, objectives, and guidelines for asset management, investment advisory contracting, fees, and utilization of consultants and other outside professionals.

Investment Property A piece of real estate that generates some form of income.

Investment Strategy The methods used by a manager in structuring a portfolio and selecting the real estate assets for a fund or an account.

Investment Structures Approaches to investing that include un-leveraged acquisitions, leveraged acquisitions, traditional debt, participating debt, convertible debt, triple-net leases, and joint ventures.

Investment-Grade CMBS Commercial mortgage-backed securities that have ratings of AAA, AA, A, or BBB.

Investor Status The position an investor is in, either taxable or tax-exempt.

Joint Liability The condition in which responsibility rests with two or more people for fulfilling the terms of a home loan or other financial debt.

Joint Tenancy A form of ownership in which two or more people have equal shares in a piece of property, and rights pass to the surviving owner(s) in the event of death.

Joint Venture An investment business formed by more than one party for the purpose of acquiring or developing and managing property and/or other assets.

Judgment The decision a court of law makes.

Judicial Foreclosure The usual foreclosure proceeding some states use, which is handled in a civil lawsuit.

Jumbo Loan A type of mortgage that exceeds the required limits set by Fannie Mae and Freddie Mac each year.

Junior Mortgage A loan that is a lower priority behind the primary loan.

Just Compensation The amount that is fair to both the owner and the government when property is appropriated for public use through eminent domain.

Landlord's Warrant The warrant a landlord obtains to take a tenant's personal property to sell at a public sale to compel payment of the rent or other stipulation in the lease.

Late Charge The fee that is imposed by a lender when the borrower has not made a payment when it was due.

Late Payment The payment made to the lender after the due date has passed.

Lead Manager The investment banking firm that has primary responsibility for coordinating the new issuance of securities.

Lease A contract between a property owner and tenant that defines payments and conditions under which the tenant may occupy the real estate for a given period of time.

Lease Commencement Date The date at which the terms of the lease are implemented.

Lease Expiration Exposure Schedule A chart of the total square footage of all current leases that expire in each of the next five years, without taking renewal options into account.

Lease Option A financing option that provides for homebuyers to lease a home with an option to buy, with part of the rental payments being applied toward the down payment.

Leasehold The limited right to inhabit a piece of real estate held by a tenant.

Leasehold State A way of holding a property title in which the mortgagor does not actually own the property but has a long-term lease on it.

Leasehold Interest The right to hold or use property for a specific period of time at a given price without transferring ownership.

Lease-Purchase A contract that defines the closing date and solutions for the seller in the event that the buyer defaults.

Legal Blemish A negative count against a piece of property such as a zoning violation or fraudulent title claim.

Legal Description A way of describing and locating a piece of real estate that is recognized by law.

Legal Owner The party who holds the title to the property, although the title may carry no actual rights to the property other than as a lien.

Lender A bank or other financial institution that offers home loans.

Letter of Credit A promise from a bank or other party that the issuer will honor drafts or other requests for payment upon complying with the requirements specified in the letter of credit.

Letter of Intent An initial agreement defining the proposed terms for the end contract.

Leverage The process of increasing the return on an investment by borrowing some of the funds at an interest rate less than the return on the project.

Liabilities A borrower's debts and financial obligations, whether long- or short-term.

Liability Insurance A type of policy that protects owners against negligence, personal injury, or property damage claims.

London InterBank Offered Rate (LIBOR) The interest rate offered on Eurodollar deposits traded between banks and used to determine changes in interest rate for ARMs.

Lien A claim put by one party on the property of another as collateral for money owed.

Lien Waiver A waiver of a mechanic's lien rights that is sometimes required before the general contractor can receive money under the payment provisions of a construction loan and contract.

Life Cap A limit on the amount an ARM's interest rate can increase during the mortgage term.

Lifecycle The stages of development for a property: pre-development, development, leasing, operating, and rehabilitation.

Lifetime Payment Cap A limit on the amount that payments can increase or decrease over the life of an ARM.

Lifetime Rate Cap The highest possible interest rate that may be charged, under any circumstances, over the entire life of an ARM.

Like-Kind Property A term that refers to real estate that is held for productive use in a trade or business or for investment.

Limited Partnership A type of partnership in which some partners manage the business and are personally liable for partnership debts, but some partners contribute capital and share in profits without the responsibility of management.

Line of Credit An amount of credit granted by a financial institution up to a specified amount for a certain period of time to a borrower.

Liquid Asset A type of asset that can be easily converted into cash.

Liquidity The ease with which an individual's or company's assets can be converted to cash without losing their value.

Listing Agreement An agreement between a property owner and a real estate broker that authorizes the broker to attempt to sell or lease the property at a specified price and terms in return for a commission or other compensation.

Loan An amount of money that is borrowed and usually repaid with interest.

Loan Application A document that presents a borrower's income, debt, and other obligations to determine credit worthiness, as well as some basic information on the target property.

Loan Application Fee A fee lenders charge to cover expenses relating to reviewing a loan application.

Loan Commitment An agreement by a lender or other financial institution to make or ensure a loan for the specified amount and terms.

Loan Officer An official representative of a lending institution who is authorized to act on behalf of the lender within specified limits.

Loan Origination The process of obtaining and arranging new loans.

Loan Origination Fee A fee lenders charge to cover the costs related to arranging the loan.

Loan Servicing The process a lending institution goes through for all loans it manages. This involves processing payments, sending statements, managing the escrow/ impound account, providing collection services on delinquent loans, ensuring that insurance and property taxes are made on the property, handling pay-offs and

assumptions, as well as various other services.

Loan Term The time, usually expressed in years, that a lender sets in which a buyer must pay a mortgage.

Loan-to-Value (LTV) The ratio of the amount of the loan compared to the appraised value or sales price.

Lock-Box Structure An arrangement in which the payments are sent directly from the tenant or borrower to the trustee.

Lock-In A commitment from a lender to a borrower to guarantee a given interest rate for a limited amount of time.

Lock-In Period The period of time during which the borrower is guaranteed a specified interest rate.

Lockout The period of time during which a loan may not be paid off early.

Long-Term Lease A rental agreement that will last at least three years from initial signing to the date of expiration or renewal.

Loss Severity The percentage of lost principal when a loan is foreclosed.

Lot One of several contiguous parcels of a larger piece of land.

Low-Documentation Loan A mortgage that requires only a basic verification of income and assets.

Low-Rise A building that involves fewer than four stories above the ground level.

Lump-Sum Contract A type of construction contract that requires the general contractor to complete a building project for a fixed cost that is usually established beforehand by competitive bidding.

Magic Page A story of projected growth that describes how a new REIT will achieve its future plans for funds from operations or funds available for distribution.

Maintenance Fee The charge to homeowners' association members each month for the repair and maintenance of common areas.

Maker One who issues a promissory note and commits to paying the note when it is due.

Margin A percentage that is added to the index and fixed for the mortgage term.

Mark to Market The act of changing the original investment cost or value of a property or portfolio to the level of the current estimated market value.

Market Capitalization A measurement of a company's value that is calculated by multiplying the current share price by the current number of shares outstanding.

Market Rental Rates The rental income that a landlord could most likely ask for a property in the open market, indicated by the current rents for comparable spaces.

Market Study A forecast of the demand for a certain type of real estate project in the future that includes an estimate of the square footage that could be absorbed and the rents that could be charged.

Market Value The price a property would sell for at a particular point in time in a competitive market.

Marketable Title A title that is free of encumbrances and can be marketed immediately to a willing purchaser.

Master Lease The primary lease that controls other subsequent leases and may cover more property than all subsequent leases combined.

Master Servicer An entity that acts on behalf of a trustee for security holders' benefit in collecting funds from a borrower, advancing funds in the event of delinquencies and, in the event of default, taking a property through foreclosure.

Maturity Date The date at which the total principal balance of a loan is due.

Mechanic's Lien A claim created for securing payment priority for the price and value of work performed and materials furnished in constructing, repairing, or improving a building or other structure.

Meeting Space The space in hotels that is made available to the public to rent for meetings, conferences, or banquets.

Merged Credit Report A report that combines information from the three primary credit-reporting agencies including: Equifax, Experian, and TransUnion.

Metes and Bounds The surveyed boundary lines of a piece of land described by listing the compass directions (bounds) and distances (metes) of the boundaries.

Mezzanine Financing A financing position somewhere between equity and debt, meaning that there are higher-priority debts above and equity below.

Mid-Rise Usually, a building which shows four to eight stories above ground level. In a business district, buildings up to 25 stories may also be included.

Mixed-Use A term referring to space within a building or project which can be used for more than one activity.

Modern Portfolio Theory (MPT) An approach of quantifying risk and return in an asset portfolio which emphasizes the portfolio rather than the individual assets and how the

assets perform in relation to each other.

Modification An adjustment in the terms of a loan agreement.

Modified Annual Percentage Rate (APR) An index of the cost of a loan based on the standard APR but adjusted for the amount of time the borrower expects to hold the loan.

Monthly Association Dues A payment due each month to a homeowners' association for expenses relating to maintenance and community operations.

Mortgage An amount of money that is borrowed to purchase a property using that property as collateral.

Mortgage Acceleration Clause A provision enabling a lender to require that the rest of the loan balance is paid in a lump sum under certain circumstances.

Mortgage Banker A financial institution that provides home loans using its own resources, often selling them to investors such as insurance companies or Fannie Mae.

Mortgage Broker An individual who matches prospective borrowers with lenders that the broker is approved to deal with.

Mortgage Broker Business A company that matches prospective borrowers with lenders that the broker is approved to deal with.

Mortgage Constant A figure comparing an amortizing mortgage payment to the outstanding mortgage balance.

Mortgage Insurance (MI) A policy, required by lenders on some loans, that covers the lender against certain losses that are incurred as a result of a default on a home loan.

Mortgage Insurance Premium (MIP) The amount charged for mortgage insurance, either to a government agency or to a private MI company.

Mortgage Interest Deduction The tax write-off that the IRS allows most homeowners to deduct for annual interest payments made on real estate loans.

Mortgage Life and Disability Insurance A type of term life insurance borrowers often purchase to cover debt that is left when the borrower dies or becomes too disabled to make the mortgage payments.

Mortgagee The financial institution that lends money to the borrower.

Mortgagor The person who requests to borrow money to purchase a property.

Multi-Dwelling Units A set of properties that provide separate housing areas for more than one family but only require a single mortgage.

Multiple Listing Service A service that lists real estate offered for sale by a particular real estate agent that can be shown or sold by other real estate agents within a certain area.

National Association of Real Estate Investment Trusts (NAREIT) The national, non-profit trade organization that represents the real estate investment trust industry.

National Council of Real Estate Investment Fiduciaries (NCREIF) A group of real estate professionals who serve on committees; sponsor research articles, seminars and symposiums; and produce the NCREIF Property Index.

NCREIF Property Index (NPI) A quarterly and yearly report presenting income and appreciation components.

Negative Amortization An event that occurs when the deferred interest on an ARM is added, and the balance increases instead of decreases.

Net Asset Value (NAV) The total value of an asset or property minus leveraging or joint venture interests.

Net Asset Value Per Share The total value of a REIT's current assets divided by outstanding shares.

Net Assets The total value of assets minus total liabilities based on market value.

Net Cash Flow The total income generated by an investment property after expenses have been subtracted.

Net Investment in Real Estate Gross investment in properties minus the outstanding balance of debt.

Net Investment Income The income or loss of a portfolio or business minus all expenses, including portfolio and asset management fees, but before gains and losses on investments are considered.

Net Operating Income (NOI) The pre-tax figure of gross revenue minus operating expenses and an allowance for expected vacancy.

Net Present Value (NPV) The sum of the total current value of incremental future cash flows plus the current value of estimated sales proceeds.

Net Purchase Price The gross purchase price minus any associated financed debt.

Net Real Estate Investment Value The total market value of all real estate minus property-level debt.

Net Returns The returns paid to investors minus fees to advisers or managers.

Net Sales Proceeds The income from the sale of an asset, or part of an asset, minus brokerage commissions, closing costs, and market expenses.

Net Square Footage The total space required for a task or staff position.

Net Worth The worth of an individual or company figured on the basis of a difference between all assets and liabilities.

No-Cash-Out Refinance Sometimes referred to as a Rate and Term Refinance. A refinancing transaction that is intended only to cover the balance due on the current loan and any costs associated with obtaining the new mortgage.

No-Cost Loan A loan for which there are no costs associated with the loan that are charged by the lender, but with a slightly higher interest rate.

No-Documentation Loan A type of loan application that requires no income or asset verification, usually granted based on strong credit with a large down payment.

Nominal Yield The yield investors receive before it is adjusted for fees, inflation, or risk.

Non-Assumption Clause A provision in a loan agreement that prohibits transferring a mortgage to another borrower without approval from the lender.

Non-Compete Clause A provision in a lease agreement that specifies that the tenant's business is the only one that may operate in the property in question, thereby preventing a competitor moving in next door.

Non-Conforming Loan Any loan that is too large or does not meet certain qualifications to be purchased by Fannie Mae or Freddie Mac.

Non-Discretionary Funds The funds that are allocated to an investment manager who must have approval from the investor for each transaction.

Non-Investment-Grade CMBS Also referred to as High-Yield CMBS. Commercial mortgage-backed securities that have ratings of BB or B.

Non-Liquid Asset A type of asset that is not turned into cash very easily.

Non-Performing Loan A loan agreement that cannot meet its contractual principal and interest payments.

Non-Recourse Debt A loan that limits the lender's options to collect on the value of the real estate in the event of a default by the borrower.

Nonrecurring Closing Costs Fees that are only paid one time in a given transaction.

Note A legal document requiring a borrower to repay a mortgage at a specified interest rate over a certain period of time.

Note Rate The interest rate that is defined in a mortgage note.

Notice of Default A formal written notification a borrower receives once the borrower is in default stating that legal action may be taken.

Offer A term that describes a specified price or spread to sell whole loans or securities.

One-Year Adjustable-Rate Mortgage An ARM for which the interest rate changes annually, generally based on movements of a published index plus a specified margin.

Open Space A section of land or water that has been dedicated for public or private use or enjoyment.

Open-End Fund A type of commingled fund with an infinite life, always accepting new investor capital and making new investments in property.

Operating Cost Escalation A clause that is intended to adjust rents to account for external standards such as published indexes, negotiated wage levels, or building-related expenses.

Operating Expense The regular costs associated with operating and managing a property.

Opportunistic A phrase that generally describes a strategy of holding investments in underperforming and/or under-managed assets with the expectation of increases in cash flow and/or value.

Option A condition in which the buyer pays for the right to purchase a property within a certain period of time without the obligation to buy.

Option ARM Loan A type of mortgage in which the borrower has a variety of payment options each month.

Original Principal Balance The total principal owed on a mortgage before a borrower has made a payment.

Origination Fee A fee that most lenders charge for the purpose of covering the costs associated with arranging the loan.

Originator A company that underwrites loans for commercial and/or multi-family properties.

Out-Parcel The individual retail sites located within a shopping center.

Overallotment A practice in which the underwriters offer and sell a higher number of shares than they had planned to purchase from the issuer.

Owner Financing A transaction in which the property seller agrees to finance all or part of the amount of the purchase.

Parking Ratio A figure, generally expressed as square footage, that compares a building's total rentable square footage to its total number of parking spaces.

Partial Payment An amount paid that is not large enough to cover the normal monthly payment on a mortgage loan.

Partial Sales The act of selling a real estate interest that is smaller than the whole property.

Partial Taking The appropriating of a portion of an owner's property under the laws of Eminent Domain.

Participating Debt Financing that allows the lender to have participatory rights to equity through increased income and/or residual value over the balance of the loan or original value at the time the loan is funded.

Party in Interest Any party that may hold an interest, including employers, unions, and, sometimes, fiduciaries.

Pass-Through Certificate A document that allows the holder to receive payments of principal and interest from the underlying pool of mortgages.

Payment Cap The maximum amount a monthly payment may increase on an ARM.

Payment Change Date The date on which a new payment amount takes effect on an ARM or GPM, usually in the month directly after the adjustment date.

Payout Ratio The percentage of the primary earnings per share, excluding unusual items, that are paid to common stockholders as cash dividends during the next 12 months.

Pension Liability The full amount of capital that is required to finance vested pension fund benefits.

Percentage Rent The amount of rent that is adjusted based on the percentage of gross sales or revenues the tenant receives.

Per-Diem Interest The interest that is charged or accrued daily.

Performance Bond A bond that a contractor posts to guarantee full performance of a contract in which the proceeds will be used for completing the contract or compensating the owner for loss in the event of nonperformance.

Performance Measurement The process of measuring how well an investor's real estate has performed regarding individual assets, advisers/managers, and portfolios.

Performance The changes each quarter in fund or account values that can be explained by investment income, realized or unrealized appreciation, and the total return to the investors before and after investment management fees.

Performance-Based Fees The fees that advisers or managers receive that are based on returns to investors.

Periodic Payment Cap The highest amount that payments can increase or decrease during a given adjustment period on an ARM.

Periodic Rate Cap The maximum amount that the interest rate can increase or decrease during a given adjustment period on an ARM.

Permanent Loan A long-term property mortgage.

Personal Property Any items belonging to a person that is not real estate.

PITI Principal, Interest, Taxes, Insurance. The items that are included in the monthly payment to the lender for an impounded loan, as well as mortgage insurance.

PITI Reserves The amount in

cash that a borrower must readily have after the down payment and all closing costs are paid when purchasing a home.

Plan Assets The assets included in a pension plan.

Plan Sponsor The party that is responsible for administering an employee benefit plan.

Planned Unit Development (PUD) A type of ownership where individuals actually own the building or unit they live in, but common areas are owned jointly with the other members of the development or association. Contrast with condominium, where an individual actually owns the airspace of his unit, but the buildings and common areas are owned jointly with the others in the development or association.

Plat A chart or map of a certain area showing the boundaries of individual lots, streets, and easements.

Pledged Account Mortgage (PAM) A loan tied to a pledged savings account for which the fund and earned interest are used to gradually reduce mortgage payments.

Point Also referred to as a Discount Point. A fee a lender charges to provide a lower interest rate, equal to 1 percent of the amount of the loan.

Portfolio Management A process that involves formulating, modifying, and implementing a real estate investment strategy according to an investor's investment objectives.

Portfolio Turnover The amount of time averaged from the time an investment is funded until it is repaid or sold.

Power of Attorney A legal document that gives someone the authority to act on behalf of another party.

Power of Sale The clause included in a mortgage or deed of trust that provides the mortgagee (or trustee) with the right and power to advertise and sell the property at public auction if the borrower is in default.

Pre-Approval The complete analysis a lender makes regarding a potential borrower's ability to pay for a home as well as a confirmation of the proposed amount to be borrowed.

Pre-Approval Letter The letter a lender presents that states the amount of money they are willing to lend a potential buyer.

Preferred Shares Certain stocks that have a prior distributions claim up to a defined amount before the common shareholders may receive anything.

Pre-Leased A certain amount of

space in a proposed building that must be leased before construction may begin or a certificate of occupancy may be issued.

Prepaid Expenses The amount of money that is paid before it is due, including taxes, insurance, and/or assessments.

Prepaid Fees The charges that a borrower must pay in advance regarding certain recurring items, such as interest, property taxes, hazard insurance, and PMI, if applicable.

Prepaid Interest The amount of interest that is paid before its due date.

Prepayment The money that is paid to reduce the principal balance of a loan before the date it is due.

Prepayment Penalty A penalty that may be charged to the borrower when he pays off a loan before the planned maturity date.

Prepayment Rights The right a borrower is given to pay the total principal balance before the maturity date free of penalty.

Prequalification The initial assessment by a lender of a potential borrower's ability to pay for a home as well as an estimate of how much the lender is willing to supply to the buyer.

Price-to-Earnings Ratio The comparison that is derived by dividing the current share price by the sum of the primary earnings per share from continuing operations over the past year.

Primary Issuance The preliminary financing of an issuer.

Prime Rate The best interest rate reserved for a bank's preferred customers.

Prime Space The first-generation space that is available for lease.

Prime Tenant The largest or highest-earning tenant in a building or shopping center.

Principal The amount of money originally borrowed in a mortgage, before interest is included and with any payments subtracted.

Principal Balance The total current balance of mortgage principal not including interest.

Principal Paid over Life of Loan The final total of scheduled payments to the principal that the lender calculates to equal the face amount of the loan.

Principal Payments The lender's return of invested capital.

Principle of Conformity The concept that a property will probably increase in value if its size, age, condition, and style are similar to other properties in the immediate area.

Private Debt Mortgages or other liabilities for which an individual is responsible.

Private Equity A real estate investment that has been acquired by a noncommercial entity.

Private Mortgage Insurance (PMI) A type of policy that a lender requires when the borrower's down payment or home equity percentage is under 20 percent of the value of the property.

Private Placement The sale of a security in a way that renders it exempt from the registration rules and requirements of the SEC.

Private REIT A real estate investment company that is structured as a real estate investment trust that places and holds shares privately rather than publicly.

Pro Rata The proportionate amount of expenses per tenant for the property's maintenance and operation.

Processing Fee A fee some lenders charge for gathering the information necessary to process the loan.

Production Acres The portion of land that can be used directly in agriculture or timber activities to generate income, but not areas used for such things as machinery storage or support.

Prohibited Transaction Certain transactions that may not be performed between a pension plan and a party in interest, such as the following: the sale, exchange or lease of any property; a loan or other grant of credit; and furnishing goods or services.

Promissory Note A written agreement to repay the specific amount over a certain period of time.

Property Tax The tax that must be paid on private property.

Prudent Man Rule The standard to which ERISA holds a fiduciary accountable.

Public Auction An announced public meeting held at a specified location for the purpose of selling property to repay a mortgage in default.

Public Debt Mortgages or other liabilities for which a commercial entity is responsible.

Public Equity A real estate investment that has been acquired by REITs and other publicly traded real estate operating companies.

Punch List An itemized list that documents incomplete or unsatisfactory items after the contractor has declared the space to be mostly complete.

Purchase Agreement The written

contract the buyer and seller both sign defining the terms and conditions under which a property is sold.

Purchase Money Transaction A transaction in which property is acquired through the exchange of money or something of equivalent value.

Purchase-Money Mortgage (PMM) A mortgage obtained by a borrower that serves as partial payment for a property.

Qualified Plan Any employee benefit plan that the IRS has approved as a tax-exempt plan.

Qualifying Ratio The measurement a lender uses to determine how much they are willing to lend to a potential buyer.

Quitclaim Deed A written document that releases a party from any interest they may have in a property.

Rate Cap The highest interest rate allowed on a monthly payment during an adjustment period of an ARM.

Rate Lock The commitment of a lender to a borrower that guarantees a certain interest rate for a specific amount of time.

Rate-Improvement Mortgage A loan that includes a clause that entitles a borrower to a one-time-

only cut in the interest rate without having to refinance.

Rating Agencies Independent firms that are engaged to rate securities' creditworthiness on behalf of investors.

Rating A figure that represents the credit quality or creditworthiness of securities.

Raw Land A piece of property that has not been developed and remains in its natural state.

Raw Space Shell space in a building that has not yet been developed.

Real Estate Agent An individual who is licensed to negotiate and transact the real estate sales.

Real Estate Fundamentals The factors that drive the value of property.

Real Estate Settlement Procedures Act (RESPA) A legislation for consumer protection that requires lenders to notify borrowers regarding closing costs in advance.

Real Property Land and anything else of a permanent nature that is affixed to the land.

Real Rate of Return The yield given to investors minus an inflationary factor.

Realtor A real estate agent or broker who is an active member of a local real estate board affiliated with the National Association of Realtors.

Recapture The act of the IRS recovering the tax benefit of a deduction or a credit that a taxpayer has previously taken in error.

Recorder A public official who records transactions that affect real estate in the area.

Recording The documentation that the registrar's office keeps of the details of properly executed legal documents.

Recording Fee A fee real estate agents charge for moving the sale of a piece of property into the public record.

Recourse The option a lender has for recovering losses against the personal assets of a secondary party who is also liable for a debt that is in default.

Red Herring An early prospectus that is distributed to prospective investors that includes a note in red ink on the cover stating that the SEC-approved registration statement is not yet in effect.

Refinance Transaction The act of paying off an existing loan using the funding gained from a new loan that uses the same property as security.

Regional Diversification Boundaries that are defined based on geography or economic lines.

Registration Statement The set of forms that are filed with the SEC (or the appropriate state agency) regarding a proposed offering of new securities or the listing of outstanding securities on a national exchange.

Regulation Z A federal legislation under the Truth in Lending Act that requires lenders to advise the borrower in writing of all costs that are associated with the credit portion of a financial transaction.

Rehab Short for Rehabilitation. Refers to an extensive renovation intended to extend the life of a building or project.

Rehabilitation Mortgage A loan meant to fund the repairing and improving of a resale home or building.

Real Estate Investment Trust (REIT) A trust corporation that combines the capital of several investors for the purpose of acquiring or providing funding for real estate.

Remaining Balance The amount of the principal on a home loan that has not yet been paid.

Remaining Term The original term of the loan after the number of payments made has been subtracted.

Real Estate Mortgage Investment Conduit (REMIC) An investment vehicle that is designed to hold a pool of mortgages solely to issue multiple classes of mortgage-backed securities in a way that avoids doubled corporate tax.

Renewal Option A clause in a lease agreement that allows a tenant to extend the term of a lease.

Renewal Probability The average percentage of a building's tenants who are expected to renew terms at market rental rates upon the lease expiration.

Rent Commencement Date The date at which a tenant is to begin paying rent.

Rent Loss Insurance A policy that covers loss of rent or rental value for a landlord due to any condition that renders the leased premises inhabitable, thereby excusing the tenant from paying rent.

Rent The fee paid for the occupancy and/or use of any rental property or equipment.

Rentable/Usable Ratio A total rentable area in a building divided by the area available for use.

Rental Concession See: Concessions.

Rental Growth Rate The projected trend of market rental rates over a particular period of analysis.

Rent-Up Period The period of time following completion of a new building when tenants are actively being sought and the project is stabilizing.

Real Estate Owned (REO) The real estate that a savings institution owns as a result of foreclosure on borrowers in default.

Repayment Plan An agreement made to repay late installments or advances.

Replacement Cost The projected cost by current standards of constructing a building that is equivalent to the building being appraised.

Replacement Reserve Fund Money that is set aside for replacing of common property in a condominium, PUD, or cooperative project.

Request for Proposal (RFP) A formal request that invites investment managers to submit information regarding investment strategies, historical investment performance, current investment opportunities, investment management fees, and other pension fund client relationships used by their firm.

Rescission The legal withdrawing of a contract or consent from the parties involved.

Reserve Account An account that

must be funded by the borrower to protect the lender.

Resolution Trust Corp. (RTC) The congressional corporation established for the purpose of containing, managing, and selling failed financial institutions, thereby recovering taxpayer funds.

Retail Investor An investor who sells interests directly to consumers.

Retention Rate The percentage of trailing year's earnings that have been dispersed into the company again. It is calculated as 100 minus the trailing 12-month payout ratio.

Return on Assets The measurement of the ability to produce net profits efficiently by making use of assets.

Return on Equity The measurement of the return on the investment in a business or property.

Return on Investments The percentage of money that has been gained as a result of certain investments.

Reverse Mortgage See: Home Equity Conversion Mortgage.

Reversion Capitalization Rate The capitalization rate that is used to derive reversion value.

Reversion Value A benefit that an investor expects to receive as a lump sum at the end of an investment.

Revolving Debt A credit arrangement that enables a customer to borrow against a predetermined line of credit when purchasing goods and services.

Revenue per Available Room (RevPAR) The total room revenue for a particular period divided by the average number of rooms available in a hospitality facility.

Right of Ingress or Egress The option to enter or to leave the premises in question.

Right of Survivorship The option that survivors have to take on the interest of a deceased joint tenant.

Right to Rescission A legal provision that enables borrowers to cancel certain loan types within three days after they sign.

Risk Management A logical approach to analyzing and defining insurable and non-insurable risks while evaluating the availability and costs of purchasing third-party insurance.

Risk-Adjusted Rate of Return A percentage that is used to identify investment options that are expected to deliver a positive premium despite their volatility.

Road Show A tour of the executives of a company that is planning to go public, during which the executives travel to a variety of cities to make presentations to underwriters and analysts regarding their company and IPO.

Roll-Over Risk The possibility that tenants will not renew their lease.

Sale-Leaseback An arrangement in which a seller deeds a property, or part of it, to a buyer in exchange for money or the equivalent, then leases the property from the new owner.

Sales Comparison Value A value that is calculated by comparing the appraised property to similar properties in the area that have been recently sold.

Sales Contract An agreement that both the buyer and seller sign defining the terms of a property sale.

Second Mortgage A secondary loan obtained on a piece of property.

Secondary Market A market in which existing mortgages are bought and sold as part of a mortgages pool.

Secondary (Follow-On) Offering An offering of stock made by a company that is already public.

Second-Generation or Secondary Space Space that has been occupied before and becomes available for lease again, either by the landlord or as a sublease.

Secured Loan A loan that is secured by some sort of collateral.

Securities and Exchange Commission (SEC) The federal agency that oversees the issuing and exchanging of public securities.

Securitization The act of converting a non-liquid asset into a tradable form.

Security The property or other asset that will serve as a loan's collateral.

Security Deposit An amount of money a tenant gives to a landlord to secure the performance of terms in a lease agreement.

Seisen (Seizen) The ownership of real property under a claim of freehold estate.

Self-Administered REIT A REIT in which the management are employees of the REIT or similar entity.

Self-Managed REIT See: Self-Administered REIT.

Seller Carry-Back An arrangement in which the seller provides the financing to purchase a home.

Seller Financing A type of funding in which the borrower may use part of the equity in the property to finance the purchase.

Senior Classes The security classes who have the highest priority for receiving payments from the underlying mortgage loans.

Separate Account A relationship in which a single pension plan sponsor is used to retain an investment manager or adviser under a stated investment policy exclusively for that sponsor.

Servicer An organization that collects principal and interest payments from borrowers and manages borrowers' escrow accounts on behalf of a trustee.

Servicing The process of collecting mortgage payments from borrowers as well as related responsibilities.

Setback The distance required from a given reference point before a structure can be built.

Settlement or Closing Fees Fees that the escrow agent receives for carrying out the written instructions in the agreement between borrower and lender and/or buyer and seller.

Settlement Statement See: HUD-1 Settlement Statement.

Shared-Appreciation Mortgage A loan that enables a lender or other party to share in the profits of the borrower when the borrower sells the home.

Shared-Equity Transaction A transaction in which two people purchase a property, one as a residence and the other as an investment.

Shares Outstanding The number of shares of outstanding common stock minus the treasury shares.

Site Analysis A determination of how suitable a specific parcel of land is for a particular use.

Site Development The implementation of all improvements that are needed for a site before construction may begin.

Site Plan A detailed description and map of the location of improvements to a parcel.

Slab The flat, exposed surface that is laid over the structural support beams to form the building's floor(s).

Social Investing A strategy in which investments are driven in partially or completely by social or non-real estate objectives.

Soft Cost The part of an equity investment, aside from the literal cost of the improvements, that could be tax-deductible in the first year.

Space Plan A chart or map of space requirements for a tenant that includes wall/door locations, room sizes, and even furniture layouts.

Special Assessment Certain charges that are levied against real estates for public improvements to benefit the property in question.

Special Servicer A company that is hired to collect on mortgages that are either delinquent or in default.

Specified Investing A strategy of investment in individually specified properties, portfolios, or commingled funds are fully or partially detailed prior to the commitment of investor capital.

Speculative Space Any space in a rental property that has not been leased prior to construction on a new building begins.

Stabilized Net Operating Income Expected income minus expenses that reflect relatively stable operations.

Stabilized Occupancy The best projected range of long-term occupancy that a piece of rental property will achieve after existing in the open market for a reasonable period of time with terms and conditions that are comparable to similar offerings.

Step-Rate Mortgage A loan that allows for a gradual interest rate increase during the first few years of the loan.

Step-Up Lease (Graded Lease) A lease agreement that specifies certain increases in rent at certain intervals during the complete term of the lease.

Straight Lease (Flat Lease) A lease agreement that specifies an amount of rent that should be paid regularly during the complete term of the lease.

Strip Center Any shopping area that is made up of a row of stores but is not large enough to be anchored by a grocery store.

Subcontractor A contractor who has been hired by the general contractor, often specializing in a certain required task for the construction project.

Subdivision The most common type of housing development created by dividing a larger tract of land into individual lots for sale or lease.

Sublessee A person or business that holds the rights of use and occupancy under a lease contract with the original lessee, who still retains primary responsibility for the lease obligations.

Subordinate Financing Any loan with a priority lower than loans that were obtained beforehand.

Subordinate Loan A second or third mortgage obtained with the same property being used as collateral.

Subordinated Classes Classes that have the lowest priority of receiving payments from underlying mortgage loans.

Subordination The act of sharing credit loss risk at varying rates among two or more classes of securities.

Subsequent Rate Adjustments The interest rate for ARMs that adjusts at regular intervals, sometimes differing from the duration period of the initial interest rate.

Subsequent Rate Cap The maximum amount the interest rate may increase at each regularly scheduled interest rate adjustment date on an ARM.

Super Jumbo Mortgage A loan that is over $650,000 for some lenders or $1,000,000 for others.

Surety A person who willingly binds himself to the debt or obligation of another party.

Surface Rights A right or easement that is usually granted with mineral rights that enables the holder to drill through the surface.

Survey A document or analysis containing the precise measurements of a piece of property as performed by a licensed surveyor.

Sweat Equity The non-cash improvements in value that an owner adds to a piece of property.

Synthetic Lease A transaction that is considered to be a lease by accounting standards but a loan by tax standards.

Taking Similar to condemning, or any other interference with rights to private property, but a physical seizure or appropriation is not required.

Tax Base The determined value of all property that lies within the jurisdiction of the taxing authority.

Tax Lien A type of lien placed against a property if the owner has not paid property or personal taxes.

Tax Roll A record that contains the descriptions of all land parcels and their owners that is located within the county.

Tax Service Fee A fee that is charged for the purpose of setting up monitoring of the borrower's property tax payments by a third party.

Teaser Rate A small, short-term interest rate offered on a mortgage in order to convince the potential borrower to apply.

Tenancy by the Entirety A form of ownership held by spouses in which they both hold title to the entire property with right of survivorship.

Tenancy in Common A type of ownership held by two or more owners in an undivided interest in the property with no right of survivorship.

Tenant (Lessee) A party who rents a piece of real estate from another by way of a lease agreement.

Tenant at Will A person who possesses a piece of real estate with the owner's permission.

Tenant Improvement (TI) Allowance The specified amount of money that the landlord contributes toward tenant improvements.

Tenant Improvement (TI) The upgrades or repairs that are made to the leased premises by or for a tenant.

Tenant Mix The quality of the income stream for a property.

Term The length that a loan lasts or is expected to last before it is repaid.

Third-Party Origination A process in which another party is used by the lender to originate, process, underwrite, close, fund, or package the mortgages it expects to deliver to the secondary mortgage market.

Timeshare A form of ownership involving purchasing a specific period of time or percentage of interest in a vacation property.

Time-Weighted Average Annual Rate of Return The regular yearly return over several years that would have the same return value as combining the actual annual returns for each year in the series.

Title The legal written document that provides someone ownership in a piece of real estate.

Title Company A business that determines that a property title is clear and that provides title insurance.

Title Exam An analysis of the public records in order to confirm that the seller is the legal owner, and there are no encumbrances on the property.

Title Insurance A type of policy that is issued to both lenders and buyers to cover loss due to property ownership disputes that may arise at a later date.

Title Insurance Binder A written promise from the title insurance company to insure the title to the property, based on the conditions and exclusions shown in the binder.

Title Risk The potential impediments in transferring a title from one party to another.

Title Search The process of analyzing all transactions existing in the public record in order to determine whether any title defects could interfere with the clear transfer of property ownership.

Total Acres The complete amount of land area that is contained within a real estate investment.

Total Assets The final amount of all gross investments, cash and equivalents, receivables, and other assets as they are presented on the balance sheet.

Total Commitment The complete funding amount that is promised once all specified conditions have been met.

Total Expense Ratio The comparison of monthly debt obligations to gross monthly income.

Total Inventory The total amount of square footage commanded by property within a geographical area.

Total Lender Fees Charges that the lender requires for obtaining the loan, aside from other fees associated with the transfer of a property.

Total Loan Amount The basic amount of the loan plus any additional financed closing costs.

Total Monthly Housing Costs The amount that must be paid each month to cover principal, interest, property taxes, PMI, and/or either hazard insurance or homeowners' association dues.

Total of All Payments The total cost of the loan after figuring the sum of all monthly interest payments.

Total Principal Balance The sum of all debt, including the original loan amount adjusted for subsequent payments and any unpaid items that may be included in the principal balance by the mortgage note or by law.

Total Retail Area The total floor area of a retail center that is currently leased or available for lease.

Total Return The final amount of income and appreciation returns per quarter.

Townhouse An attached home that is not considered to be a condominium.

Trade Fixtures Any personal property that is attached to a structure and used in the business but is removable once the lease is terminated.

Trading Down The act of purchasing a property that is less expensive than the one currently owned.

Trading Up The act of purchasing a property that is more expensive than the one currently owned.

Tranche A class of securities that may or may not be rated.

TransUnion Corporation One of the primary credit-reporting bureaus.

Transfer of Ownership Any process in which a property changes hands from one owner to another.

Transfer Tax An amount specified by state or local authorities when ownership in a piece of property changes hands.

Treasury Index A measurement that is used to derive interest rate changes for ARMs.

Triple Net Lease A lease that

requires the tenant to pay all property expenses on top of the rental payments.

Trustee A fiduciary who oversees property or funds on behalf of another party.

Truth-in-Lending The federal legislation requiring lenders to fully disclose the terms and conditions of a mortgage in writing.

TurnKey Project A project in which all components are within a single supplier's responsibility.

Two- to Four-Family Property A structure that provides living space for two to four families while ownership is held in a single deed.

Two-Step Mortgage An ARM with two different interest rates: one for the loan's first five or seven years and another for the remainder of the loan term.

Under Construction The time period that exists after a building's construction has started but before a certificate of occupancy has been presented.

Under Contract The period of time during which a buyer's offer to purchase a property has been accepted, and the buyer is able to finalize financing arrangements without the concern of the seller making a deal with another buyer.

Underwriter A company, usually an investment banking firm, that is involved in a guarantee that an entire issue of stocks or bonds will be purchased.

Underwriters' Knot An approved knot according to code that may be tied at the end of an electrical cord to prevent the wires from being pulled away from their connection to each other or to electrical terminals.

Underwriting The process during which lenders analyze the risks a particular borrower presents and set appropriate conditions for the loan.

Underwriting Fee A fee that mortgage lenders charge for verifying the information on the loan application and making a final decision on approving the loan.

Unencumbered A term that refers to property free of liens or other encumbrances.

Unimproved Land See: Raw Land.

Unrated Classes Usually the lowest classes of securities.

Unrecorded Deed A deed that transfers right of ownership from one owner to another without being officially documented.

Umbrella Partnership Real Estate Investment Trust (UPREIT) An organizational structure in which a REIT's assets are owned by a holding company for tax reasons.

Usable Square Footage The total area that is included within the exterior walls of the tenant's space.

Use The particular purpose for which a property is intended to be employed.

VA Loan A mortgage through the VA program in which a down payment is not necessarily required.

Vacancy Factor The percentage of gross revenue that pro-forma income statements expect to be lost due to vacancies.

Vacancy Rate The percentage of space that is available to rent.

Vacant Space Existing rental space that is presently being marketed for lease minus space that is available for sublease.

Value-Added A phrase advisers and managers generally use to describe investments in underperforming and/or under-managed assets.

Variable Rate Mortgage (VRM) A loan in which the interest rate changes according to fluctuations in particular indexes.

Variable Rate Also called adjustable rate. The interest rate on a loan that varies over the term of the loan according to a predetermined index.

Variance A permission that enables a property owner to work around a zoning ordinance's literal requirements which cause a unique hardship due to special circumstances.

Verification of Deposit (VOD) The confirmation statement a borrower's bank may be asked to sign in order to verify the borrower's account balances and history.

Verification of Employment (VOE) The confirmation statement a borrower's employer may be asked to sign in order to verify the borrower's position and salary.

Vested Having the right to draw on a portion or on all of a pension or other retirement fund.

Veterans Affairs (VA) A federal government agency that assists veterans in purchasing a home without a down payment.

Virtual Storefront A retail business presence on the Internet.

Waiting Period The period of time between initially filing a registration statement and the date it becomes effective.

Warehouse Fee A closing cost fee that represents the lender's expense of temporarily holding a borrower's loan before it is sold on the secondary mortgage market.

Weighted-Average Coupon The average, using the balance of each mortgage as the weighting factor, of the gross interest rates of the mortgages underlying a pool as of the date of issue.

Weighted-Average Equity The part of the equation that is used to calculate investment-level income, appreciation, and total returns on a quarter-by-quarter basis.

Weighted-Average Rental Rates The average ratio of unequal rental rates across two or more buildings in a market.

Working Drawings The detailed blueprints for a construction project that comprise the contractual documents which describe the exact manner in which a project is to be built.

Workout The strategy in which a borrower negotiates with a lender to attempt to restructure the borrower's debt rather than go through the foreclosure proceedings.

Wraparound Mortgage A loan obtained by a buyer to use for the remaining balance on the seller's first mortgage, as well as an additional amount requested by the seller.

Write-Down A procedure used in accounting when an asset's book value is adjusted downward to reflect current market value more accurately.

Write-Off A procedure used in accounting when an asset is determined to be uncollectible and is therefore considered to be a loss.

Yield Maintenance Premium A penalty the borrower must pay in order to make investors whole in the event of early repayment of principal.

Yield Spread The difference in income derived from a commercial mortgage and from a benchmark value.

Yield The actual return on an investment, usually paid in dividends or interest.

Zoning Ordinance The regulations and laws that control the use or improvement of land in a particular area or zone.

Zoning The act of dividing a city or town into particular areas and applying laws and regulations regarding the architectural design, structure, and intended uses of buildings within those areas.

INDEX

V

vacation home 72
value 86
Veterans Administration (VA) loans 102

Z

zero-down 102
zero-down loan 166
zoning and code verification 39

ABOUT
THE AUTHOR

Jeff Haden bought his first
home while still in college;
since then he's invested
extensively in residential and
commercial properties in five states.
He has also written extensively on
real estate investing, mortgages,
and personal finance. A graduate
of James Madison University, he is
also President of BlackBird Media,
an advertising agency and book
publishing services provider.

MORE GREAT TITLES FROM ATLANTIC PUBLISHING

THE REAL ESTATE INVESTOR'S HANDBOOK: THE COMPLETE GUIDE FOR THE INDIVIDUAL INVESTOR

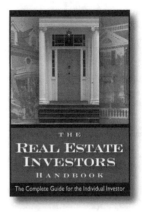

This book is a must-have for beginning investors, real estate veterans, commercial brokers, sellers, and buyers. This comprehensive step-by-step proven program shows beginners and seasoned veterans alike the ins and outs of real estate investing. This book is a road map to successful investing in real estate. Real estate appreciates at a rate far greater than the rate of inflation, builds equity, provides a steady return on investment, provides cash flow, and can offer substantial tax benefits. This handbook is the resource for novices and pros alike; it will guide you through every step of the process of real estate investing. You will uncover secrets that expert real estate investors use every day. This comprehensive resource contains a wealth of modern tips and strategies for getting started in this very lucrative area.

432 Pages • Item # RIH-02 • $24.95

THE FIRST-TIME HOMEOWNER'S HANDBOOK—A COMPLETE GUIDE AND WORKBOOK FOR THE FIRST-TIME HOME BUYER: WITH COMPANION CD-ROM

In this new book you will find vital information and great strategies that will allow you to find your dream home faster and feel confident about the purchase. You will learn to avoid some of the most prevalent—and potentially dangerous and expensive—mistakes made by first-time home buyers. With the help of this comprehensive new guide, you will learn how to find the best opportunities, negotiating, financing, budgets, needs and wants, credit reports, home-buying timeline, the process of building a house, manufactured homes, real estate and mortgage glossaries, setting values, home warranties, homeowners insurance, creative financing, buying with little or no money down, closing, moving plans, walk-throughs, closing and settlement inspections and more.

288 Pages • Item # FTH-02 • $21.95

THE RENTAL PROPERTY MANAGER'S TOOLBOX— A COMPLETE GUIDE INCLUDING PRE-WRITTEN FORMS, AGREEMENTS, LETTERS, AND LEGAL NOTICES: WITH COMPANION CD-ROM

This book and will teach you how to professionally manage your rental property. Maximize your profits and minimize your risks. Learn about advertising, tenants, legal rights, landlord rights, discrimination, vacancies, essential lease clauses, crime prevention, security issues, as well as premises liability, security deposits, handling problems, evictions, maintenance, recordkeeping, and taxes. The CD-ROM contains dozens of forms, sample contracts and more.

288 Pages • Item # RPM-02 • $29.95 with Companion CD-ROM

To order call 1-800-814-1132 or visit www.atlantic-pub.com

MORE GREAT TITLES FROM ATLANTIC PUBLISHING

THE PRE-FORECLOSURE REAL ESTATE HANDBOOK: INSIDER SECRETS TO LOCATING AND PURCHASING PRE-FORECLOSED PROPERTIES IN ANY MARKET

The Pre-Foreclosure Real Estate Handbook explains everything you need to know to locate and purchase real estate bargains from banks, public auctions, and other sources. Whether you are a first-time homeowner or an experienced property investor, *The Pre-Foreclosure Real Estate Handbook* is a tremendous guide for buying pre-foreclosed homes in any market. You will learn the simple formula (developed from real-life experience) that can build massive wealth through real estate foreclosures. This book is a resource for novices and pros alike; it will guide you through every step of the process including finding properties, negotiating, and closing on your first deal. Exhaustively researched, it will arm you with hundreds of innovative ideas that you can put to use right away. This book gives you the proven strategies, innovative ideas, and case studies from experts to help you get more with less time and effort.

288 Pages • Item # PFR-02 • $21.95

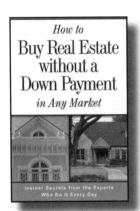

HOW TO BUY REAL ESTATE WITHOUT A DOWN PAYMENT IN ANY MARKET: INSIDER SECRETS FROM THE EXPERTS WHO DO IT EVERY DAY

This book explains everything you need to know to locate and purchase real estate with no down payment from individuals, banks, and other sources. Whether you are a first-time homeowner or an experienced property investor, this is a tremendous guide for buying real estate. You will learn the simple formula that can build wealth through real estate, with no money down. This proven formula works even if you have no real estate experience, bad or no credit, or very little money. This formula has been developed out of real-life experience. You will learn how to make smart real estate investments and use those investments to help you achieve financial success.

288 Pages • Item # BRN-02 • $21.95

FAST REAL ESTATE PROFITS IN ANY MARKET: THE ART OF FLIPPING PROPERTIES— INSIDER SECRETS FROM THE EXPERTS WHO DO IT EVERY DAY

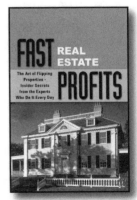

In real estate markets everywhere, real estate "flippers" have discovered that a small down payment, a little paint, some cleaning, and some time can net them tens (even hundreds) of thousands of dollars in profits, possibly tax-free. Finally there's a comprehensive, no-nonsense book that teaches you everything you need to build wealth through flipping properties quickly, legally, and ethically. You don't need great credit, a real estate license, or large sums of capital or experience to get started. There has never been a better time to invest in real estate. **288 Pages • Item # FRP-02 • $21.95**

To order call 1-800-814-1132 or visit www.atlantic-pub.com

MORE GREAT TITLES FROM ATLANTIC PUBLISHING

THE COMPLETE GUIDE TO INVESTING IN REAL ESTATE TAX LIENS & DEEDS: HOW TO EARN HIGH RATES OF RETURN—SAFELY

Tax lien certificates and deeds are not purchased through a broker; you purchase these property tax liens directly from the state or county government (depending on the state). This type of investment was created by state law, and state law protects you as the investor. Investing in tax liens and deeds can be very rewarding. Tax liens can be tax deferred or even tax-free. You can purchase them in your self-directed IRA. Interest rates vary but average between 4% and 18%. The interest rates are fixed by local governments, essentially a government-guaranteed loan. This sounds great, but what is the catch? There really is none, except you must know what you are doing! This groundbreaking book will provide everything you need to know to get you started on generating high-investment returns with low risk, from start to finish. **288 Pages • Item # CGI-02 • $21.95**

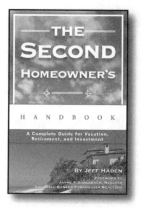

THE SECOND HOMEOWNER'S HANDBOOK: A COMPLETE GUIDE FOR VACATION, INCOME, RETIREMENT, AND INVESTMENT

There is no better time than now to buy that second home you've been thinking about for getaways, vacations, investment, or retirement. Low interest rates, tax savings, rising appreciation, and effortless financing make it simple to profit from a second home. This book explains how to invest profitably in a vacation or future retirement home. Your second home can be for living, to re-sell, or even rent. This comprehensive guide presents proven tactics to make your second home a smooth and profitable transaction. You will learn precisely what to look for in a real estate investment, buying prospects, and how to make your current home groundwork for potential real estate investments, how to find the best opportunities, negotiating, financing, budgets, credit reports and more. **288 Pages • Item # SHO-02 • $21.95**

PRIVATE MORTGAGE INVESTING: HOW TO EARN 12% OR MORE ON YOUR SAVINGS, INVESTMENTS, IRA ACCOUNTS AND PERSONAL EQUITY: A COMPLETE RESOURCE GUIDE WITH 100s OF HINTS, TIPS & SECRETS FROM EXPERTS WHO DO IT EVERY DAY

This book provides detailed information on how to put money to work in a relatively safe private mortgage investment with a high return of 12 to 15 percent (or more) in most cases. Private mortgages have grown into a multi-billion-dollar industry. This market allows investors to earn substantially higher yields—while offering the security of real property to back the loan. **288 Pages • Item # PMI-01 • $29.95**

To order call 1-800-814-1132 or visit www.atlantic-pub.com

MORE GREAT TITLES FROM ATLANTIC PUBLISHING

ONLINE MARKETING SUCCESS STORIES: INSIDER SECRETS FROM THE EXPERTS WHO ARE MAKING MILLIONS ON THE INTERNET TODAY

Standing out in the turmoil of today's Internet marketplace is a major challenge. There are many books and courses on Internet marketing; this is the only book that will provide you with insider secrets. We asked the marketing experts who make their living on the Internet every day—and they talked. *Online Marketing Success Stories* will give you real-life examples of how successful businesses market their products online. The information is so useful that you can read a page and put the idea into action—today!

With e-commerce expected to reach $40 billion and online businesses anticipated to increase by 500 percent through 2010, your business needs guidance from today's successful Internet marketing veterans. Learn the most efficient ways to bring consumers to your site, get visitors to purchase, how to up-sell, oversights to avoid, and how to steer clear of years of disappointment.

We spent thousands of hours interviewing, e-mailing, and communicating with hundreds of today's most successful e-commerce marketers. This book not only chronicles their achievements, but is a compilation of their secrets and proven successful ideas. If you are interested in learning hundreds of hints, tricks, and secrets on how to make money (or more money) with your Web site, then this book is for you.

Instruction is great, but advice from experts is even better, and the experts chronicled in this book are earning millions. This new exhaustively researched book will provide you with a jam-packed assortment of innovative ideas that you can put to use today. This book gives you the proven strategies, innovative ideas, and actual case studies to help you sell more with less time and effort.

288 Pages • Item # OMS-02 • $21.95

To order call 1-800-814-1132 or visit www.atlantic-pub.com